Thinking Outside the Crime and Justice Box

Thinking Outside the Crime and Justice Box

Diane Dimond

Creators Publishing
Hermosa Beach, CA

Thinking Outside the Crime and Justice Box
Copyright © 2016 Diane Dimond

Cover art by Peter Kaminski

FIRST EDITION
Creators Publishing
Hermosa Beach, California 90254
310-337-7003
ISBN 978-1-945630-27-9
CREATORS PUBLISHING

This book is dedicated to all Americans so they may better understand how our crime and justice system operates -- and fails to operate.

The system is an intricately woven organism, comprised of law enforcement on the front lines and judicial deciders and enforcers on the inside. It is an arrangement populated by fallible human beings and, as such, it should remain open to public inspection, always fluid and ever-evolving to keep up with the needs of citizens and not its own inhabitants. For too long this most important segment of society was left to operate autonomously. As a result, parts of it became arrogant, stagnant and bloated by their own indifference to those they were designed to serve.

Anyone with common sense -- everyone who has been intimately involved in the justice system -- knows it could be better. Within this book some observations about how to make it more efficient, understanding and humane to the population that needs it most.

~~~

Contents

~~~

Acknowledgments

First and foremost, I must thank all those whose names and stories appear on the following pages. By speaking to me and allowing your stories to be told, you have opened eyes and hearts about what is both right -- and wrong -- with our system of justice. I am forever in your debt.

This book would never have been possible without the warm journalistic embrace of Kent Walz, editor-in-chief of the Albuquerque Journal, and his managing editor, Karen Moses. As I looked for ways to broaden my horizons past the small box of television, the Albuquerque Journal provided the first home for my weekly crime-and-justice columns and made syndication possible. A heartfelt thanks to Kent and Karen for recognizing the need for this hometown girl's unique blend of reportage and commentary on the issues that fascinated me most. To Editorial Director Dan Herrera and writer D'Val Westphal: I send a warm appreciation for all you've done to make the column a long-running success. I am forever grateful to you all.

In 2009, Creators Syndicate enthusiastically offered a way to distribute my columns to a much broader, nationwide audience. Special thanks to both Richard and Jack Newcombe for recognizing the dearth of writing about the state of the nation's crime and justice system and taking a gamble on the idea that through human stories we reach a better understanding about both the good and the bad of it. To Margo Sugrue and Mary Ann Veldman, thanks for all your sales efforts in a time when newspapers and news sites face particular challenges. Tons of appreciation, too, to Managing Editor David Yontz and my dedicated editors, Courtney Davison and Alissa Stevens, who (thank goodness!) insert all missing commas and eliminate my all-too-frequent dashes -- among other editorial fixes.

Lifelong supporters also deserve very special acknowledgment: Wayne Kabak, the only agent I've ever had and a dear man who has always encouraged me and believed in me.

My daughter, Jenna Lamond, and her beautiful and loving family. My son-in-law, Jaime, and their three incredibly intelligent children, Ruby, Luke and Owen. You help my life be complete.

And finally, the man I feel indescribably lucky to have met all those years ago, my life partner and husband, Michael Schoen. He never fails as my frontline proofreader, illuminating critic and best friend. I love him with all my heart.

~~~

Foreword

Of all the millions of words written by journalists each week a relative few routinely delve into the life-altering issues of crime and justice. That is why I write.

Most crime stories you learn about center on a particular incident. They often tend to be a cursory look at an event or issue, rather than truly informative. Usually they are a quick who-what-when-where-why rendition of an event found in the morning newspaper or on the evening news. There is often very little follow-up, and most offer no perspective along with the dry facts. That is why I write.

My columns go beyond the headlines to dissect, discuss and point out flaws in the ways the system currently works -- always mindful of the human condition. When a rape kit lies on a shelf untested for years it not only allows a predator to roam free; it is also a slap in the face to the sexual assault victim. When we endorse tough-as-nails mandatory sentencing guidelines, we wind up with massively overcrowded prisons and the mind-numbing statistic that by 2013, 1 in every 100 American adults had been incarcerated. A citizen with a prison record might as well go to the head of the unemployment line.

The consequences of our crime and justice policies matter. And we need to understand the beginning, the middle and the end of how we got where we are. So many times, shortsighted or partisan politics are the genesis. Too many times, well-meaning strategies go awry and, as history shows, we stick with them far too long.

Conversely, the public needs to know about those who selflessly dedicate their careers to keep the rest of us safe. Like the brilliant homicide detective in Kansas -- the "Dick Tracy of Wichita" -- who spent decades tracking down the infamous BTK serial killer. Or the forensic sculptor in Philadelphia whose uncanny ability to take the fleshless human skulls of unidentified bodies and perfectly reconstruct the faces helped scores of families find peace.

I've long been keenly interested in all things having to do with crime and justice. I try to share what I learn and make each column different. Sometimes I simply tell you a story. Sometimes I'll share my opinions, praise or criticism. Other times I'll hold a mirror up to our society and invite you to form your own opinion. I hope this compilation of some of my favorite columns gives you something new to think about.

It's a complicated world out there, full of situations of good versus evil, right versus wrong. I figure it's my job is to point them out. This is why I write.

~ Diane Dimond

~~~

CHAPTER 1
Our Fascination With Murder

"In films murders are always very clean. I show how difficult it is and what a messy thing it is to kill a man." ~ **Alfred Hitchcock, film director**

Since biblical times and the tale of Cain and Abel people have been captivated by stories of murder. How could someone take the life of another, we ask ourselves. What was the method of death and what did the killer do with the dead body?

One murder could possibly be explained away as an accident or a heat-of-the-moment mistake. But there is no clear-cut explanation for a serial killer, the person who makes it their business to kill ... and kill again and again. Given their erratic and sometimes years-long activity there is no way to know how many active serial killers there are in the United States at any given time. And that captivates us as well. Could we be living next door to one?

Mass murder represents only a tiny fraction of the shamefully high occurrences of deadly gun violence in America, yet we are both frightened and riveted each time we hear about a case. Primarily because there is little defense against the chillingly random nature of such an event. These singular explosions of rage occur in darkened theaters, public parking lots, shopping malls, fast-food restaurants, on university campuses and even inside elementary schools.

I use my columns to repeatedly question why - given the shocking and repetitive carnage - society hasn't demanded a better and more readily available mental health system. Surely, those who turn guns on innocent children and adults are mentally sick, right? Moreover, if the horrific cold-blooded killing of 20 elementary school students in Newtown, Connecticut, didn't shock us into demanding change, what will?

I believe we devour stories of murder because deep down we wonder if we could ever be capable of such a thing.

Let's Remember All the Victims

June 25, 2011

How wonderful to see the recent photos of a smiling Rep. Gabrielle Giffords as she left the hospital five months after being viciously shot in the head by 21-year-old Jared Loughner.
Our hearts went out to Giffords and to the families of the 19 other victims, six of whom died.

But what about the family of Jared Loughner? Did you stop to think about them? The pain and suffering of Jared's parents makes them victims, too. And, in the end, if Jared is declared fit to stand trial, Arizona's death penalty might be used to take away their only son.

It is easy to forget about the plight of the families of those who commit these murders -- Tucson, Virginia Tech, Columbine, Oklahoma City, to name just a few of the most infamous. When families are remembered, it is often with pointed fingers of blame and condemnation.

Whether the offense makes national headlines or not, these ghastly crimes have two things in common: Nearly all involve shooters who have been clinically diagnosed with mental illness (Loughner is a paranoid schizophrenic). And, second, their families will never shake the shock, guilt and embarrassment of having a relative who kills.

In addition, these families have usually struggled for years trying to manage their loved ones' psychological deterioration, only to be told by medical experts to take them home, give them their medication and hope for the best. When the worst arrives, these folks are often left on their own to cope. Victim-assistance programs don't consider that the killer's family might need help, too.

You likely never heard of Bill Babbitt, but as he told me his story the other day, we both cried.

"It is the epitome of suffering," he said as he told me about his little brother, Manny. "I've lost the love and support of much of my family over it." You see, Bill was the first to realize his brother had caused someone to die, and he turned him in to police.

The story of Bill, now a 68-year-old war veteran living in California, is too rich in detail to adequately fit in this small space, but the summary is this: Manny's mental problems began in 1962, when his bike collided with a car and the boy was thrown into the air. He escaped death but was never "right" after that.

At 17, Manny joined the Marines. He wasn't bright enough to pass the written test, but during the Vietnam War the military needed every good man.

Handsome Manny did two tours of duty and was so badly wounded during the bloody 77-day siege at Khe Sanh that his seemingly lifeless body was rescued from an active battlefield and med-e-vaced out among a pile of corpses. Manny had sustained another major head wound.

Once home, post-traumatic demons set in, and Manny was sent by the VA to two different mental institutions. Finally, big brother Bill brought him to live at his house. Bill could tell from the frequent nightmares that his brother still was not "right."

One rainy night in December 1980, Manny was out drinking with friends, some PCP laced marijuana was passed around, and on the walk home Manny's demons returned.

The wet weather reminded him of Vietnam, a wide street morphed into the airstrip back in Khe Sanh, and a loud TV set blaring a war movie sent him over the edge. He opened the homeowner's unlocked screen door, as if to get closer to the war action, and encountered 78-year-old Leah Schendel. There was a violent scuffle, and the elderly grandmother died of a heart attack. He wouldn't remember, but Manny grabbed a piggy bank and some rolls of coins as he fled.

Bill and his wife found the unexplained money, along with a cigarette lighter bearing Schendel's initials. After reading about their neighbors death, the Babbitts knew what they had to do to get Manny the help he desperately needed. Bill turned in his own brother, and as the squad car pulled away, he told me: "I ran alongside and said, 'Manny, Manny ... please forgive me!' And he said, 'Billy, I already have forgiven you.'"

Manny didn't get the mental health treatment he needed. He got a bad lawyer who never mentioned post-traumatic stress or head injuries during the trial, and on May 14, 1982, Manny was found guilty and sentenced to death.

Upon hearing of his situation, the U.S. Marines sent officers to San Quentin prison, where they pinned a Purple Heart on Manny as he stood shackled before them. He was executed one day after his 50th birthday. His brother Bill was on hand to watch.

"It seems like it was just yesterday," he told me through tears, "or just an hour ago." Being a victim often lasts a lifetime.

This is the other side to the too-frequent stories we hear about "mad gunmen" who seemingly kill for "no reason." There is almost always a reason. And most often its family members who plead the loudest for help. Let's remember them, too.

America's Serial Killers -- How Many Are There?

Jan. 14, 2012

It was a small but horrifying item in the Los Angeles Times. "Police are asking for the public's help in identifying what they call a 'serious, dangerous serial killer operating in Orange County.' Police believe one person is responsible for stabbing three middle-aged homeless men. He is (considered) extremely dangerous to the public."

Another serial killer, I thought. And then the question: How many serial killers are out there in America?

John Douglas, a former chief of the FBI's Elite Serial Crime Unit and author of "Mind Hunter" says, "A very conservative estimate is that there are between 35 and 50 active serial killers in the United States" at any given time. Often, Douglas told me, they will, "kill two to three victims and then have a 'cooling-off' period between kills." That period can be days and in some cases (such as the BTK Strangler, Dennis Rader, convicted of killing 10 people from 1974 to 1991) even years."

But others who study serial killers (defined as someone who kills three or more people) think there are many more of these demented predators out there than the FBI admits -- maybe as many as a hundred of them actively operating right now.

Why don't we know the exact figure? Because serial killers are a secretive and often nomadic bunch.

Right before his execution in January 1989, the widely traveled Ted Bundy, described as a charismatic killer, admitted to 30 murders across half a dozen states from Washington to Florida.

Andrew Cunanan killed at least five people during his wanderings through Minnesota, Illinois, New Jersey and Florida, including fashion designer Gianni Versace in Miami.

The FBI knows death travels, and five years ago it set up the Highway Serial Killings Initiative. The bureau reveals it has "a matrix of more than 600 victims and potential suspects in excess of 275." Since the bodies were found off major highways, top suspects are long-haul truckers who may pick up prey in one state and dump the body several states away.

I know this is disturbing to read, and you may wonder: "Why should I care? I'm not going to hitchhike at a truck stop!"

Well, realize that lots of serial killers stay close to home and their victims are random. The aforementioned Rader found all his victims in Kansas, not far from the Wichita home he shared with his wife and two kids. Rader, the president of his local church, knocked on his victims' doors, and they simply let him in.

John Wayne Gacy met many of his 33 victims (all young men and boys) at charity events where he appeared dressed as a clown. After luring them to his house and murdering them, he stuffed them under his Cook County, Ill., home.

Gary Leon Ridgway, the so-called Green River Killer, was convicted of strangling 49 random women he met in Washington. He confessed to killing 71, but authorities believe the number of victims could be over 90.

Jeffrey Dahmer of Milwaukee admitted to killing and cannibalizing 17 young men and boys before he was arrested. Dahmer's mother, Joyce, once told me her son wished doctors would come study him in prison to help figure out what drove him to do it.

We who write about crime are told that law enforcement nationwide is doing a better job of communicating with each other about suspected serial killers. Indeed, the item I read about the homeless murders was a milestone. In the past, detectives were loath to tell the public about a serial killer on the loose for fear of spooking people. Now, they've come to realize that knowledge is power, and citizens' information can be a huge help in solving crimes.

Hardly a state in the union hasn't had a serial killer. California, Texas and Florida seem to have more than their fair share. And mass graves have been found all around the country. Two examples: The 11 bodies of young women and an infant found on the isolated West Mesa outside Albuquerque, and an eerily similar case thousands of miles away in Long Island, N.Y., where authorities unearthed 10 bodies -- eight women and a toddler, along with a man dressed in women's clothes.

These are among the serial killer dumping grounds that have been found. Many others may go undetected forever.

The best thing we can do is be vigilant. Know that many victims of serial killers put themselves in harm's way. Most are women who have some contact with the sex trade or illegal drug underworld. And if they have children, they are in grave danger, too.

Dr. Maurice Godwin has studied serial killers for years, and one in-depth analysis of 107 of them revealed important information. Godwin found that 55 percent of serial killers began having trouble in childhood and had criminal juvenile records. Forty-five percent had been convicted for a previous sex crime.

As with so many criminals, it goes back to their early formative years, and the best lesson we can learn is that when we find a troubled child, we best help them. Failure to do so could result in another serial killer walking among us.

We Need to Shift Thinking on Mass Murder

Dec. 22, 2012

In a study just presented to Congress, the Congressional Research Service concludes, "The estimated total number of firearms available to civilians in the United States (is) approximately 310 million: 114 million handguns, 110 million rifles and 86 million shotguns." Think about that. That translates to about one firearm for every man, woman and child in America. Mindboggling.

To my mind, however, it is not about the numbers so much as it is about the mental health of the person using the gun. Now, hold that thought a moment.

Millions of words have been written about the horrific tragedy at the Sandy Hook Elementary School in Newtown, Conn. Many of the stories contain a call for more gun laws. Keep in mind that the guns that 20-year-old Adam Lanza used were legally purchased by his mother in a state that has some of the toughest gun control laws in the country.

To be certain, America should explore more restrictive laws on where guns are sold, what types of guns are available, more uniform background checks and how bulk ammunition is purchased. But to limit the national discussion to passing more laws is a foolish mistake.

We must have a serious dialogue about mental health services and what has been afforded -- or not afforded -- to those who have caused such unspeakable carnage. Experts may argue, but I believe anyone who takes guns into a school, mall, movie theater or any other public place and opens fire must be, by that very act, mentally sick.

Mother Jones magazine reports these killing sprees are on the rise. Over the last 30 years, America suffered through some 62 incidents of mass murder by firearms. There were three last year resulting in a total of 40 people injured or killed. This year, there have been seven mass shootings with a shocking 138 victims. Something is radically wrong.

However, let's be honest. The vast majority of gun owners in America act very responsibly. They keep their firearms safe and use them only for sport, hunting or their constitutionally protected right to defend themselves and their families. Since the right to bear arms is included in the very fabric of our country, there is no way some 300 million guns are simply going to disappear.

So, what do we do to try to keep firearms out of the hands of the mentally ill? Well, first, when a person is declared mentally ill, the court must immediately place the name on a mandatory do-not-sell gun registry.

Families burdened by an unstable family member must not keep guns in the house -- period.

And by no means should a family follow the lead of the late Nancy Lanza and take the mentally disturbed relative (in her case, her son Adam) to the shooting range as a way of spending family time together.

Next, we have to realize that what was trendy in the '60s and '70s doesn't work now. We shut down psychiatric hospitals and deinstitutionalized patients by sending them out into the world with a prescription and a prayer. It didn't take long to see that community-based treatment wasn't feasible. Today, there are simply not enough psychiatric beds in hospitals or specialized clinics to keep up with the demand.

The result of our past action can be seen sleeping in tattered clothing on street corners and aimlessly pushing shopping carts along alleyways. Worse yet, we systematically toss the mentally deranged into prisons, where treatment options are nil.

Perhaps most important, we have to set up a new system to help the ever-growing number of desperate families looking for treatment for their troubled children. Ever since the elementary school shooting there have been a number of heart-wrenching personal essays published from parents of disturbed children with absolutely nowhere to go. One, titled "I Am Adam Lanza's Mother" has gone viral.

The mother of an academically gifted 13-year-old relates how her son scares her to death. "A few weeks ago," she wrote, "Michael pulled a knife and threatened to kill me and then himself after I asked him to return his overdue library books. His 7- and 9-year-old siblings knew the safety plan -- they ran to the car and locked the doors before I even asked them to."

Imagine living like that, knowing that someday your boy will be too physically strong for you to hug into submission.

Imagine asking a social worker about options and being told, as this mother wrote: "He said that the only thing I could do was to get Michael charged with a crime. 'No one will pay attention to you unless you've got charges.'" She concludes the essay by declaring, "No one wants to send a 13-year-old genius who loves Harry Potter and his snuggle animal collection to jail."

I know I don't think that's a suitable option.

Make no mistake: Today's troubled kid could be tomorrow's next mass murderer. Adam Lanza's mother complained and worried about how to help her painfully awkward son, and while people are now careful to say, we are not sure mental illness was a factor in the deaths of those 20 small children and seven adults. What else could it possibly have been?

No sane person does what Adam did. Or what Michael does to his family on a regular basis. If helping the mentally ill isn't a priority now, then when?

Murderabilia -- Our Fascination With Serial Killers

June 29, 2013

Do you collect anything? My dear Aunt Isabel used to collect little spoons that she proudly displayed in a wall cabinet. Grandma collected teacups. I began a collection of beautiful hand bells. Well, some people collect items that are much more macabre -- items that have a connection to notorious serial killers.

How macabre? Would you believe these collectors buy serial killers' autographed photos, artwork and handwritten letters sent to people outside prison walls? Even an envelope bearing a handwritten return address commands a pretty penny. The murderer's fingernail clippings, dirty socks or any other object that can be authenticated as genuine merit a place of honor on some people's mantle. But those are not the most shocking serial killer items up for sale on the Internet.

Andy Kahan, the Houston Police Department's victims' rights advocate, has dedicated much of the last 15 years to following -- and fighting -- this bizarre form of commerce. Kahan told me he got interested in making sure serial killers could never profit from their crimes after reading an article about Arthur Shawcross, who sold paintings and poems out of his cell in upstate New York. This serial killer had sexually abused, mutilated and killed at least 14 people (including two children) in the '70s and '80s. Some Shawcross paintings sold for nearly $600.

"I thought to myself, 'This is just not right,'" Kahan said. His research led him to eBay, where items from several notorious killers were being sold. Kahan vowed to spread the word about the morbid practice and actually bought up some of the most bizarre offerings to use during lectures on why there should be a law against the practice. He called these odd collectibles "Murderabilia," and the name has stuck.

Kahan bought hair from Charles Manson that had been fashioned into a swastika, dirt from a crawlspace tomb at John Wayne Gacy's house and an action figure of cannibal killer Jeffrey Dahmer that is marketed with this little ditty: "Open me up for a sure delight and see what I ate for dinner last night." Unzip the doll and mock body parts fall out. Among the most disgusting thing for sale, according to Kahan, was a bag of rocks and dirt taken from the Texas road where a black man named James Byrd was dragged to his death by three white supremacists in 1998.

"From a victim's perspective, selling murderabilia is about the most nauseating and disgusting thing that could happen," Kahan told me. "It is like being gutted all over again by the justice system."

Kahan has made it his life's calling to rid the internet of this ugly profit-making booty.

EBay finally gave in to his persistent calls and lobbying and has now banned the sale of murderabilia from its site. Kahan works hard to get states with the most serial killers in prison to pass "Notoriety for Profit" laws to make sure none of the money goes to the criminals. So far, Alabama, California, Florida, Michigan, Montana, New Jersey, Utah and Texas have done so.

Many people think the so-called Son of Sam laws prohibiting murderers from profiting by selling their life stories are still in effect, but they were declared an unconstitutional violation of free speech by the U.S. Supreme Court in 1991. The Notoriety for Profit laws are designed to follow the money, and therein lies the difference.

In the meantime, there are still grisly offerings out there: calendars, trading cards, T-shirts and even snow globes glorifying the grisly crimes of these killers. A handwritten recipe card from Dorothea Puentes for her tuna casserole is one of the coveted finds. Puentes ran a rooming house in Sacramento, Calif., in the '80s and killed at least nine of the elderly boarders who dared to complain that she was cashing and keeping their Social Security checks. Then there are the gravestone chips from Wisconsin serial killer Ed Gein's final resting place. His repulsive story was the inspiration for the movies "Psycho" and "Silence of the Lambs."

After the purveyors of murderabilia found the eBay door closed, sellers simply started their own websites and their ghastly business flourishes. As Kahan says: "I have no problem with those who are collecting the stuff. My problem is someone profiting from it. It is blood money, plain and simple."

While some of the convicts have entered into shady "trades" with sellers -- mailing out their personal items in return for small gifts or money deposited into their prison accounts -- many of the killers had no clue that what they were sending from prison was then being sold at auction sites.

"(David) Berkowitz had no idea his things were being sold and is violently opposed to it," Dr. Scott Bonn told me. "After having been born-again in 1987 ... he thinks it is a sacrilege." As an author and professor of criminology, Bonn befriended the so-called Son of Sam killer as part of his research for an upcoming book called "Why We Love Serial Killers."

So, why are we so fascinated by them? And what prompts people to collect these awful souvenirs? Bonn believes the media elevates these larger-than-life ghouls to morbid rock-star status. They become celebrity monsters.

"It's an adrenalin rush, and we love to have the crap scared out of us," Bonn said. "That, and we're riveted to the dark side of humanity. ... They define the outside parameters of what one human being can do to another."

Indeed, but I still don't want a bag of dirt from a crime scene on the shelf with my bells.

The 40th Anniversary of the Year of Fear

March 29, 2014

There is no subject that brings in more reader reaction than when I write about serial killers. The answer to why we are so fascinated by these multiple murderers is mercurial, depending on who you ask.

Dr. Scott Bonn, a professor of criminology at Drew University says: "Serial Killers seem to be for adults what monster movies are for children. It's exciting -- it's arousing," to learn about their exploits.

Dr. Casey Jordan, a criminologist, behavioral analyst and attorney in private practice says we are captivated by stories about serial killers because "We wonder to what extent they are just like us."

I would take it one step further and say we are riveted by details about serial killers because we wonder if we might ever reach a point where we could do what they do.

I read as much about the topic as I can, and during recent research about serial killers I discovered an intriguing set of facts dating back four decades. You might say this is the 40th anniversary of the "Year of Fear."

In the '70s, the U.S. experienced a frightening uptick in the number of active serial killers. In that decade, according to the serial killer information center at Radford University, there were 450 individual serial killers at work. Over the previous decade, the number stood at 156.

What caused the spike? Were there that many more vicious and deranged predators roaming the country, or did law enforcement become better able to identify those who killed over and over again?

Two years earlier, the FBI allowed a visionary special agent named Howard Teten to establish what would ultimately become the Behavioral Science Unit. Teten devised a groundbreaking analytical approach, now known as psychological criminal profiling, to try to identify unknown killers. His agents dedicated themselves to studying high-volume kill areas around the country and meticulously logged similarities between the cases. They analyzed the lifestyle, physical attributes and location of victims, the way the killers committed the murders and exactly how they left their victims. Patterns emerged. There was a swath of the county where pretty brunette coeds were repeatedly reported missing. Some hospitals experienced an extraordinary number of unexplained deaths. Bodies were found with both similar and unique wound patterns. Victims had been left in similar provocative positions. All similarities were put together like pieces of a big, ugly puzzle. Agents began to know the "how" and "where" of multiple murders, but not the "who." Not yet.

Although the exact date is unknown, this is the time the FBI began to use the term "serial killer" as opposed to the less precise "murder without motive" designation they used back then.

My research also led to a startling revelation I never knew about: 1974 was the year in which some of America's most notorious and prolific murderers began their reigns of bloody terror.

Ted Bundy committed his first murder in January 1974.

Dennis Rader (BTK-Bind-Torture-Kill) first murdered in January 1974.

John Wayne Gacy killed the second of his 34 victims in January 1974.

Coral Eugene Watts murdered the first of an estimated 90 victims in 1974.

Paul John Knowles went on a killing spree, murdering 18 people in 1974.

What was it about 1974?

Retired FBI special agent Jim Clemente worked in the FBI's Behavioral Analysis Unit (the modern day name of Agent Teten's original BSU) for the last 12 years of his 20-year career at the bureau. He told me: "At the time, the BAU had no idea how devastating a year 1974 would turn out to be. Some of the most brilliant and prolific serial killers would launch their destructive careers at that time. But it would be decades before they were all brought to justice."

As FBI agents were building their multiple puzzles, the elusive Bundy would murder upward of 36 people over the next four years. Rader killed until 1991. Gacy wouldn't be caught until late 1978. Watts continued his bloody spree for more than eight years. The handsome Knowles was on a rapid path of destruction. His murder binge ended after five months when a police officer shot him dead.

Surely, there were news reports about some of these murders and missing people left behind in the frenzy of serial killing. But in 1974, the nation's attention was scattered. Vietnam was still ongoing. There was a frantic worldwide nuclear arms race underway. Watergate was toppling the administration of President Richard Nixon. Even though the daughter of multimillionaire Randolph Hearst was kidnapped that year, most Americans didn't notice that the nation's crime rate was on the rise.

But the FBI knew the murderous score and, worried about creating public panic, kept the information quiet. Also in 1974, agents were well-aware of a murderous maniac operating in San Francisco who signed taunting, cryptic letters to police with the moniker "Zodiac" and someone else was systematically picking up military men along Southern California freeways and dumping their dismembered bodies along major highways.

The takeaway from this look back at history is that since that peak of serial killing madness in the '70s and '80s (there were 603 serial killers identified in the '80s), the numbers have decreased every single decade since. In the '90s there were 498 serial killers; in the 2000s there were 275. So far in this decade there are just 67 active serial killers registered on the reliable Radford University site. It's a testament to the perseverance of the FBI and to all law enforcement that studied and implemented FBI special agent Teten's revolutionary criminal profiling protocol.

Serial killers may still hold a place of fascination for many of us, but here's hoping their number continues to dwindle.

Murder -- Especially Jodi Arias' -- Can Be Mesmerizing

April 6, 2015

In the summer of 2008, Jodi Arias stabbed her boyfriend nearly 30 times, slashed his throat, shot him in the head and left him in the shower of his Mesa, Arizona, home. Eleven days later, the attractive 28-year-old was arrested, and the public became transfixed by her case.

Nearly seven years after the vicious murder, Arias has yet to be sentenced* on the finding that she is guilty of the first-degree premeditated murder of Travis Alexander. Two separate juries have deadlocked on whether she should be executed for the crime. Now, under Arizona law, the death penalty is off the table. Later this month, a judge will finally announce her sentence -- likely life in prison.

Legions of court-watchers remain fascinated by her case. And I want to understand why this murder, of all the murders in America, has commanded so much public attention.

"If she was a homely, overweight Korean man, we'd never have heard about her," Dr. Scott Bonn, a professor of sociology and criminology told me during a conversation from his office at Drew University. He believes Arias was demonized by the media from the beginning.

To put it bluntly, he said, "Pretty young white girls who sing in the choir are just not supposed to hack up their boyfriends."

But she did. She ultimately admitted to committing the murder, saying it was self-defense. But she first told police she wasn't at Alexander's home when he died. She also once claimed masked intruders suddenly broke in, assaulted her and murdered Alexander.

What a liar! Is that why so many people worldwide were mesmerized by her case? Was the attraction her ability to tell such baldfaced lies?

Bonn, who teaches courses on sociology and criminal behaviors, thinks it goes deeper than that. It's not about Jodi; it's about us.

Two very different camps of people have persistently followed the case, and they either viscerally hate or love this convicted killer, their feelings fueled by massive and exploitative TV coverage. HLN's Nancy Grace led the charge, and when her ratings soared other TV outlets jumped on the Arias bandwagon.

Those who see Arias as the devil incarnate have long demanded her execution, and when one juror -- juror number 17 -- deprived them by refusing to vote for the death penalty, the 33-year-old mother of three's identity and home address were plastered across the internet. She has received death threats and police protection.

But others continue to passionately support Arias. They proclaim her innocence and viciously attack the late Alexander, calling him a domestic abuser and pedophile, repeating Arias' unsubstantiated claims at trial that she had been victimized by Alexander and once caught him looking at child porn. They fervently believe the claim of self-defense.

Why do so many of us expend so much psychic energy either loving or hating defendants like Arias? Why does anyone bother to spend time vilifying witnesses or reporters or threatening jurors? Bonn says the fixation stems from society's angry and fearful nature.

"Since 9-11 ... We're waiting for the next shoe to fall; we don't know who to trust anymore," he said. "So we go around believing the world is full of evil. ... We're looking for justice these days, and if Jodi is put to death, then we feel justice is returning."

Dr. Kristina Randall, a psychotherapist who works with troubled young women, writes that Arias supporters are likely damaged souls who identify with the killer's claims of abuse by Alexander. Female supporters, she writes, may be "hating themselves for not being able to end their abuse and now celebrate the fact that ... Jodi's victory is now their victory." Male supporters of this convicted killer may be on her side because "They watched their father abuse their mother, couldn't stop the abuse and now celebrate Jodi's achieving what they could not."

Maybe the mesmerized just lead boring lives and need something to fill the void.

Bonn, author of a recent book on serial killers, has written to Jodi Arias to ask her to participate in a book about how her legal process has proceeded over the years under the white-hot glare of unrelenting media coverage. If she says yes, his readers may get a glimpse of what it's like to be on the receiving end of a justice system that struggles mightily, yet fruitlessly to stay detached from public opinion.

*UPDATE: On April 13, 2015, Arias was sentenced to a sentence of natural life in prison with no possibility of parole. In announcing the sentence Judge Sherry Staples made note of the pre-planning and savage, cruel nature of the murder.

An Open Letter to Peter Lanza

March 15, 2014

"With hindsight, I know Adam would have killed me in a heartbeat, if he'd had the chance. ... The reason he shot Nancy four times was one for each of us: one for Nancy; one for him; one for Ryan; one for me." ~ Peter Lanza, father of mass killer Adam Lanza

Dear Mr. Lanza,

First, may I tell you how deeply sorry I am for the loss of your son, Adam? As a mother myself I cannot imagine my child committing suicide and the never-ending pain that action must bring with it. Here's hoping you know how many people have prayed for your family since the terrible tragedy in December 2012.

I'm writing to say how glad I am that you finally spoke publicly about your youngest child. Like you, many of us hope that speaking out about your son's mental illness will help other struggling families with afflicted children. I wonder how many of them fear their children might turn dangerous, too.

While reading the New Yorker article about you, I had to smile when you described Adam as "just a normal little weird kid," who was intellectually curious and loving. Then, I felt sadness for you and your ex-wife, Nancy, as the writer described Adam's increasing self-isolation -- smelling things that weren't there, washing his hands obsessively and showing antisocial behavior. When you had to tell his elementary school teachers to watch him for seizures, I guess you knew that Adam was more than a little "weird."

From reading the story, it seems Adam's 2005 diagnosis of Asperger's syndrome gave you some hope of finding meaningful solutions for your son. I realize you and your ex-wife had separated back in 2001, but I was glad to read that you stayed close to 13-year-old Adam and his big brother, Ryan.

So what the hell happened, Mr. Lanza? Why, on the morning Adam walked into his mother's bedroom and pumped four bullets into her face and then gunned down 26 innocent children and their teachers at Sandy Hook Elementary had you not spoken to him in two years? I don't mean to be disrespectful here, but you were the grown-up in this equation -- the male figure in your son's life -- and you let weeks, months and years go by without communicating face-to-face though he was obviously troubled?

I read that he was angry with you after a dispute about how many classes he should take. That was all it took to shut him down -- forever?

You said when Adam refused to see you: "I was hurt. I never expected that I would never talk to him again. I thought it was a matter of when." But two whole years went by!

You knew Adam never accepted the Asperger's diagnosis and that he was prone to fanciful thinking. He wanted to take college courses. He wanted to join the military. You knew your wife had a lifelong hobby of shooting and that there were guns in the home.

If you weren't responsible for Adam, who, besides his dead mother, was?

I'm not asking to be rude; I'm asking to understand how a parent can become so clouded in thinking about a mentally ill child's behavior so as to allow that youngster to dictate the rules of the house. How does that even happen?

Sadly, I have to assume that similarly burdened parents are reacting the same way when they can't find good-quality mental health care solutions for their kids.

The author of the article, Andrew Solomon, wrote about you, saying, "He constantly thinks about what he could have done differently and wishes he had pushed harder to see Adam."

I truly wish you had pushed harder, too, Mr. Lanza. If only you had gone back to that big, beautiful, yellow home nestled behind the knoll in Newtown, Connecticut, you might have noticed, for example, that your 20-year-old, 6-foot-tall son weighed only 112 pounds at the end.

I checked the official Body Mass Index and was astounded to learn that Adam's BMI was 15.2. People in the "underweight" category have a BMI of 18.5. Your son fell into the "starvation" and "anorexia" group. A study I read says prolonged semi-starvation brings on severe emotional instability, hysteria, antisocial behavior and depression - conditions it sounds like Adam already suffered. I have to believe if you had only seen him in that haunted-looking state you would have done something, right?

If you had gone to visit Adam during those last two years you might also have noticed that he had covered the windows in his bedroom with thick, black plastic. You might have noticed his stack of violent video games, the newspaper articles he collected about school shootings or the photos he had of dead humans wrapped in plastic. A check of his computer might have brought up his spreadsheet about mass murders, the rights of pedophiles or the selfies he took while holding guns to his head. Your ex-wife might have finally admitted that he was refusing to eat or talk to her, communicating only via email from behind his bedroom door.

I'm sure you've probably read that lengthy report by the Connecticut State Attorney's Office about your son's mass murder, Mr. Lanza. It concludes Adam was a kid immersed in his own spiraling and destructive hell, and your ex-wife was intent on trying to manage it all herself. So, how did you envision your son's future?

You got it right, I fear, when you described Adam's final, fatal actions by saying, "You can't get any more evil." You wished he had never been born and admitted: "How much do I beat up on myself about the fact that he's my son? A lot."

I am truly sorry for your loss, Mr. Lanza, but it is the parents of those 20 murdered children and the families of the six dead teachers I mourn for the most. They had everything to live for. Inaction by you, Nancy and the nation's mental health system ensured Adam was lost long ago.

I pray that this nation wakes up and comes to the realization that we either help the helpless like Adam or be condemned to suffer their sometimes inexplicable and explosive wraths.

Another Massacre, Another Meaningless Blame Game

June 2, 2014

In the aftermath of a terrible tragedy we always look for someone or something to blame. In the case of the Isla Vista, California, massacre in which six college students were murdered and 13 others were wounded, the blame game started almost immediately. Most of the criticism was misdirected.

This mass murder was not due to the lack of strict gun laws. It was not the fault of violent video games. It wasn't that the killer had an uncaring or inattentive family. It didn't happen because the killer's therapist or school counselor failed to decipher a madman's inner turmoil. And it wasn't because law enforcement somehow failed.

There is only one reason so many people died: Twenty-two-year-old Elliot Rodger was a young man of privileged means who was possessed by a demented, murderous and conniving mind. Period. For three years, he meticulously concocted his hideous plan and documented it in a lengthy manifesto. All the while, he appeared weird and standoffish (according to classmates), but never dangerous.

Evil is sometimes like that. It can hide in plain sight.

The father of one of the dead, Christopher Michaels-Martinez, tearfully declared that the carnage was the fault of "craven, irresponsible politicians and the NRA."

My heart goes out to that man. However, respectfully, that conclusion is nonsense. California politicians have passed some of the nation's toughest, most restrictive gun and ammunition laws in the nation despite intense lobbying from the National Rifle Association.

Besides, Elliot Rodger didn't rely on just his three (legally obtained) guns as he carried out his sick strategy. He began the spasm of violence by rendering his two roommates and a visitor defenseless with hammer blows to the head. He is then believed to have slit their throats with a knife and a machete, just as he had outlined in his manifesto. Evidence bags bearing these three weapons were seen being carried from his apartment. Rodger then jumped in his late-model BMW and used it as a weapon, terrorizing pedestrians and bicyclists, injuring four.

To blame just one of the various weapons Rodger used -- the guns -- while ignoring the others overlooks the fact that it was his demented bloodlust that drove the action, not any particular weapon. Were the guns an expeditious means to his awful endgame? Yes. But I'll bet that if Elliot had somehow been denied firearms he would have devised other fast-acting weapons to use, such as explosives or poison.

There will always be those who must find fault after such a murderous spree, as if to say all horrible incidents can be avoided if we just pass enough laws. We all know that's not true, because those possessed of a mentally disturbed and criminal mind are obsessed.

They let nothing stop them from their goal. Think Timothy McVeigh, Ted Kaczynski or Eric Rudolph, three delusional killers who used bombs to blast their way into infamy.

Many of the critical comments I've heard since the California killings have been directed at the Santa Barbara County Sheriff's Department. They should have done more. They should have searched Rodger's apartment. They should have watched his online videos. So goes the criticism. Let's use our common sense here.

Rodger had three contacts with the department over the years. He once called deputies complaining that his roommate had taken $22 worth of candles from his room. No charges were filed. Officers were once called in after a drunken Rodger provoked an incident in a bar. In an area where many of the 22,000 UC Santa Barbara students routinely drink too much and cause a scene, Rodger's actions hardly made him a standout. And finally, about a month ago, his mother became concerned about disturbing videos her son had posted on the internet and called for help.

A source inside the Sheriff's Office tells me they get welfare calls from worried parents "All the time ... and from locations across the country," and officers dutifully follow up on each call.

In Rodger's case, deputies reported that when they located and spoke to him, he was "courteous and polite." He calmly answered all their questions and gave them no reason to think he was a danger to himself or others. The officers had no warrant to enter and search the property, and even if they had found his stash of guns and ammunition, so what? He was an adult, and he owned them legally. Can you imagine the outcry if sheriff's deputies pushed their way into peoples' homes on a whim?

As the Sheriff's Office source told me: "We can't violate someone's rights because we have a feeling. It doesn't work that way." Nor can a deputy arrest someone for posting free speech online.

The fault for the Isla Vista massacre lies not with the weapons used but with the man involved. The arrogant and delusional Rodgers had been festering and plotting toward this point for years. His hatred for the human race apparently began in middle school. It was there, this 22-year-old virgin wrote in his manifesto, that a younger classmate refused to return his affections. It was there he began to despise all the rest of us for our happiness. While his parents have indicated their son had been in therapy for many years, it was obviously not enough to ease his tortured mind.

Too bad we can't channel all the energy that goes into finger-pointing and demanding more laws and channel it into a way to help the truly sick who walk among us. They are the roots of the problem. Until we can figure out a way to identify, isolate and treat sick minds like Elliot Rodger's, we will continue to suffer the gut-wrenching and deadly aftereffects of their maniacal breaks with reality.

Why the Colorado Theater-Shooter Trial Is So Important

April 27, 2015

Here comes another headline-grabbing criminal trial. James Holmes, now 27, stands accused of murdering 12 and wounding 70 in a mass shooting at an Aurora, Colorado, movie theater in July 2012. Opening statements in the capital murder case are set for Monday.

Ho-hum, you say? I beg to differ.

This trial is massively important for anyone who wants to understand what possesses young men to grab guns, randomly shoot and kill total strangers and then plead not guilty by reason of insanity. It promises to give us a rare glimpse into the troubled mind of a mass shooter. All too often mass shooters turn the gun on themselves or force a suicide by cop. And we are left with nothing but questions.

Why did they do it? How did they pick their victims? Had they sought mental health treatment, and were they turned away for lack of space? If the shooter wanted to die, why did he kill so many others in the process?

All too often we accept unsatisfactory explanations like "He was just evil, I guess." If that's the case, I want to understand where that evil seed was planted and how it was nurtured.

Or if, as Holmes' defense team maintains, this was a case of uncontrollable mental illness, I want to know why no one noticed or offered him help before it was too late. If Holmes, an honored neuroscience student pursuing his Ph.D, is so mentally ill that he sought to destroy strangers who had simply gathered to watch a midnight showing of a Batman movie, then why is the state of Colorado seeking the death penalty? Is that what we do to sick people?

Ah, back to the importance of this trial. It is up to a court of law to decide whether Holmes suffered a psychotic break that awful summer evening, or whether he knew exactly what he was doing.

Among the evidence the jury will surely hear is how young he stockpiled mail-ordered ammunition, manufactured 30 homemade hand grenades and brought in gallons of gasoline to booby trap his apartment to inflict maximum damage on the investigators he knew would come.

Did those actions reveal his coherent premeditation?
The jury will also hear that before the shooting, one of his University of Colorado psychiatrists had reported to campus police that Holmes had made "homicidal statements." He had sent text messages to a fellow student mentioning dysphoric mania and warning her to stay away -- "because I am bad news." An expert witness is likely to explain that schizophrenia and other mental illnesses mostly take hold of young men around the ages of 18 to 25 -- just like Holmes.
The trial is also an important window into how our criminal justice system works.

Guess how much this process has cost so far? An analysis done from public records shows that as of February 2015 this case has gobbled up $5.5 million in public money. That doesn't include the bill for Holmes' public defenders. The probable final tab? Ten million or more.

One more lesson about a death penalty trial. If the defendant is found guilty, there is a built-in guarantee of years of appeals -- years more for victims' families and survivors to have to testify at hearings and relive the horror.

Arlene Holmes, the defendant's mother, has published a small prayer journal she's kept since the shooting (proceeds are to go to mental health services) in which she repeatedly says there is no need for a trial.

"He could go to prison for life. What good does the death penalty do?" she writes. Thoughts no mother in her position can be criticized for thinking.

She also reveals her crash course in the law and mental disorders, admitting she thought her son was just "very shy" -- until the shooting.

"I thought what my son did was completely insane," she says. She continued: "He did what no sane man would do. But the law says a man who knows murder is wrong, then murders anyway, is sane."

It is doubtful Holmes will take the stand in his own defense, but a boatload of information about his personal life, his scholastic failures in the months before the shooting and his overall mental state will be revealed -- a rare glimpse into the motivations and mind of the man police say carried out a premeditated mass murder. Its information we need to understand.

Withholding a Name Won't Stop the Next Mass Shooting

June 15, 2015

For those of us who have never lost a child to a violent crime, we cannot possibly know a grieving parent's pain. But we know that out of pain can come a convoluted way of thinking.

It isn't easy to question the motives of the heartbroken parents who decide they hold the key to stop future tragedies. It isn't popular to ask them whether they are acting out of grief or common sense when they point the finger of blame and demand change. But that's exactly what I'm doing.

There is a campaign called No Noteriety that is advanced most energetically by Tom Teves and Caren Teves, the devastated parents of Alex Teves, 24, one of a dozen people who lost their lives during the 2012 mass shooting inside an Aurora, Colorado, movie theater. Another 70 were wounded.

No Noteriety supporters believe, as the website states, that the individuals who carry out these murderous rampages are motivated by "the quest for notoriety," and that such criminals should be deprived of being "the media celebrity they so crave."

(And the proof of that is where?)

The Teves' have issued a challenge to the media to stop reporting the names of shooters like Holmes, who meticulously planned and carried out the theater shooting that took their son's life. They also don't want TV, newspapers or magazines to show his photograph.

No Name. No Photo. No Noteriety. That is the group's motto. They believe that the mere mention of a shooter's name or a glance at a shooter's mugshot glorifies the shooter and creates copycat killers.

Tom Teves takes it one step further, saying the media has "blood on its hands" for reporting such details in the past.

"You guys need to be responsible for what you do," he told KUSA 9News on the year anniversary of the theater shooting. "You guys could change overnight. All you have to do is have the courage to stop."

Now it's my turn.

No reputable reporter can cover a case -- especially a criminal trial -- without mentioning the defendant's name. How can we fail to show the photograph taken of deranged-looking, red-haired Holmes just a few hours after that horrific mass shooting? His appearance and state of mind at the time goes directly to his current insanity defense.

Journalists are trained in the who-what-why-where-when of a story. Facts are our lifeblood. How are we supposed to do our jobs and still satisfy the demands of those who have embraced the No Noteriety movement?

I have spent a career reporting on victims of murder, childhood sexual abuse, rape and domestic abuse. It never once dawned on me that I should leave the perpetrator's identity out of my story.

What the No Noteriety folks are asking creates a slippery slope. If the media agrees to keep mass shooters' names and photos out of their stories for fear it could influence a future tragedy, where does it stop? Do we keep secret the names of corrupt politicians on trial because it might give other crooked officials an idea? Shall we stop mentioning the names of bank robbers, domestic abusers or child molesters? Do we keep the names of all murderers out of our stories, or just the ones who go on these random, mass-killing sprees?

It is so easy to blame the messenger instead of focusing on the aspects of today's society that are harder to change. My list: The ease in which determined individuals can buy guns and online ammunition, their mental health status and the widespread practice of prescribing too many mind-altering drugs to too many patients.

Investigative authors Stephen and Joyce Singular wrote "The Spiral Notebook," a new book about the uptick of these acts of mass violence. They conducted years of research on the topic and engaged a forgotten segment in the conversation: millennials. They asked young people why so many of their generation turn to this kind of violence.

"They came of age when the future seemed quite limited," the Singulars wrote. "Climate change, economic collapse, Y2K, global terrorism -- there's always another apocalypse around the corner." And to add to this skewed upbringing, the authors noted, the movie industry kept churning out terrifying films.

"They were filled with superheroes who wielded power by killing as many others as they could."

Seems there are a lot of possible stimuli that go into creating these monstrous mass killers. Blaming the news media is a cop-out.

~~~

CHAPTER 2
Fighting Crime With Forensic Science

"Every human being carries with him from his cradle to his grave certain physical marks which do not change their character, and by which he can always be identified -- and that without shade of doubt or question. These marks are his signature, his physiological autograph. ... This autograph consists of the delicate lines or corrugations with which Nature marks the insides of the hands and the soles of the feet." ~ **Mark Twain, "The Tragedy of Pudd'nhead Wilson," 1894**

In Mark Twain's day, the art of fingerprinting was in its infancy. I've often wondered what ol' Samuel Clemens would have thought about how the skill of identifying individual "autographs" developed into today's fascinating science of forensics.

Forensic science (the legally recognized method of gathering and examining information about the past) is used in accounting, astronomy, geology and many other disciplines. For law enforcement purposes, the tiniest bits of evidence are often the most crucial for conviction. A minute blood drop, a single strand of hair and even microscopic skin cells can be studied by qualified scientists to either help identify or rule out a criminal suspect. Fibers from clothes or carpet, the crust left from a dried tear or droplet of sweat, a chip of paint from a car or wall, or a computer hard drive can put a criminal at the center of a crime and go a long way toward convincing juries to convict.

Forensics has always captivated me -- its successes and its failures, the mysteries and cold cases it can solve. And if the evidence goes against a defense attorney's client, it is always entertaining to watch the attorney skate around the facts in court.

Crime scene investigators meticulously collect forensic evidence, but for various reasons this crucial material isn't always processed. Sometimes suspects plead guilty and there is no need to test the evidence. But often, crime labs simply don't have the budget to get all the work done. That's a shame, because locked inside those evidence envelopes could be the clue to catching a criminal and getting him or her off the street.

A Little Swab Will Do Ya

April 25, 2009

What if a policeman approached you and ordered you to open wide for a DNA mouth swab test? Suppose you were pulled over on suspicion of driving while intoxicated, check fraud or skipping child support payments, and you suddenly found yourself on the business end of a Q-tip. Would you submit or refuse and ask for your lawyer?

It's not so far-fetched a scenario. Both the FBI and police officials in at least 15 states have recently ratcheted up efforts to collect DNA samples from nearly all those who pass through their systems, whether they're hardened criminals or merely a suspects. It used to be these tests were administered only to those actually convicted of a crime. But somewhere along the line, authorities determined that creating a bigger suspect pool of known people who have had run-ins with the law was a good thing. In short, they figured it was better to have too many DNA samples than not enough. Suddenly, a suspect in, say, a burglary case could be run through the DNA database to see if he were wanted for something much more serious like rape or murder.

It's a good thing when police catch the bad guy, right?

Those in favor of swabbing all suspects point out that DNA samples have helped convict and remove from the streets thousands of criminals. It's also helped exonerate more than 200 people who were wrongly convicted. They say that coupled with other evidence, DNA is the capper to making an airtight case.

Those against the idea point to the Fourth Amendment to the U.S. Constitution, which guards against unreasonable searches and seizures, including body searches. They fret that America is becoming a genetic-surveillance society with a sort of swabs-are-us mentality. They have filed lawsuits to protect against what they see as an invasion of privacy.

Courts have generally upheld laws calling for the compulsory collection of DNA from convicts. The reasoning has been that once citizens commit a criminal act, they have given up their rights. But, courts have not fully considered this expansion of DNA testing to those not yet found guilty of a crime. You can take it to the bank, however, that those lawsuits are being prepared as you read this.

The field of forensic science goes way back. Even before it had such a fancy name, in the year 700, the Chinese were studying distinct fingerprint patterns on documents.

In England in 1784, a man named John Toms was found guilty of murder after a torn paper in his pocket matched a wad of paper in his pistol. In 1835, Scotland Yard was analyzing flaws in bullets to pair up with murder weapons.

As the commercial used to say, "We've come a long way, baby!" One of the latest jaw-droppers in the forensic science field is called "touch DNA." It has only been around a few years. It is a process whereby the scientist can return to any item a perpetrator has touched and, likely, lift the smallest skin cells from which DNA can be extracted.

Scientists used the technique recently in Boulder, Colorado, when they reviewed evidence in the cold case of little JonBenet Ramsey. Using the touch DNA process, they were able to lift microscopic skin cells off the long johns she was wearing the night she was murdered. An "unexplained third party" intruder has now been identified as belonging to that DNA. And this latest genetic material matches other male DNA previously gathered from a single blood drop found in Ramsey's underwear. The hard part, of course, will be to find the person with whom this mysterious DNA matches.

Maybe the fiend who took Ramsey's life will pop up in America's newly expanded DNA database someday. It's a sure bet that other elusive criminals will. Think about it. If we can put away repeat offenders, not only will countless outstanding crimes be solved, but other citizens might be spared from becoming victims.

I wonder if those against expanded DNA tests are also against other crime-fighting techniques already in widespread use. Is taking a suspect's fingerprints or blood a violation of privacy? How about if police ask for a Social Security number or home address, or listen in on a suspect's phone calls? All these tactics and more have been used for decades to help keep the rest of us safe.

I have a problem with authority figures ordering me to do something I think is unfair. I worry about government encroachment on my rights. But if I'm not guilty of anything, and if submitting to such a test would save others from pain or death, why wouldn't I help the police effort? I look at it like giving blood. Give, and you could save a life.

Toxicology Reports Don't Lie

July 25, 2009

Imagine the hushed, sterile atmosphere of an autopsy room. A body arrives, and a team of forensic experts quietly get to work trying to determine cause of death. Scientific evidence is gathered to determine whether a crime was committed to cause the death, whether it occurred from natural, unavoidable causes or whether it was death by suicide.

In many cases, such as that of retired NFL quarterback Steve McNair, the cause of death is pretty obvious. McNair was found sprawled on the couch in his condo, shot twice in the head and twice in the chest. Nearby was the body of his 20-year-old mistress and a gun underneath her. It was quickly ruled a murder-suicide.

But other deaths are not so clear-cut. Take the case of 50-year-old infomercial scream-seller Billy Mays. After he was found dead in his bed by his wife, we heard that he'd violently bumped his head in an airplane just hours earlier. It was thought that his sudden death had something to do with the hit on the head. But forensic science proved it wasn't so. Once the medical professionals opened Mays' chest, they immediately discovered a diseased heart was to blame, an affliction Mays was apparently unaware he had.

And then there are the full-blown forensic investigations like the one surrounding entertainer Michael Jackson, who was suspected of dying from an overdose on a hospital-strength anesthesia called Diprivan and, perhaps, a cocktail of other drugs. Cases like Jackson's demand a full toxicology and histology workup, or in layman's terms, a full examination of blood, tissue, hair and organ samples to determine if someone should be charged with a crime.

All this scientific sleuthing takes time to accomplish, and in the meantime, families of the dead anxiously await the final verdict.

Autopsy blood workups are routine. The sample is usually taken from deep inside the heart chamber, and tests determine what compounds are present in the bloodstream. Some drugs like cocaine break down quickly in the body and are hard to detect. But most drugs stop metabolizing when the person dies, so the traces found in the bloodstream are indicative of what was present at the time of death. The forensic investigators also examine urine, bile and tissue samples from the liver, heart, spleen and kidneys.

The information gathered fits together like pieces in a cause-of-death puzzle.

Hair is especially revealing. It holds on to what the body has ingested like rings on a tree. Scalp hair usually grows about half an inch a month. The longer the hair, the more information can be found. A 6-inch hair will reveal a full year's worth of clues. Traces of each drug used will be stored in the hair shaft. The coroner will be able to identify every one, be they prescription or illegal, and when they were used. If the person is bald, shorter hair from the armpits or the groin area can be used. They will just yield less information.

But there is nothing as telling as what scientists can deduce from studying the brain. Unlike other organs from which samples can be taken immediately, the brain requires special handling. The entire brain mass must be submerged and hardened in formaldehyde for about three weeks before samples can be taken. Once gathered, a neuro-forensic pathologist usually needs four to six weeks to unravel telltale evidence of what happened to the person during life.

If the decedent was beaten as a child, contusions on the brain will show as dead tissue called necrosis spots. If the person suffered a drug overdose (or multiple drug overdoses), the scientist will be able to see evidence of that and determine when the overdose(s) occurred. If the decedent suffered strokes, there will be visible scar tissue.

When families receive a negative cause-of-death determination from the coroner, they are often in denial. They don't want to believe their family member could have committed suicide or died of a drug overdose.

Media leaks about the state of Jackson's body at death have been excruciating. The almost 6-foot-tall performer was reported to have weighed just 112 pounds. The skin on his arms, neck and legs was said to have been pockmarked with old and new needle punctures. All evidence indicates he died from a fatal overdose of several different drugs.

If that is the final judgment on what killed Michael Jackson, something tells me the Jackson family will never accept it. It will be more comforting to believe some outside force killed their loved one. It's much harder to accept the fact that someone you cherished slowly and deliberately shortened his own life.

Searching the Family DNA Tree to Solve Crime

April 2, 2011

What if I told you there was a powerful crime-fighting tool that could help find, convict and put away violent criminals that most of our 50 states are NOT using? Your first question would likely be, "Why not?!"

That's what I'd like to know.

We all get how important the discovery of DNA has been in identifying rapists, murderers and other criminals over the years. But DNA technology has now graduated, and for the most part states just haven't kept up.

Colorado has been leading the way in a process called familial DNA search. Crime scene scientists and police investigators who have used it swear by its usefulness. The state has offered up special computer software it developed, along with its experts, to train others to use the new forensic technology -- for free.

Here's how it works. When DNA is taken from a crime scene, it is run through a computer program called CODIS (short for combined DNA Index System) to see if there is a match. If the owner of the suspect DNA has ever given a sample to law enforcement, the sample is in the CODIS database. But what if the forensic scientist doesn't find a match within CODIS? Are they dead in the DNA water? Not anymore.

With the new Colorado software, scientists can search CODIS again. The second time, they can look for DNA that is genetically similar to the crime-scene sample, sometimes so similar that scientists can determine blood relatives. The DNA might come from a parent, sibling, child or even a cousin or uncle. Armed with the DNA family connection, detectives staring at a cold case file suddenly find a whole new group of people to question.

Sounds like a fantastic new tool! Yet, familial searching is only being routinely used in Colorado and California.

In Colorado, the method has helped identify 10 subjects wanted on a variety of charges.

In California, a serial killer suspect in Los Angeles was identified using this method. Police called him the "Grim Sleeper" because he seemed to go dormant in between the murders of at least 10 women over more than 20 years. Saddled with an ice-cold case, California authorities decided to run DNA samples collected from saliva left on the bodies through a familial DNA search. Voila! They identified a young man named Christopher Franklin who was in the system for doing time on a felony weapons charge. Further investigation led police to 57-year-old Lonnie David Franklin, Christopher's father.

Once police had him as a suspect, an undercover detective posing as a waiter collected the elder Franklin's plate, utensils and leftover food from a restaurant, and the DNA sample taken from a piece of pizza crust matched the DNA left on the bodies of the dead women long ago.

The case suddenly came back to life. Franklin is now awaiting trial on multiple charges of murder.

The state of Illinois is thinking about using the familial DNA method to help solve a cold case from 2008 involving the mysterious murders of five women who worked at a Lane Bryant clothing store.

Both Pennsylvania and Virginia have already taken up Colorado's generous offer to share the familial DNA software. Officials in both states are studying possible legal ramifications before plunging into this brave new world. They understand there are cautions regarding familial DNA.

The state of Maryland, for example, has flat-out rejected the idea because, as the chief of forensics for the public defender's office declared, it would have placed half the state's African-American families under possible scrutiny because of the sheer number of black men who've been arrested and have given DNA samples in the CODIS system.

This promising new technology couldn't be approved fast enough for Dan and Gil Harrington, a Virginia couple who have been agonizing over who might have murdered their beautiful daughter, Morgan. She disappeared after leaving a concert in October 2009. That is, until her badly decomposed body was found months later in a field nine miles south of Charlottesville.

DNA found on Harrington's body was ultimately linked to the person who committed a brutal rape in Fairfax, Virginia, some 90 miles away, four years earlier. Who who would rape and murder young women? The Harringtons believe a familial DNA search might hold the clue, and they don't understand what's taking so long to do it. I don't understand, either.

The American Civil Liberties Union commented after the Grim Sleeper suspect was arrested to warn that a familial DNA search is not the "silver bullet" that prosecutors suggest. The ACLU worries that privacy concerns and civil-rights concerns have not been adequately addressed, and they worry that blacks might be unfairly singled out.

The district attorney of Denver said it best in a recent debate when he reminded that while African-Americans account for 13 percent of the population, they were the victims in nearly half of America's homicides in 2005.

Don't they deserve the best forensic investigations have to offer, too? And let's not forget that DNA evidence also exonerates innocent people.

I vote for every state to adopt familial DNA search techniques ASAP!

Failure to Test Is a Failure of Justice

July 30, 2011

The evidence had been there all along. It had been sitting on a shelf inside a cold storage facility at the Houston Police Department for 12 years. After a determined detective tracked it down and sent it off to the lab for testing, the state of Texas realized it had a found a serial rapist.

The criminal's name is Roland Ali Westbrooks, and his story highlights why every state in the union should make testing of backlogged rape kits a top priority.

For more than two decades, law enforcement has had the ability to take even the tiniest specks of evidence from a rape victim -- bodily fluids, stray hairs, fingernail scrapings -- and match the DNA findings to information stored in a national database called CODIS. Every time a rape kit is processed, the DNA print is supposed to be entered into CODIS. And the reason for this is simple: Rapists rape repeatedly. They hardly ever have just one victim.

One study on serial offenders puts the average number of a rapist's victims at seven, while another study puts it at 11. To put this in perspective, realize that if we get just one of these perps off the street, we've prevented future crimes. Every year in America there are roughly 200,000 reported rapes, and it is not just women who are attacked. Ten percent of all rape victims are men.

We know that the first time Westbrooks struck was in August 1995. It was a nighttime home invasion, and his victim was a complete stranger -- a teenager girl alone in her bedroom. Houston police say as he put a pillow over the 16-year-old's face and threatened to kill her if she screamed. The girl reported the attack immediately and submitted to a complete rape examination. Like tens of thousands of other rape kits nationwide, her evidence package was never processed, and no one was ever arrested for her brutal assault.

After a cold case detective re-opened the teen's case earlier this year and ordered the DNA in her kit to finally be processed, Westbrooks was identified as her rapist. The good news was that he was already in jail! The bad news was that he was in prison because he had been convicted of another rape, a crime that occurred in 1997 -- two years after he attacked the teenager. That attack might never have taken place if the 16-year-old's rape kit had been tested in a timely manner. Police suspect Westbrooks had more victims and are investigating that now.

To be sure, states have made some progress in winnowing down their backlog of rape kits. When I first wrote about this topic in 2008 there were 400,000 bundles of untested evidence. Today, the best estimates put the national number at about 180,000. But that's still way too many.

Sometimes lab work isn't necessary, as police have already gotten a confession, or the victim withdraws the complaint. But in too many other cases it becomes a matter of indifference, inconvenience or finances. Each test costs about $1,500.

In most jurisdictions, it is still up to the discretion of the investigating detective whether to order a full lab analysis of a rape kit. Usually the victim is never told whether her evidence has been processed or relegated to a shelf to gather dust.

I can think of no other crime where police have definitive evidence of a crime and fail to process it. I think it is unconscionable.

Information from these kits, entered into CODIS, would likely mean numerous outstanding sex crimes could be solved. Perpetrators could be identified, taken off the streets, or, if they're already behind bars, slapped with a longer prison sentence, just like Westbrooks. More importantly, victims could finally feel a sense of justice.

It's already happening in Texas. The popular Texas-based blog Grits for Breakfast (gritsforbreakfast.blogspot.com) reports that when "Tarrant County tested their entire backlog, they identified five serial rapists by matching the results to CODIS." Imagine, five dangerous criminals were able to be scooped up just by testing evidence that was already there!

May I be so blunt as to ask, what the heck we are waiting for? And don't tell me it's a matter of money. The money spent on processing these kits would be far less than what we would have to pay out to investigate and prosecute these rapists' future crimes.

I call for a nationwide initiative to examine every relevant kit. Let's get every state to dedicate one group of lab technicians to examine the most recent kits so as to stop currently active rapists. A second group should examine the oldest kits, keeping an eye out for the ones that might come up against a statute of limitations problem. Let's get that information into CODIS and see how many more perps we can get off the streets.

The perfect tool is already sitting there. If we would just use it! Anybody with me?

Laws to Catch Up With Science

Sept. 17, 2011

Many years ago, I was assigned to cover a story about a certain sperm donor, a newly graduated doctor in Kansas who had donated on such a frequent and regular basis that he was suspected of being the biological father of 500 children. You read that right, 500 children!

My research led me to learn that professors and medical mentors had often urged their male med school residents to donate sperm as a way to put a little money in their pockets and help propagate future generations of intelligent children. The belief was that if the sperm came from a person smart enough and driven enough to study to be a doctor, well, all of mankind could benefit from the children they would sire.

An elitist viewpoint, to be sure, but a prevalent one back in the early '90s.

A problem arose following this particular Kansas doctor's years of donating when it was learned that many of the recipients lived within a small radius. The children who resulted from this man's donations began to grow up within miles of each other, and as they matured into teenagers, attending the same schools, churches or sport camps, they began to become attracted to one another, pulled together by an unexplainable and invisible magnet of familiarity. Some of the teens began dating and were sexually attracted to one another. Accidental incest was a real possibility -- if it hadn't already happened -- I was told.

In some instances the children did not know of their test-tube beginnings. In almost all other cases, the parents were completely unaware of how many siblings their sons or daughters might have or that that their children could be romantically interested in their own half-sister or half-brother.

I reported back then that the sperm bank was urgently trying to locate all the recipients of this particular doctor's donations and make a geographic registry of where his offspring landed. Oh, if they had only been so diligent from the beginning!

Flash forward to today, some two decades later, and the law still hasn't caught up with the science.

There are still no cohesive federal or state laws regulating how many times an in vitro fertilization clinic can disseminate one man's sperm or in what geographic area it should be offered.

Clinics continue to rake in profits, but children born of this procedure have little more than a donor number to hold on to when they wonder about their paternal beginnings.

Sperm banks and IVF clinics keep secret such vital information as the father's name, address and where he can be reached if a specific health problem crops up for the child later in life.

And now, some donors are complaining about the system, too, saying they were hoodwinked about the number of children that might result from their donation.

"We have more rules that go into place when you buy a used car than when you buy sperm," Debora Spar, the author of "The Baby Business: How Money, Science and Politics Drive the Commerce of Conception," said to MSNBC. "It's very clear that the dealer can't sell you a lemon, and there's information about the history of the car. There are no such rules in the fertility industry right now," she says.

Since each donor has a unique tracking number, inquisitive parents have started independent registries online to track how many kids are born to particular donors. One woman found her IVF baby had more than 150 brothers and sisters! Others discover more than 50 offspring in their child's donor group.

The sudden realization that they have half-siblings or several dozens of half-siblings has to be confusing to many of the estimated 30,000 to 60,000 IVF babies born in the United States each year. Some families decide to try to meet their IVF relatives. Others choose never to tell their children about their biological beginnings.

Scientists worry about America's sperm donation system for a different reason. There is the possibility, they say, that our collective gene pool could be becoming skewed. If a popular donor has a defective gene that causes a rare disease, that disease will be a silent, ticking time bomb spreading more quickly and widely through the general population than it would otherwise.

I recently did some research on that Kansas doctor whose story I reported so many years ago. He is still in the same area and apparently has a successful psychiatry practice. I wonder if he ever stops to think about the psychological impact he's had on however many children he fathered.

Whether that doctor has stopped to rethink the ramifications of our current sperm donation system or not, I think it's high time some forward-thinking lawmakers do. We're way overdue for some laws governing this field.

Fooling with Mother Nature almost never turns out well.

Your Body Telegraphs Your Lies

July 24, 2012

So, have you heard the stories about how to beat a polygraph test? Ever read any of the odd suggestions on the internet?

Among them: Silently count backward from 100 during the test to distract your brain; learn to control your breathing; put a tack in your shoe or bite down hard on your tongue to elicit a pain response; and -- the one that makes me laugh the hardest -- contract your anal sphincter muscle to confuse the machine.

Do any of these methods work? According to the experts, they do not. In fact, if used they can actually make innocent people look guilty.

Jack Trimarco is one of the country's pre-eminent polygraph analysts. He was with the FBI for 21 years, heading up the Los Angeles Polygraph Unit, and he figures he's conducted some 2,500 lie detector tests all over the world. Trimarco is the guy both cops and defense attorneys want to call in to get to the truth.

In the absence of DNA or some other conclusive evidence, a polygraph test -- given by an experienced examiner -- can be very valuable to a district attorney struggling with the decision of whether to file charges against a suspect.

I ran into Trimarco recently at the annual conference of the California Association of Licensed Investigators in San Diego, California.

"There are all these anti-polygraph internet sites out there," Trimarco explained to a room full of CALI members who had signed up to hear his presentation. "And they offer to tell you all the secrets of how to beat the test for $70."

Trimarco called such sites "terrible frauds" out to take worried peoples' money. "We professionals already know all the tricks they peddle and can spot them a mile away," he said in his quiet, but confident way.

Since the first modern-day lie detector machine was used back in 1921, the technology has evolved considerably, so much so that Trimarco is willing to reveal at least one major weapon polygraphists use today to detect those who try to cheat by using the "countermeasures" described above. It's called the "movement pad" or "pressure pad," and the person taking the test sits on it.

"It detects any muscle movement that could be a countermeasure," Trimarco told me. "If a person deliberately bites their tongue or squeezes their sphincter their physiology will change. When a person tells a lie their physiology changes, and they can't help it," he said.

The subject's sweat glands will activate, their blood pressure will jump and then decrease immediately, their respiration will change. And all this happens over the course of just a few seconds.

In other words, your body telegraphs your lies.

Pam Shaw, the president of the American Polygraph Association, admits: "Every test can be beaten. But under polygraph, (that happens) under very, very narrow conditions."

Shaw says people who are required to take a polygraph to get or keep a job, or to prove to law enforcement they had nothing to do with a crime, understandably, get nervous before the test. Many hit the internet to research the polygraph process and run through horror stories about those who claim they were declared guilty when they were not. After reading the sometimes cockamamie-sounding suggestions to manipulate the test, their anxiety might cause them to resort to using countermeasures.

Shaw told me during a phone conversation: "They feel they have to enhance the outcome ... and what really happens? What really happens is truthful people end up hurting themselves." And Shaw's best advice to those facing a polygraph test? "Let your body do what it does naturally," she says.

Polygraph testing has always been controversial, but at this point it is not going away. The real problem, according to those in the upper echelon of the industry, is not the machine's reliability, but those barely trained, uncertified operators who try to pass themselves off as experienced. Charlatan examiners posing as pros can be found nationwide, especially in states like California, where, for some reason, lawmakers refuse to acknowledge or certify qualified polygraphists.

Currently, only one state -- New Mexico -- has fully embraced the idea that polygraph results are admissible in court, but only if examiners follow strict certification guidelines. Most other states will allow the results to be presented to a jury if -- and it's a big if -- both sides of a case agree to do so. In the real world, that rarely happens. In federal court the judge decides if polygraph results are allowed.

Still, lots of employers, police departments and federal agencies require lie detector tests. If you are one of those who must take one, Trimarco has a warning for you, should you think you might be able to manipulate the results: "The only way to give an experienced, licensed polygrapher a run for their money is for the (test-taker) to be an experienced, licensed polygraph examiner themselves."

Open Up DNA Databases to All

Jan. 26, 2013

The scene: A criminal courtroom anywhere in America.

The players: A judge, a prosecutor, a defense attorney and the accused.

The assumption: that all parties involved enjoy a level playing toward the twin goals of discovering the truth and finding justice.

The fact: In many criminal cases the prosecution holds the key to what could be the most important evidence of the trial: DNA. Prosecutors in most states have exclusive access to CODIS, the national database of more than 11 million DNA samples, which is considered to be the gold standard in forensic-based investigations. CODIS is used in two ways: to match a known suspect to a crime and to find an unknown suspect who may have been entered into the system years earlier.

Surely you've seen TV cop shows where a lab technician simply punches a bit of information into the computer to try to find a match with DNA gathered from a crime scene. CODIS results are easy and remarkably fast to get, and widely considered to be extremely accurate.

So, why doesn't everyone get to have access to the system? Consider that we, the American taxpayers, have paid out multimillions of dollars (ever since the DNA Identification Act was passed in 1994) annually to build this massive database of DNA samples. But if we find ourselves in trouble and our lawyer discovers DNA evidence that needs to be checked out, we're not allowed access? Does that sound fair to you?

Over the last decade or so, there have been dozens upon dozens of reported cases where an attorney for a convict -- a person who has always maintained their innocence -- has dug deep into the case file and found untested DNA that could exonerate their client. But often when they return to court to ask for the right to test the new evidence, they are told judges don't have the power to force prosecutors to retest.

Prosecutors are duty-bound to turn over to the defense all the evidence they have, but sometimes they fail to do so. Sometimes they don't even realize what their own investigators have missed.

Currently there are only nine states with laws that grant defense attorneys access to DNA databases. I think the rest of the country should join Colorado, Georgia, Illinois, Maryland, Mississippi, New York, North Carolina, Ohio and Texas. That one side gets to keep such important information all to itself means there is not the level playing field our criminal justice system demands.

Almost every state has a law permitting some post-conviction DNA testing (although the Supreme Court ruled a few years ago that it is not a constitutional right), but it is done at the discretion of the prosecutor, and they very rarely jump at the chance to reopen a convict's case.

Each of them would likely declare that they are in the business of "finding justice," yet there are cases on record where, to cite just one, a new DNA test showed that the semen found in a 16-year-old rape victim did not match that of the Long Island, N.Y., man convicted of the crime. Well, after the revelation, the prosecutor continued to insist he had convicted the right man and that the girl had engaged in consensual sex. The victim's mother and best friend swore she was a virgin.

As University of Virginia Law Professor Brandon Garrett says, "(Prosecutors) are attached to their convictions, and they don't want to see their work called into question." Hey, who wants to take one out of their own win column, right?

Now, look. I'm not naive enough to think that every defense attorney petitioning for a new DNA test will be on the up-and-up. Yes, some might be on a fishing expedition on behalf of their client. But, as with everything in the justice system, standards can be established for retesting, and a balance sheet can be kept of offending attorneys. Believe me, none of them want to be reported to their state ethics board for reprimand or suspension.

Government and judicial watchdog groups maintain that hundreds, and maybe thousands, of prisoners could substantiate their innocence if only they could tap the CODIS system. Some convicts say they falsely confessed to crimes they did not commit after being deprived of sleep and enduring day-long interrogation sessions. (This happens more often than you think.) Other prisoners maintain they were wrongly convicted and just want a chance to prove it.

Groups like The Innocence Project estimate that in the last 15 years some 300 prisoners have been given access to DNA databases and won their freedom.

I cannot confirm the 300 figure, but what if someone you loved was unfairly convicted? Wouldn't you want them to have every chance to prove their innocence? It might cost a bit more to fully open the database to both sides, but if it frees innocent people, isn't it worth it?

It won't surprise you to learn that the National Association of Criminal Defense Lawyers is all for the idea of opening up the CODIS system. The group's president, Steven Benjamin, says, "Science doesn't belong to the government, but they act like it does."

But guess what: Even the National District Attorneys Association agrees with the idea. The NDAA's executive director, Scott Burns, has said, "It seems like there should be laws for it, and I agree that the defense should be given the information."

Well, OK then. Let's really start leveling the playing field, shall we?

What's Really in That Coffin?

Feb. 17, 2013

The worldwide headlines say it all.

In the United Kingdom: "Pathologist 'Stockpiled Children's Organs.'" In Canada, the headline reads, "Ontario Service Has 4,000 Autopsy Organs, Unmatched to Families." This shocking headline appeared in Las Vegas, Nevada: "Misplaced. Thrown away. Stolen. Sold? Nobody Knows What Happened to Richard Boorman's Missing Organs." And in New York one read, "Parents Shocked to Learn Examiner Kept Son's Brain."

The cleverest headline for this macabre topic: "The Great Brain Robbery."

It is the last thing grieving next-of-kin should have to worry about. But if burying an intact body is important to a family's religious, moral or ethical beliefs, they should ask the funeral home to make sure all their loved one's organs are in place.

Now, I understand that student doctors and pathologists need to study, hold and dissect human organs to become good physicians. But I always thought those organs were donated. That's why I checked the donor box on the back of my driver's license, right? But that's not always the case. Sometimes medical examiners hold back organs of the dead and their families have no idea.

If pressed for an answer, a pathologist would likely justify the action by explaining it is for the advancement of science. But what about the rights of the dead?

It has been revealed that a medical examiner's office in New York kept the brains of more than 9,200 people over the last eight years. From that finding came two particular stories I will never forget.

First was the case of Jesse Shipley, who died in a horrible car accident at the age of 17. Two months after his funeral, Shipley's Staten Island classmates happened to be on a field trip to the local morgue. There, in a glass jar on a shelf, floated a human brain with the label JESSE SHIPLEY. That is how Shipley's parents came to realize they had buried their son without his brain: Tearful classmates told them.

The Shipley case changed the rules in the Empire State. Henceforth, medical examiners are required to fully inform next of kin if any organs were held back for examination. Families can then choose to postpone the funeral until all tests are complete and the organs are returned or to proceed with burial or cremation.

The second case involved a woman named Cindy Bradshaw. Her attorney, Daniel Flanzig, told me her sorrowful story. Last May, Bradshaw buried her stillborn son, who died from an abnormality in the umbilical cord and placenta. Just hours after little Gianni's funeral, the medical examiner's office called to inform her (under the Shipley regulation) that it still had the baby's brain.

Too little effort, too late.

"Why did they keep the brain?" Flanzig asked. "They already knew the cause of death. Our research shows the baby's brain was retained for the purposes of research," he said.

Indeed, there is an abundant supply of adult brains available for autopsy, but a newborn's brain is a rare commodity for pathologists to study.

Different states have different procedures for medical examiners to follow, and not all require the upfront honesty that New York has tried to instill. Aggrieved families can sue in civil court, claiming their common-law right of sepulcher (the right to find "solace and comfort in the ritual of burial," as one judge explained) has been violated, but none of these missing-organ cases is considered to be a crime. Only the black-market sale of organs rises to the level of a felony criminal case.

There are those who might think: "Well, the person is dead. What does it matter?" Please, don't tell that to Mary Jane and Dan McCann of Fairfax County, Virginia. I spoke to an agonized Mary Jane McCann last week and wrote about the McCanns' sad case last year. For four years now, they have tirelessly fought the Baltimore, Maryland, medical examiner's finding that their 16-year-old daughter, Annie, committed suicide by drinking Bactine. (The honor-roll student carried a small bottle of Bactine to cleanse her newly pierced ears.)

The makers of the antiseptic and other prominent medical examiners pooh-pooh the idea that Bactine could cause death. In reviewing McCann's autopsy seven months after her burial, her devoutly Catholic parents were shocked to find that her brain and heart had not been interred with her.

As her parents put it, "The state has no right to abort our effort at a Christian burial by carelessly losing our Annie's brain and heart -- her very essence."

To make matters worse, they still can't find out if Annie McCann was raped. The Baltimore police say they must get that information from the medical examiner's office. The ME then refers them back to the police. It's a Catch-22, Baltimore style.

This may not be an important issue in your life -- not yet, anyway -- but for countless Americans like the Shipleys, the Bradshaws and the McCanns, it has left a gaping wound in their souls.

I think it is time for a uniform set of standards that requires each state and every medical professional who deals with the dead to be responsible for restoring deceased patients to their pre-autopsy condition. If an organ must be held for further examination -- a brain, for example, must harden in a formaldehyde solution for several weeks before it can be biopsied -- then full notification to the family must be made.

Withholding organs without permission may not constitute a crime, but in my book it's a crime against nature.

DNA and Death Row

Nov. 23, 2013

In this time of economic strain, anyone who doesn't look at ways to cut their personal or professional budget is just not being responsible. The same goes for the justice system.

For nearly two decades, lawyers working with death-row inmates have spent countless hours, court time and tens of millions of dollars fighting for access to DNA testing. These attorneys work right up until execution time to win court orders for DNA tests on crime-scene evidence or DNA of the condemned prisoner.

I could never figure out why so much time and money was spent fighting for condemned peoples' last chance to establish their innocence. Don't we want to make sure we're executing the right person? Now that DNA technology has become so advanced, isn't that one extra step the necessary and honorable thing to do?

Since 1992, when the Innocence Project was founded, which was designed to help prisoners who could be exonerated through DNA testing, more than 300 convicts have been set free, including 18 who were on death row.

Some might see the death-row DNA fight as a stalling tactic used by crafty lawyers for an obviously guilty person. That might certainly be true in some cases. But ask the 18 death-row inmates exonerated by the Innocence Project if their final DNA fight was worth it.

Most states have statutes allowing access to post-conviction DNA testing, but none are automatic and almost all of them come with strict restrictions or absolute deadlines for use. District attorney's offices routinely fight defense requests for DNA testing -- as if to say each of their prosecutions were perfect and never needs review. What are they afraid of?

Well, here's an idea that could reap double dividends. First, Congress needs to get past its partisan paralysis and pass a federal law mandating automatic DNA testing of inmates who have been sentenced to die. Test each of America's 3,125 death-row inmates whose DNA has never been collected, and register the DNA with the national database CODIS -- no questions asked.

The argument, of course, will be that DNA tests are costly. Really? Compared to what? Research shows they average between

$350 and $1,800, depending on the laboratory used. Compare that to the accumulated big-ticket costs of lawyers, judges, prosecutors and court staff and it's easy to see that paying a bit up front could actually save taxpayer dollars in the long run. It could also save an innocent person's life.

Most importantly, mandated DNA tests could more quickly identify innocent inmates, which, in turn, could alert police to the fact that there is still a dangerous criminal on the loose. It's estimated that the exonerated spend about 13 years in prison before they are released.

That's too many years to allow a guilty party to roam the streets preying on others.

Another budget point: The longer you keep a wrongfully convicted person in prison, the more the state is liable to pay out in compensation. Isn't it smarter to spend a bit of money today (on DNA tests) and spare the state a potentially large payout later?

About half the states have no actual statute for compensation on the books, but that doesn't mean they don't pay out huge sums. In California, for example, a state law awards up to $100 for each day a wrongfully convicted person spent in prison. (Multiply that by the average 13 years and it totals about $475,000. Realize that many of the exonerated have languished in prison for 25 years or more. For a quarter century of wrongful imprisonment a California inmate could receive more than $912,000.) Missouri is less generous, offering $50 for each day, but that's still a nice nest egg for a newly released prisoner. In Florida an exonerated person can get $50,000 for each year spent behind bars, with a maximum of $2 million.

Here's that second dividend I mentioned: DNA testing could help solve cold cases and provide answers to families that have been waiting years for news on what happened to their loved ones.

While there are some wrongfully convicted inmates in prison, most of the people who populate death row didn't get there by being choirboys. A vast majority committed multiple crimes before winding up where they did -- crimes that range from burglary and robbery to bank robbery and murder. By including their DNA in the CODIS network, law enforcement agencies around the country could tap into it to see if there's a connection to their cold cases.

There has been a recent push to take DNA from all newly arrested citizens, and those results wind up in the national database automatically. But there are prisoners who have been incarcerated for decades who never got the cheek-swab test for DNA.

Can you imagine the backlog of criminal cases that might be solved if each and every prisoner were included in the CODIS system? A study of 41 serial rapists, for example, showed that before they were imprisoned, they admitted they had collectively raped 837 times and attempted the crime against more than 400 others. If DNA was left behind at the crime scenes, those open cases could be closed and victims could be assured their attacker was behind bars.

Yes, it would take money to accomplish such an all-inclusive prisoner DNA system. But I maintain there's nothing more important than good, solid information, a guide to identifying the known criminal element. It would be money much more wisely spent than endless court fights because it would reap definitive evidence that would go toward the common good.

It's way past time for justice-system bean counters to think outside the box.

Pets Help Solve Crimes

April 5, 2014

As far as crime laboratories go, they don't look very impressive. And they usually have a permanent staff of just three forensic scientists and a few interns. But the work that comes out of the Veterinarian Forensic Lab at the University of California, Davis is important, and it has changed the way crimes are investigated and prosecuted worldwide.

The lab has been called the "CSI of the four-legged world," and it is the nation's first laboratory dedicated to animal DNA profiling. It's accredited by the prestigious American Society of Crime Lab Directors because the VFL conducts animal-related forensic tests as rigorously as any lab dealing with human DNA.

Simply put, the VFL uses animal DNA to help solve a variety of crimes -- from burglary to animal abuse to sexual assault to murder. They analyze crime scene evidence that decades ago might have been overlooked by detectives. Today, investigators automatically collect any animal fur or hairs, feces, urine stains and tissue samples found at a crime scene. They also take mouth swabs from pets after they defend their owners against attackers.

The case that helped establish the lab came from New Hampton, Iowa, in 1999. A sexual assault victim was not able to pick her attacker out of a police lineup. But she remembered that as she stood near the man's truck to answer his request for directions, her dog lifted his leg and urinated on one of the tires. Two days later, police found the truck, swabbed the tire and the lab (then the foremost test center for blood-typing cattle) was able to place the suspect where he insisted he had never been -- alongside the victim. That conviction convinced everyone of the need for a full-time animal-DNA testing lab.

The VFL's director, Beth Wictum, told me the lab handles about 100 cases every year. She's particularly proud of the lab's work on a grisly triple homicide case out of Indiana. The suspect insisted he did not stand at the spot where three workmen were shot execution style. But police found a shoe print left behind in a poop patty and scooped up the evidence for evaluation. The lab was able to genetically match the droppings to the property owner's dog and a pencil eraser-sized specimen taken from the suspect's shoe. Bingo! The suspect was convicted and is serving life in prison.

On Christmas Eve 2002, Kevin Butler became the victim of a deadly home invasion. When two men stormed into Butler's Dallas apartment and began to beat him, his prized cockatoo -- named Bird for basketball great Larry Bird -- tried to come to Butler's rescue. He repeatedly dove down on the attackers, clawing at their skin and pecking at their heads. Sadly, police found Bird dead on the kitchen floor, stabbed to death with a fork.

But in the blood trails Bird created and on the valiant pet's beak they found human DNA. The lab matched the specimens to the prime suspect and helped put Butler's murderer behind bars for life. Director Wictum says her forensic team is "often asked to test cat and dog hairs from blankets, rugs and sheets that are wrapped around homicide victims." Such a cold case out of Florida is Wictum's current favorite.

The body of Shantay Huntington was found in a wooded area of Loxahatchee, Florida, wrapped in a shower curtain. Crime scene investigation agents found dog hairs on the curtain and sent them to the VFL for testing. The lab identified the hairs as matching a family of dogs that were raised by Liliana Toledo. When questioned, she pointed the finger at Guillermo Romero, her former brother-in-law, who she described as terrifying and violent. He was raising two of the Akita puppies. When police got a DNA sample from Romero it also matched DNA on the curtain. Case solved.

Besides its work in the U.S., the VFL has worked on criminal investigations in several countries including Japan, Ireland, Canada, Australia and Argentina. Scotland Yard approached the lab to help solve the death of a bouncer who was stabbed outside a pub. Drops of nonhuman blood had flummoxed the Brits.

"We did the testing," Wictum said during a radio interview, "and we were able to match the blood on the sidewalk to the suspect's dog, which had apparently had his ear nicked during the altercation." It was the first time dog DNA was used in a U.K. trial.

Bereft pet owners often contact the lab to find out how their beloved Fluffy or Fido died. Wictum remembers one particular case in which a woman was sure that a certain neighbor's dog had killed her cat. DNA tests of the cat's wounds proved the culprit was a bobcat.

The lab works on lots of dog-on-human attack cases, many of them involving children. In fact, one such case was upgraded to a homicide after the female victim was taken off life support and died. But the staff at VFL knows firsthand that what humans do to animals can be just as vicious.

Law enforcement in Florida had its eye on a suspected serial animal abuser and sent items to the lab for testing. Police believed this man had started out torturing hamsters, graduated to shooting razor arrows at livestock and then began killing goats and llamas in hideous ways. The lab was able to link the suspect to the grisly crimes when they identified the blood on his shirt as being from a llama. After the arrest, the lead detective breathed a sigh of relief.

"He told me that they were going to keep an eye on him once he got out of prison because he was looked to be at high risk for eventually killing people," Wictum said.

All of us with pets have a special bond -- a special way of communicating with our beloved animals. Now, thanks to the Veterinarian Forensic Lab, whether the animal is the victim, the perpetrator or simply a witness to a crime, they can communicate with the courts as well.

~~~

CHAPTER 3
Inside the Courtroom

"Justice has nothing to do with what goes on in a courtroom; Justice is what comes out of a courtroom." ~ Clarence Darrow, lawyer, circa 1925

"Money will determine whether the accused goes to prison or walks out of the courtroom a free man." ~ Johnnie Cochran, lawyer, circa 1995

Today, it's simplistic to think that every defendant in every courtroom will get an equal shot at justice. Yes, that's the foundation upon which our judicial system was built, and back in Clarence Darrow's day it might have been more likely. But a lot has changed since then.

Now there are dream teams of defense lawyers, jury consultants who can pluck the most desirable jurors from a jury pool and massive, state-sponsored prosecutions that roll over defendants not wealthy enough to take on the United States of America.

Back in 1924, when Darrow famously won life sentences (instead of death sentences) for two wealthy, spoiled brats named Leopold and Loeb charged with murdering another teen, he netted about $30,000. In 1995, Johnnie Cochran and his team helped O.J. Simpson walk away from double murder charges and earned millions of dollars. They also enjoyed millions more from writing books and giving speeches about their triumph, and the resulting publicity attracted even more wealthy clients who needed a dream team to get them out of trouble.

The idea that there is "green justice" in America -- the theory that whichever side has the most money wins -- is alive and well. Still, I find it fascinating to watch courtroom action, especially the faces of jurors who sit in judgment of their fellow citizens. Courthouses are like cauldrons -- all types of humanity are stirred together in one pot and served up into individual courtrooms to state their case.

How to Make 8K a Day

April 27, 2008

I know a man connected to the justice system who makes $8,000 a day.

You read that right. When he shows up in a courtroom for a client, his very presence and whispered advice to the lead attorney are worth $8,000 per day. And that's on top of lots of other services he's already charged for. He is a jury consultant.

This man has also been a good, confidential source of information for me in the past, so I cannot tell you his name. But I bring this up because I want Americans to understand what our system of justice has evolved into.

The consultant's firm offers a soup-to-nuts menu of services, and clients decide how much they want to spend. It goes without saying all the clients are wealthy. You and I would never be able to afford such "justice."

You're surely asking what the jury consultant does for all that money. Well, the minute a beleaguered client hires him the consultant's firm gets to work. Workers study and then travel to the trial location. They conduct intricate door-to-door surveys of the community and get to know the ethical, religious, family and occupational backgrounds of the potential jury pool, carefully noting every response.

The firm also works backward to fully understand how much publicity the client's case has already gotten in local media. If it has been extensive, then extra canvassing can be ordered up to try to gauge public opinion. Does the community already think the client is guilty? Would asking the court for a change of venue be the smartest course of action? If the answer is yes and the court agrees to move the trial, then the firm picks up and replants its costly door-to-door activities at the new trial location.

Charting all this information is an enormous amount of work, but it comes in handy later if the client chooses other services from the firm's a-la-cart menu.

Once the jury consultants understand the moral fiber of the locale in which their client will be tried for, say, murder or a major white-collar crime (think Enron), the big honcho, the 8K guy, gives his learned opinion about what type of juror should be chosen. He might decide more women should be seated or older, more professional men would be more likely to decide in the client's favor.

And as if that isn't enough service for you, hold onto your hats! In some of the biggest cases jury consultants hire people called "shadow jurors." Remember those door-to-door surveys? Well, once the real jury is seated the consultant can reach back into the extensive information files and pluck out people in the community that very nearly match the real jurors.

In other words, if juror No. 1 is a civil engineer and the father of two teenagers, the firm will find a virtual clone and hire that person for up to $500 a day to sit anonymously in the courtroom every day. If juror No. 5 is a young mother with an accounting background, they'll find another person from the community just like her and have her sit in, too. Sometimes as many as six or eight of these shadow jurors are hired to listen carefully to the proceedings.

At every break in the trial the shadows will huddle with defense attorneys to give real-time feedback on what they've seen and heard. They might tell the lawyer that he or she is turning off the jurors by being too harsh or loud. They may suggest certain lines of questioning the lawyer hadn't even thought about. It's the closest a lawyer can get to getting inside the minds of the jurors.

Hiring a jury consultant doesn't automatically mean the wealthy accused will get off. Just ask Martha Stewart, who hired one of the most expensive jury firms around and lost anyway. During her five months in a West Virginia prison for lying about a stock transaction, she certainly must have asked herself whether her final six-figure bill was worth it.

But consider the case of murder defendant Robert Durst. He admitted to killing, beheading and hiding parts of his elderly Texas neighbor's body and was found not guilty. No matter that Durst had a long history of mental instability; no matter Durst had been a suspect in another murder. The jury, handpicked by one of the top jury consultants in America, found that Durst had acted in self-defense. Again, you and I could never afford such "justice."

The Impact of Victim Impact Statements

May 22, 2010

Imagine being in a room with the person who murdered your child. How would you react? What would you want to say to the killer?

Every day in America, grieving families congregate in courtrooms to watch justice meted out to those who've robbed them of their loved ones. Before the sentence is passed upon the accused, judges offer family members a chance to give a victim impact statement. It's the most dramatic, heart-wrenching moment of the entire judicial process.

Such a day played out recently in a San Diego, California, courtroom with a registered sex offender named John Gardner. He'd been out on parole less than five months after serving six years for sexually attacking a 13-year-old girl. At 31 years old, Gardner was living with his mother when he began preying on other young girls.

Gardner ultimately confessed to abducting, raping and murdering 14-year-old Amber Dubois and 17-year-old Chelsea King and brutally attacking another young woman, who testified about how she lived through the ordeal.

"Look at me!" King's mother, Kelly King, demanded of Gardner as she began reading her victim impact statement to the court. There was a long pause as Gardner, wearing his prison greens, slumped at the defendant's table, kept his chin low, but sheepishly glanced up for a split second.

And then, in a soft, eloquent voice, King compared the "wretched piece of evil" that is Gardner to her beautiful dead daughter: "She was a funny, a fun-loving girl, a gifted musician, a fiercely competitive athlete with a thirst for life. She couldn't wait to start college! I can never adequately articulate what you plundered from us and our community. You should burn in hell."

Brent King told the killer what it was like to be Chelsea's father. "I loved feeding her, playing with her, changing her diapers, just being her dad," he said. He called Gardner a coward for knowing he had a problem and ignoring it. King said he hoped Gardner lived every day of the rest of his life in prison in fear of fellow inmates. "You do not deserve a peaceful moment on this earth or the next life," he said.

Both Kings blamed a judicial system that allowed a dangerous predator to be freed.

Gardner's mother, a psychiatric nurse, knew what her son was capable of but did nothing to monitor or stop him, they said.

As I watched this play out, I wondered if I would have the strength to be so articulate in that circumstance. Or would I dissolve into a puddle of tears, unable to speak a word?

The statements given by the parents of Amber Dubois really tore my heart. They waited 13 months with no news about what had happened to their precious daughter. It was only after Gardner was arraigned on charges of murdering Chelsea King that he finally led police to Dubois' body and the awful truth was revealed.

Maurice Dubois compared Gardner to a mountain lion whose predilection to kill came naturally, so it was no surprise the murders began so soon after he was released from parole.

"(You) ... heartlessly discarded our beautiful 14-year-old girl, Amber," he said. "You will burn in hell for the acts you have committed. I just hope that day is an agonizingly long way away and that you have to suffer as much as we all have."

Then, Amber's mother, Carrie McGonigle, stepped forward to address the court. Her attorney had told me privately that she had been so consumed with knowing about her daughter's last moments on Earth that she requested and got a face-to-face meeting with John Gardner in prison. No details have been released, but can you imagine sitting down to talk with your child's killer?

McGonigle began saying, "After 15 months of the most agonizing pain, worry and grief, I'm supposed to address the court," She continued: "On Feb. 13, 2009, (Amber) innocently walked to school. I kissed her goodbye and said I loved her, not knowing it would be the last time. You took my best friend."

Amazingly, tears rolled down John Gardner's cheeks. Perhaps it was because he'd already met with McGonigle and she'd somehow gotten through to his perverted, criminal sense of right and wrong.

In courtrooms around America the victim-impact-statement scene plays out in varying degrees every day. Victims' families hope that somehow confronting the guilty will bring them some sort of vindication or peace. For some, it does.

McGonigle said the most remarkable thing to Gardner at the end of her message to the court that day. She said, "I forgive you, but I will never forget what you stole from me."

I know I'd never have the courage to say that.

Time for Professional Jurors?

May 21, 2011

Having spent the better part of the last two weeks watching an excruciatingly long jury selection for a capital murder case I'm left wondering, is it time for the United States to begin using professional jurors?

During the last couple weeks, I've watched intently as prospective jurors took the stand to explain to the court the financial hardship that leaving work to judge another would bring to their lives. Some of them work for employers who grant paid leave for jury duty, but often it covers only a day or two. Many others worked for struggling small businesses or are self-employed, and they explained that every day they didn't show up at work would result in lost profit or a day's pay docked off their paycheck.

The questioning of the jurors -- called "voir dire" -- to determine their suitability to serve was emotional and sometimes embarrassing. Yet many of those who were hoping hard not to be picked told the judge they recognized their civic duty and felt badly that they were unable to serve.

Besides harsh financial hardships jurors can face from serving jury duty during this economically topsy-turvy time, there is the issue of laypersons trying to decipher intricate legal language and instructions. For the most part, today's jurors have no training in the law and wouldn't know a dictum from a disjunctive allegation. They're given a super-crash course in the law applicable to their particular case, but overall the system isn't friendly.

During trial, jurors are not allowed to pass notes to the judge or raise their hands to ask a question if they don't understand something. And, let's admit, for most of us much of what lawyers say in court is mumbo-jumbo. In addition, some states don't allow jurors to take notes in court or have a copy of their instructions in the deliberation room. They are often put into the deliberation room with no idea how to even begin to talk about a verdict.

Add to this confusing realm the possibility that panelists might be exposed to grisly crime scene photos or autopsy photos of small children. In rare trials they might be asked to vote on whether the defendant should be put to death for the crime they committed. Some citizens can take the strain and bounce back from judging others, while others come away shell-shocked.

All in all, jury duty is an awesome responsibility, and it has been known to change the lives of those who serve.

I can't help thinking there might be a better, less intrusive way for all of us to have access to fair, impartial, educated panels to hear court cases about anything from murder and medical malpractice to organized drug kingpins and corporate fraudsters.

Now, if you're thinking professional jurors wouldn't constitute a "jury of your peers," realize that nowhere in the U.S. Constitution are we promised that. We are not guaranteed a panel that looks just like us -- Barbie the teacher, Bob the carpenter or Diane the journalist. The Constitution simply ensures American citizens a "right of trial by jury."

So who's to say that a jury can't be composed of a group of people whose occupation is that of a professional juror? The requirement could be for them to take a one- or two-year study course before being assigned to hear cases. Courts would save the paltry daily sums they currently pay jurors and put them into a pot to pay these pros a living wage.

Another idea that has been floated is for retired judges, lawyers or law professors to serve as jurors, as they are already educated in the ways of the courtroom. Critics of this idea worry that these legal eagles will overthink the cases they hear or exert undue influence over other professional jurors of lesser status.

Look, nothing is perfect. Our current system certainly is not, which we see in the increasing number of cases overturned when new DNA evidence is found. So isn't it time to take a serious investigative look at ways that would possibly make it better?

I ran the idea of turning retired legal types into jurors by a dear friend of mine. He startled me by asking, "What percentage increase in the conviction rate do you think there'd be with professional jurors?" He believes the legal fraternity would act like judges as well as jurors in their minds, and he predicted the conviction rate would jump considerably.

I'm not so sure. But then again, neither is anyone else -- because we've never fully tested the idea.

I just remember the haunted looks I've seen on the faces of many jurors I've encountered covering court cases throughout my career.

Some have told me in post-trial interviews they found it hard to concentrate in the unfamiliar territory of a courtroom. During the proceedings they worried about their jobs, families and peace of mind.

If there are citizens better suited for this job, people who could more keenly focus on the job at hand, don't we owe it to everyone involved in the system to try them out?

Bravery in the Witness Box

June 16, 2012

They're all different, the men who come forward to tell their stories of childhood sexual abuse. But they all share a debilitating, horrorific memory.

Psychologists say it is difficult for any victim of childhood molestation to reveal what happened to them. But it is particularly tough for young males because it goes to the very core of their budding manhood. Often, males choose to keep it secret rather than seek help to deal with the emotional problems that always occur.

So, when these victims muster up enough courage to speak, I think it's time we start praising them. They are the ultimate moral whistleblowers in our society, helping to keep children safe by identifying, convicting and removing child molesters from our midst.

I also think it's time we understand what happens when these brave souls finally begin to talk. They reveal only when they feel safe, and they disclose details of their abuse in stages.

In every criminal trial I've covered involving an accused pedophile, defense attorneys pounce on the accusers, saying their stories have evolved once they began talking to the authorities -- child protective services workers, police officers and grand juries. They criticize because they know the victims are vulnerable in the beginning.

When the accusers disclose, they may say at first that only fondling occurred. The next time they are interviewed they will divulge more -- if they feel safe with the interviewer. They may subsequently admit there was oral activity or actual penetration. As time passes and they are able to mentally distance themselves from their molesters, the full story flushes out.

In court, however, the accusers are routinely attacked for not divulging the whole story from the very beginning. It's just not fair, and it's counterintuitive to the way the real-life world of victim reporting works. Experts will confirm that abused and untrusting people never sit down and blurt out the whole story of their horrible experience, in part because they don't understand it themselves in the beginning. They ask themselves: "Why didn't I scream, 'NO!' from the get-go? Why did I voluntarily return to the abuser? Why didn't I seek protection from someone at home or school? What is the matter with me?" Think about your deepest, darkest secret. Can you imagine how difficult it would be to repeatedly tell strangers about it? These victims have to tell theirs to detectives, mental health workers, prosecutors and, ultimately, jurors.

I've watched this legally sanctioned witness attack (disguised as cross-examination) occur yet again, at the Bellefonte, Pennsylvania, trial of former Penn State University assistant football coach Jerry Sandusky. This is not to say I think accusers shouldn't face tough questioning. Of course they should. But manufactured red herrings should be excluded.

I wish every child sexual abuse trial could begin with an easy-to-understand testimony from a mental health professional so jurors could really understand a victim's reporting mentality. Jurors should be made aware that evolving facts in a victim's sworn statement should be put into perspective.

And one more thing that, frankly, all of us need to understand: There is no single way a victim is supposed to act. You can't always see on the outside how a person is suffering on the inside. At the Sandusky trial, there are no actual "victims" until the jury declares there are victims. There are only accusers at this stage of the game, and Sandusky is to be considered completely innocent.

But I was struck by the different demeanor of everyone who took to the witness box. Some were feisty during their testimony; some were so quiet they were told to speak up so the jury could hear them. And then there was the 18-year-old young man who just graduated from high school and has been waiting three long years -- and has testified at three grand jury proceedings -- for justice so he can get on with his life. The moment he stepped into the courtroom, observers could tell from his tortured body language he was a damaged soul. He sobbed through his testimony and spoke of the anxiety attacks he suffers. I was among those in the gallery left wondering if he will ever mature into a complete and happy adult. He is a hero in my book.

We like to think we've got a handle on child molesters and their victims so we can wave our hands and declare that we need hear no more about it. Cases like the Sandusky trial are "too ugly to hear," as I heard one network news executive say recently, as if it's just not fashionable to discuss.

That is nonsense. This is very important stuff for generations to come. We can stamp out the cyclical scourge of pedophilia if we put our minds to it, but that will never be achieved if we keep burying our heads in the sand because it's "too ugly."

The pretty part of it comes when we realize we have a justice system that is more primed now than ever to deal with these cases. Let's encourage everyone to understand it and use it so that everyone benefits.

Only Adults Can Stop Pedophiles

June 30, 2012

It was the most raw and emotionally brutal court case I've ever sat through: the Commonwealth of Pennsylvania v. Jerry Sandusky. Eight young men ranging in age from 18 to 28 testified about their loss of innocence at the hands of a serial pedophile who plucked his prey out of the ranks of his own charity. The powerful and often tearful testimonies came at us rat-a-tat-tat. Observers felt smacked in between the eyes at the end of every day.

In the end, Sandusky was found guilty of 45 out of 48 charges of sexual abuse. I suppose you could call it a victory for the damaged young men who climbed into the witness box and sobbed, gasping for breath as they told their gut-wrenching stories. But really no one wins. Not even if the victims get a monetary settlement from Penn State University, the institution that first learned of Sandusky's proclivities back in 1998 and still let him roam the campus and locker rooms with his young targets in tow. Talk about enablers!

I began reporting on high-profile suspected pedophiles 19 years ago when I became the first to tell the world that California police had targeted Michael Jackson as a possible molester of boys. I followed the Jackson story for more than a decade, and as I sat in the Sandusky courtroom, I marveled at the parallels.

Although a jury found Jackson not guilty on all counts, his behavior and that of Sandusky, in my opinion, are classic case studies of how a serial, predatory pedophile acts.

Both men were famous -- one admired on an international stage, the other in his community and the world of sports. Both men projected an aura of truly caring about children. With a full-scale amusement park, zoo and movie theater, Jackson outfitted his Neverland Ranch to be the quintessential child magnet.

Sandusky, as we learned through testimony, designed his own boy cave in the basement of his home, complete with games, a dartboard, a pool table, an air hockey table, a television and a water bed. Both men focused on boys from single-parent homes, where beleaguered mothers were grateful to have who they saw as a positive father figure for their boys.

When questioned about their constant proximity to other peoples' young sons, both Jackson and Sandusky professed that the world did not understand their actions, that they "truly love" all children. And they made a point to sprinkle a few girls among the crowd of boys to cover up their secret lust.

When their actions were exposed, both men very publically turned on the very people they claimed they loved so much, the children, calling them liars, money-grubbers and conniving manipulators who were out to hurt a great man for some unexplained reason.

It was sickening to watch years ago, but it was even more sickening sitting in that courtroom the last couple of weeks and realizing the general population still doesn't know how to spot a pedophile on the prowl.

I get weary wondering how long it will take to convince people that pedophiles really are the people you don't think they could ever be. They are the most charming, personable, charitable and kid-friendly people you could meet. They pay their taxes, go to church, have respectable jobs and cloak themselves in acts of charity. They tell you they just want to help you by being a positive influence in your child's life.

Remember, pedophiles are on the hunt all the time, and it is their charm that gets them past the parents so that they can prey. When they get caught, they rely on authorities comparing their "upstanding" lives to the lives of the single parent and troubled kid who is making the allegations. Too often detectives have believed the perpetrators' version of events, and they are left alone to violate again.

I don't want to turn parents into monsters of suspicion, but the only way to stop pedophiles from targeting children is for grown-ups to learn how to identify them. If an overly friendly person has a "special place" they take kids, if they are always surrounded by either all boys or all girls, or if they take kids home to watch movies (a typical grooming tool is to "mistakenly" show pornography to a child to gauge the reaction), if the child comes home in an uncharacteristically somber mood or with wet hair or clothes - get suspicious. The warning signs are often there; the adults just need to pay attention.

Parents: You can educate your children about the difference between a good touch and bad touch, but again, these serial predators are so masterful at what they do that your child will already be victimized by the time they realize what kind of touch they've just received.

Look, we know the damage childhood sexual abuse causes. Victimized kids grow into angry, troubled adults. So when do we break the cycle? How do we let all children know they must never keep such a secret? We've launched successful campaigns to encourage people to fasten their seat belts while driving or quit smoking; we set up a nationwide system to make sure terrorists don't board airplanes. So why can't we come up with a cohesive plan to educate people and stamp out predatory pedophiles?

We can -- if we make it a priority.

Why We Dislike Lawyers

July 2, 2011

Question: What's the difference between a lawyer and a shark? Nothing.

OK, look. Right off the bat I want to say that I work with a lot of lawyers, and I consider many of them good friends. But we've all heard the jokes, and let's face it: The public's general perception of lawyers' honesty and integrity is pretty rotten. The latest Harris poll on the subject puts attorneys way down at the bottom of the list with members of Congress, car salesmen and, yes, journalists.

However, since lawyers are the crux of our justice system, I think it is important that we take a closer look at the way some of them operate. Why is it so many of us curl our upper lip at the very mention of dealing with a lawyer?

Maybe it's the sheer number of them these days. Maybe it's because we believe they make so much money on other peoples' misery. Or maybe it's that so many of us are forced to turn to lawyers these days to handle things that used to be settled with a handshake and a good word.

Despite what we see on TV dramas like "Law and Order" and "The Good Wife," most lawyering goes on in a stealthy way. It is done out of plain sight -- in boardrooms and depositions, in front of secret grand juries and in the confines of the prosecutor's office. When engaged in their profession, lawyers speak a different language and follow a set of rules most of us will never understand. It is human nature not to trust what we don't know, what we can't see or what we can't hold in our hands.

For the last six weeks, I've been closely covering a capital murder trial, the case of Florida vs. Casey Marie Anthony, taking place in Orlando, Florida. As I watched the defense lay out its presentation it struck me that there is another, more basic reason why we think the way we do about lawyers: They often destroy innocent people in the name of defending their clients.

To watch defense attorneys Jose Baez and Cheney Mason conduct their case on behalf of Anthony has been painful. Of course, they have every right (and duty) to do what they can to ensure their client gets a fair trial, especially since she is facing a possible death sentence. But they do not have the right to vilify and destroy bystanders to the murder of 2-year-old Caylee Anthony. This scorched-Earth, take-no-prisoners behavior should not be allowed.

During the defense's opening statement, Baez promised the jury it would hear evidence that there was no murder, that in fact the little girl drowned in the family pool. He blamed Anthony's grandfather, George Anthony, for discarding her body. There has been no evidence presented to back up that claim.

Baez also told the jurors that repeated sexual molestation of Casey Marie Anthony by both her father and her brother, Lee, had turned her into a trained liar, who naturally kept secrets. He promised to provide evidence to explain why his client let 31 days go by before finally admitting her daughter was gone. So far, the jurors have heard exactly the opposite -- clear denials that any sort of sexual abuse ever took place.

What the jury have heard are testimonies from more than a dozen of Anthony's friends and co-workers that showed she was a known liar and thief long before her daughter went missing.

Baez's opening statement also smeared the reputation of a man named Roy Kronk, a county meter reader who found the victim's skeletonized remains in the woods six months after she was last seen. He reported that the tiny child's skull was still wrapped in duct tape.

The defense lawyer called Kronk a "morally corrupt individual" and promised evidence that would show he had stolen Anthony's remains after she drowned in the Anthonys' pool and then waited for the reward money to grow. Kronk has come and gone from the witness box, and no such evidence was presented against him.

While I have highlighted the Casey Anthony case here, it is far from the only trial in which lawyers have made reckless claims on behalf of their clients, leaving human despair in their wake. Believe me, it happens all the time, in courthouses across the country.

The question for all of us -- including honorable lawyers who read this now -- is, what do we as a society do with attorneys who deliberately demolish the reputation of others in their quest for their client's acquittal? If they make promises to a jury at the expense of others and don't follow through, shouldn't there be some sort of penalty? Wouldn't you or I face consequences if we repeatedly lied about important issues at our job?

Most other professions have a code of behavior. I submit that criminal defense attorneys should be held to one as well.

Perjury Should Be Punished -- Always

July 23, 2011

Let's talk about perjury -- the act of taking an oath to tell the truth and then lying through your teeth. Perjury is illegal, and you can be fined and thrown in jail for it.

I don't know about you, but my parents instilled in me a sense of honesty. I get the shakes at the mere thought of telling a lie after taking an oath. I don't think I could do it. I would be like that person on television who suddenly blurts out: "OK, I told my boyfriend I wanted to see him dead! I'm sorry!" when I really had nothing to do with the murder in question.

I recently witnessed what I believe to be an act of perjury while covering the Casey Anthony case in Florida. The lie will go unpunished, and that bothers me, because that's the justice system saying, in effect, "OK, never mind. That oath you took really doesn't matter."

Here's what I saw: Casey Anthony was accused of knocking out her 2-year-old child with chloroform and causing her death by binding her airways with duct tape. She was also suspected of conducting more than 80 searches for "chloroform" and "how to make chloroform at home" on the family computer in March 2008.

Her mother, Cindy, stunned court-watchers last month when testifying that she was the one who had been doing searches about chloroform on the home computer on the dates in question. She explained she had typed in "chlorophyll," but the computer automatically corrected her search to "chloroform." She claimed she was doing the searches to know if their dog's illness was caused by him eating too many chlorophyll-filled bamboo leaves in the backyard.

The prosecution called computer experts, who testified that they found absolutely no "chlorophyll" searches on the family hard drive. An executive from Gentiva, the company where Anderson worked, testified that her password-protected work computer showed she was actually logged in on the dates in question. Her work terminal was active all day and reflected her usual workload.

In other words, it appeared that Anderson's motherly instinct kicked in and she lied, thinking it would somehow help her daughter dodge the charge of premeditated murder, which carried the death penalty as punishment.

I know this may seem like a small point compared to the whole hoopla about Casey Anderson's murder acquittal, but I was upset to hear that the state of Florida decided not to pursue perjury charges against Cindy Anthony.

I understand she's been through a lot, losing her granddaughter and all, but the system cannot allow lies to told in courts of law to pass with no penalty. It matters because it undermines our whole system.

It's bad enough when someone gets away with perjury in court. It may be even worse when someone lies to Congress after swearing to tell the truth. I'm talking, of course, about the case against former Major League Baseball great and suspected liar Roger Clemens.

In Feb. 2008, Clemens was called to Capitol Hill to appear before a House committee that was looking into doping by professional athletes. Congressmen had before them a long-anticipated report about the problem, written by the well-respected former Sen. George Mitchell.

Clemens' name was mentioned in the report 82 times, tying him to the use of both steroids and human growth hormones. Under oath, Clemens' longtime trainer, Brian McNamee, said he injected Clemens with performance-enhancing drugs as early as 1998, when he played for the Toronto Blue Jays. In addition, the pitcher's good friend, former New York Yankee Andy Pettitte, swore he had spoken with Clemens about his use of illegal drugs. He went home and told his wife all about the conversations.

So, what did Clemens say when he testified to Congress? He said: "I'm not saying Sen. Mitchell's report is entirely wrong. I am saying that Brian McNamee's statements are wrong. Let me be clear. I have never taken steroids or HGH." And he said Pettitte had "misremembered" their talks. Clemens was charged with six felony counts of lying to the federal government and obstruction of Congress.

However, the federal prosecutors bungled the Clemens trial earlier this month by showing a videotape to the jury that included mention of Andy Pettitte's wife, Laura's, comments about Clemens' doping confession. Before the trial, the judge had ruled that testimony was hearsay, and therefore could not be mentioned. After the video was played, a mistrial was declared, and now there's real doubt about whether prosecutors will press forward or drop the charges.

Unlike Cindy Anthony, who apparently lied to try to save her daughter from lethal injection, the perjury allegations against Clemens go to an entire industry: Major League Baseball, the league of the American pastime. The MLB has taken great strides to try to clean up its image the last few years, and I applaud that. Now, it's the justice system's turn.

I say in the name of justice -- another American pastime -- there must be a second trial for Roger Clemens. Perjury should never go unpunished.

Watching the Justice System Up Close

May 26, 2012

When they first sit down together, they look uncomfortable. They're all strangers. They could be a group of people who've gathered for a mandatory driver's ed class or in response to some ad about job training. They sit stiffly, their eyes looking straight ahead, afraid to look at the person sitting next to them.

But after a day or so, they invariably come together as a cohesive group. When they file in the room and the person in charge says, "Good morning," they begin to respond more robustly, sometimes even boisterously as the days progress -- like smiling kids singing a strung-out version of "Gooood Morrrrn-ing!" They gel together.

They become a jury that will decide the fate of a fellow citizen.

They are black, white, Hispanic, Asian and all sorts of other mixed races. Some are young enough to still wear a scrunchie in their hair or old enough to shuffle into the room. Like the judge, they sit in an elevated box to signify that they, too, will judge, in the end. These jurors are anointed with the oil of civic duty, and while they may be annoyed by the inconvenience in the beginning, they always walk away proud of what they did.

I'm proud, too, as I watch this process unfold every time I attend a trial. I know it sounds corny, but watching this time-honored process -- American citizens giving up their time to perform this most important civic service -- is awesome. But it isn't a pleasant duty. Jurors can be kept away from their daily life for weeks, and it isn't easy to pass judgment on others.

This is exactly what George Washington, James Madison, Benjamin Franklin, Alexander Hamilton and the other 35 forward-thinking Founding Fathers had in mind when they signed the U.S. Constitution in 1787. And here we are, centuries later, still adhering to one of their ideals of a more perfect union. Awesome.

Back in the day, it really was a "jury of peers" that sat in judgment, even though that phrase does not appear anywhere in the Constitution. It was the farmers, blacksmiths and cattle ranchers who were closest to the defendant who decided the defendant's fate.

Today, jurors usually have no neighborhood ties to the case. The trial I most recently attended, for the case of the U.S. v. Johnny Reid Edwards (aka John Edwards), the jurors were chosen from a pool of citizens plucked from 27 counties within the Middle District of North Carolina.

The jurors had never met one another, but fate brought them together to pass judgment on no less than a former U.S. senator and two-time presidential candidate. Again, awesome.

At the Edwards federal trial in Greensboro, North Carolina, I watched closely as the white man in seat No. 2 made friends with the black woman next to him. He was a financial consultant, she was a customer service representative, and they likely had little in common. The young, black woman in seat No. 7 works in human resources, and the 60-something white man on her right is a retired railroad worker.

In the back row, the last three seats were occupied by two black men -- a retired police/fire department employee and a mechanic -- and a white man -- a corporate vice president. They appeared engaged and respectful of one another.

As I watched the jurors' relationships grow, through frequent smiles and thoughtful gestures, I daydreamed about how juries are wonderful microcosms of equality -- citizens of all races, sexes and ages working together, for a common purpose. I wondered if these jurors would exchange contact information at the end of the trial (as some have been known to do) and stage verdict anniversary parties to stay in touch.

Greensboro has a history of bringing people together in the name of justice. Just three blocks from the federal courthouse is the famous Woolworth's lunch counter, where four black college students defied the convention of the day and sat down to be served on Feb. 1, 1960. The International Civil Rights Center & Museum now occupies the same building.

Franklin McCain, one of the four brave students, was recently quoted, saying: "We had no notion that we'd even be served. What we wanted to do was serve notice, more than anything else that we were going to be about trying to achieve some of the rights and privileges we were due as citizens of this country."

Nothing embodies the rights of an American citizen more than the guaranteed privilege of a jury deciding their justice. We may not always agree with a jury's final verdict, but we must respect it, and continue to honor the process that embodies our system of justice.

Jury service is the great equalizer, and a reminder that no one is above the court-sanctioned judgment of another. If you have never sat in on a jury trial, pick one and go. It's a real eye-opener.

Let All Jurors Ask Questions

Mar. 30, 2013

I have sat in many courtrooms during my career and studiously watched the faces of jurors listening to evidence in cases ranging from murder and rape to assault and political corruption.

I've strained to see if I could get a clue as to what their ultimate verdict might be. It is journalistic gold to be able to report that a juror was seen crying, wincing or rolling his or her eyes in response to specific testimony. Rarely, however, have I seen a juror telegraph his or her feelings. Most appear to take their jury service very seriously.

That said, I have also caught some jurors yawning and looking bored. A few times a juror appeared out-and-out asleep and not just "resting their eyes," as they would explain later. Nearly every juror I've spoken to at the finish of a case has admitted there were times during trial that they simply did not understand what was going on or the importance of certain testimony. More than one has told me it's as if lawyers and judges speak an entirely different language than the rest of us.

I've always wondered why jurors aren't allowed to play a more active role in the trial process. If we count on our fellow citizens to pass judgment, don't we want them to fully understand the proceedings and the facts of a case?

That's why I've been so entranced watching the current headline-making, televised murder trial of Jodi Arias, 33, in Phoenix, Arizona. Arizona is one of the few states with a specific law giving jurors the right to ask their own questions if something isn't clear. Panelists write down what they want to know, and if their inquiry passes legal muster, the judge poses it to the witness. (Arkansas, Colorado, Florida, Indiana, Iowa, Kentucky and North Carolina have similar laws.)

In a rare move, the defendant herself took the stand, so jurors got to pose questions directly to Arias. She is charged with brutally stabbing and shooting her boyfriend, Travis Alexander, to death after their stormy love affair fizzled.

During her testimony, Arias described what she said was the final furious physical attack she endured at the hands of the abusive Alexander. She says she dashed to Alexander's closet to get his gun so she could defend herself. The meek-looking Arias maintains she has no memory of stabbing her lover, yet she remembers that she cleaned up the murder scene, ditched the gun in the desert and began concocting multiple alibis -- three different ones.

This jury had plenty of pointed questions for this defendant:

--"How did you have time to get the gun down if he was right behind you?" asked one juror. Arias answered, "I just had the sense that he was chasing after me."

--"If you shot Alexander first (before the stabbing), how did the bullet casing land in blood?" Arias' answer seemed to indicate that in the struggle the bullet casing probably got moved around.

--"Why did you call the cops on your ex-(boyfriend) who shook you but you never called the cops on (Alexander)?" Because, Arias said, her past experience with 911 was "negative."

In all, about 200 juror questions were posed to Arias. And while some like those above went directly to the substance of the case, many seemed almost silly, asking about Alexander's Spiderman underwear and why she appeared so calm in pre-trial TV interviews.

One of the main arguments against allowing jurors to ask questions is that they might decide on a verdict based on the answers they get to their particular questions, not on the totality of evidence.

Some lawyers fret about a judge allowing an inappropriate question that will later be used to appeal the verdict. Many attorneys fear losing control of their case if jurors wander into territory that flies in the face of their trial strategy. And there is always the chance that one smart-alecky juror will dominate the questioning and alienate others, who might then disengage from the testimony.

Another frequent complaint? That it just takes too much time. In the Arias case, it certainly has. This trial is now in its third month!

The defendant was on the stand 18 days. Her psychologist, Richard Samuels, slogged through five days as a witness. After he testified that Arias suffered from post-traumatic stress disorder and dissociative amnesia, jurors let loose with more than 100 questions for him, including this doozie: "How can we be certain that your assessment of Ms. Arias is not based on her lies?"

Last year about this time, Texas Chief Judge Leonard Davis heard an important and complicated corporate damages case and decided to experiment with allowing jurors' questions. (Other states allowing this at the judge's discretion are Georgia, Pennsylvania and Michigan.)

At the conclusion of the trial, Davis announced that the questions only added about 15 minutes per witness, and he saw no downside to applying the idea at future trials. Even all 11 lawyers involved reported their support and enthusiasm for the process. Independent research by Professor Nancy Marder, director of IIT Chicago-Kent's Jury Center, also concludes that when all the pros and cons are weighed, "justice is fully served when a jury is informed and understands all the mechanisms."

It's time for all states to allow jurors to become fully involved in the judicial process. I say it's the very best way to keep them awake, interested and actively engaged in finding justice.

A Judge Takes a Stand

April 6, 2013

We often hear people associated with the criminal justice system complain about how it works -- or fails to work. Prosecutors, defense attorneys, police officers and social workers all cite specifics that they believe tip the scales of fairness.

Very rarely -- if ever -- do we hear from a judge. The ethics of their profession mandate they remain mum about public policy issues while on the bench. Even after they retire, the public rarely gets the benefit of their insight. I think that is a shame. Who better to help teach the public about how politician's laws, sometimes crafted and passed with headlines in mind, actually affect citizens?

This is a story about not one, but two judges from different states who came together to pro-actively help a woman they believed had been given a raw deal at sentencing. Their actions speak volumes about our justice system and prove there really is no such thing as one-size-fits-all sentencing.

In 2003, Denise Dallaire, a college graduate, was convicted for possessing and selling a relatively small amount of crack cocaine in Rhode Island. Seven years earlier, she had been arrested on a similar charge. (She explained she really wasn't into drugs herself, but enjoyed the money she could make selling them). When Dallaire attended college in Connecticut, she had once thrown a glass and injured someone in a bar fight and had been arrested.

By the time Dallaire came before Senior U.S. District Judge Robert Lagueux to face the last charge at age 26, she had three strikes against her. Under mandatory sentencing laws, she was automatically considered a career criminal. Lagueux made it clear at sentencing that his hands were tied. He was forced by law to pass a stiff sentence.

"This is one case where the guidelines work an injustice," he said that day in 2003. "And I'd like to do something about it, but I can't." Lagueux sentenced Dallaire to 15 years in prison. That moment bothered the judge for all the years Dallaire served her time at the federal prison for women in Danbury, Connecticut.

Over the last decade, Dallaire has been an exemplary inmate. She has made thousands of blankets, hats and pillows to donate to children suffering from cancer, and she organized fellow inmates to decorate and sell Christmas trees on behalf of cancer charities.

Dallaire admitted she deserved prison and that she had made "a lot of stupid and ridiculous decisions" in her early life. She seemed resigned to her fate and said she looked forward to her release in 2018. She had no possibility of early release.

At Danbury Prison, Dallaire met another judge, U.S. District Court Judge John Gleeson from Brooklyn. Every year, Gleeson makes a pilgrimage to the prison so as to remind himself where he sends defendants. The judge takes his New York University Law School students and law clerks with him. Gleeson got to know Dallaire and told The New York Times he came to realize her case was a textbook example of how mandated sentences do more to ruin lives than protect society.

"There are a lot of people like Dallaire doing bone-crushing time under the old sentencing regime," Gleeson said. "We need to try to find ways to help them."

It is important to note that just two years after Dallaire was sentenced the U.S. Supreme Court ruled that mandatory sentencing guidelines, originally designed to target drug kingpins, were unconstitutional. Congress agreed and has twice passed laws to reduce sentences for crack cocaine convictions like Dallaire's.

Gleeson wants to start what he calls "The Mercy Project," wherein pro bono lawyers would help the hundreds of prisoners (thousands, by some estimates) languishing under antiquated sentences. With that in mind, Gleeson convinced a friend, a top New York lawyer named Jonathan Polkes, to seek a presidential pardon for Dallaire. Part of the process required them to go back to Judge Lagueux to sign on to the idea.

Lagueux earnestly wanted to help Dallaire, but didn't think the pardon idea would work. Instead, he pointed out a procedural flaw that he, himself, had made at sentencing that could be exploited. Lagueux suggested bringing the case back to Rhode Island on the basis of his self-reported mistake.

Last month, Dallaire was brought before the now 81-year-old judge who had sentenced her so many years earlier.

"I felt bound by those mandatory guidelines, and I hated them," Lagueux explained to the sobbing prisoner before him. "I'm sorry I sent you away for 15 years," he said.

The judge then instructed that Dallaire be released on time served. He told her to hurry home to her sick mother in Groton, Connecticut. She was able to be with her mother for her final 11 days. As for her future, Dallaire says she wants to dedicate her life to helping others who are serving long sentences like she did win commutation.

Certainly, mandatory sentencing has helped lock up many real career criminals for a long time. But over-sentencing the undeserving doesn't keep us safer. Keeping them in prison long after the law that put them there has been struck down only adds to our mammoth prison costs. And every year that ticks by eats away at the prisoner's chance for reclaiming a productive life on the outside.

I like Judge Gleeson's idea of a selective Mercy Project to review the sentences of prisoners caught in the cracks like Dallaire. Any other justice-seeking judges out there interested?

Who Judges the Judges?

Oct. 12, 2013

There is something special about a courtroom -- sacrosanct, almost. In the hushed quiet, there is the inevitable not-too-comfortable spectator seating that discourages people from becoming too relaxed. There is the official bar that separates onlookers from the lawyers -- a bar that civilians are not allowed to cross. There are bailiffs to keep the peace. And, of course, there is the elevated bench upon which the honorable judge sits in his or her ceremonial black robes. When it comes down to it, this is their stage. They run the show. Respect for judges is a cornerstone of our judicial system.

But what happens when the judge acts erratically, or even criminally? Who judges the judge?

In San Diego, California, Superior Court Judge Patricia Cookson isn't in any legal trouble – yet. But her behavior has caused quite a stir. After presiding over a murder trial in which Danne Desbrow, 36, was found guilty and sentenced to life in prison, Judge Cookson did something no lawyer there had ever seen. She called up the convicted killer's longtime girlfriend and married the couple! According to the bride, Destiny, they then enjoyed a homemade wedding cake baked by the judge herself, served up on paper plates with plastic forks.

Short of a successful Ethics Committee complaint, Judge Cookson is expected to remain in her position with her $179,000 salary until 2018. When she runs for re-election, voters might decide to judge the judge for her baffling act of rewarding a just-convicted murderer with a special ceremony and a cake and vote her off the bench. But experience tells me voters have short memories.

In Montana, District Judge G. Todd Baugh has a better chance of the electorate booting him to the curb. He's up for re-election next year. This is the judge who sentenced a former high school teacher -- the admitted rapist of a 14-year-old girl -- to serve just one month in prison after the accused man violated the terms of his no-jail parole. Stacey Rambold, 54, never had a full-blown trial because his young victim, Cherice Moralez, committed suicide before the case got to court. Compounding the family's pain was what Judge Baugh said about their dead daughter during his clumsy justification of the short sentence.

"It wasn't this forcible, beat-up rape," Baugh explained. And he declared that the girl seemed "older than her chronological age" and was "as much in control of the situation" as the much-older teacher. There was an immediate uproar from activists who saw the judge as biased against females and Hispanics.

Judge Baugh has apologized for his comments, but not for the sentence, and has declined calls for him to resign.

In Las Cruces, New Mexico, District Judge Michael Murphy ultimately chose to resign and then got what some believe was a sweetheart plea deal from prosecutors.

Murphy was caught on audiotape discussing how judgeships were awarded only to those candidates who first made a sizeable contribution to the sitting governor's political party. Murphy described how he had paid $4,000 to win his appointment to the bench from the governor in 2006. In addition, Murphy was heard on tape making graphic and disparaging remarks against Mexicans, gays and Jews.

Judge Murphy was about to be judged by the state Judicial Standards Commission, but he resigned before any action was taken. For two years, he fought felony and bribery charges, and in the end, he was allowed to plead guilty to only one misdemeanor. Murphy agreed never to run for public office again and got a one-year probation.

Tell me, please, how judges who dodge justice help maintain confidence in our legal system. Oh, that's right -- they don't. And those who facilitate such deals are complicit in the erosion of the public's trust. That's right, I'm talking to you prosecutors, defense attorneys and fellow judges who sign off on such plea deals.

There have been times when corrupt judges finally get the book thrown at them. In Luzerne County, Pennsylvania, two veteran judges were convicted for a years-long "Kids for Cash" scandal. President Judge Mark Ciavarella and Senior Judge Michael Conahan ultimately pleaded guilty to accepting $2.6 million in kickbacks after sending youthful defendants to private juvenile detention facilities in which they had a financial interest. The more inmates shipped there, the more money each judge pocketed. Thousands of juveniles were sent away in the scheme, oftentimes for trivial infractions. A 13-

year-old was locked up for throwing a piece of meat at her mother's boyfriend. A 15-year-old served time for mocking an assistant principal on a Myspace page. An 11-year-old was incarcerated for calling the police after his mother locked him out of the house.

Both former judges have been disbarred and are each currently serving 87 months in prison. But the point is, it took five years for this ugly child abuse scheme to end. During all that time there were prosecutors, public defenders, social workers and court employees who were eyewitnesses to what was happening.

It is way past time for the court system officials to take a good, hard look at policing themselves and their personnel, and that includes the judges in charge of the nation's courtrooms. Every state's oversight body for judicial standards needs to step up to the plate in a timely manner, even if it's just to remind a judge that baking a cake for a convicted murderer is not entirely ethical. Bar associations across the country need to tell members that the duty of a lawyer includes reporting wrongdoing within the system.

American's confidence in both the civil and criminal justice systems is under 30 percent, according to the latest national polls. Can we afford for it to go lower than that?

Update:

At this writing, Judge "Birthday Cake" Cookson remains on the bench in San Diego, California. Her annual salary has been increased to $181,292. In July 2014, District Judge G. Todd Baugh was officially censured by the Montana State Supreme Court for his victim-blaming comments and suspended from the bench for 31 days. In April 2015, Judge Baugh received a lifetime achievement award from his local bar association. The Pennsylvania "kids for cash scandal" Judges Ciavarella and Conahan remain in separate federal prisons.

Jurors Urge Another Look at Their Verdict

Nov. 9, 2013

Sometimes the justice system just doesn't work.

The prosecutor could be more interested in winning than finding the truth. The defense attorney might be inexperienced and botch things. Maybe the judge makes rulings that keep crucial evidence from the jury.

Was the trial of 19-year-old Tyra Patterson of Dayton, Ohio, one of those flawed cases? Six of the jurors who sat in judgment of Patterson now say that if they knew back then what they know now, they likely would not have found her guilty of aggravated robbery and murder.

But you decide.

On a September evening in 1994, Patterson and her good friend, Becca Stidham, were in her apartment smoking marijuana with two young men they had recently met. They climbed into a car owned by one of the young men to run an errand. Along the way, the young man spotted his girlfriend walking her dog and stopped to talk. Two other women also approached the car, and one of them -- identified as LaShawna Keeney -- had a gun. According to Patterson, Keeney "was acting crazy." She and Stidham said they had not met the three women before that night.

There was a lot of conversation and milling about, and suddenly it was clear that the three women were verbally harassing five young women sitting in a nearby, parked Chevrolet Chevette. They were punching them through the windows and stealing things from them. Some items fell to the ground.

Patterson and Stidham realized they needed to get out of the area. As they scooted away, Patterson bent down and impulsively scooped up one victim's necklace. When they heard a single gunshot behind them, they broke into a run toward home.

They did not realize that 15-year-old Michelle Lai had just been murdered.

At trial, the prosecution made it sound as if Patterson was in cahoots with the three women at the scene that night and referred to the perpetrators as "the Patterson group." Patterson's public defenders never corrected that misconception.

Stidham would have offered testimony supporting Patterson's innocence, but for unknown reasons, the defense never called her as a witness.

The jury never heard about the sworn statement from the shooter, LaShawna Keeney, who said: "Tyra actually tried to stop the robbery. She walked up to me and told me to leave the victims alone." The woman with the dog also said in an affidavit, "I remember Tyra trying to stop the robbery by telling LaShawna to leave the victims alone."

The jury never heard a word about it.

Most unbelievably, Patterson's team never had the jury listen to the 911 tape of her calling police almost immediately after she reached her apartment.

"I heard a gunshot. Please hurry up and come," Patterson tells the operator.

Attorney David Singleton, the Director of the Ohio Justice and Policy Center, has taken up Patterson's cause pro bono. He wrote to the Ohio Clemency Board about the 911 call: "(It) was powerful evidence that the state's theory was wrong, that Tyra Patterson was not acting in concert with the criminals, but instead tried to get police help for the victims."

It should not go unmentioned that Patterson endured a hellish, poverty-ridden childhood in a single-parent household and no one, not even state officials, noticed when she stopped going to school in the sixth grade.

She was forced to quit the one job she ever had (at a Wendy's) because she had never learned to count change.

Yet, Patterson knew the day after the shooting that she must go to police and tell them what she saw. At one point, after Patterson mentioned the necklace to police, she says officers began to scream at her and threaten her with prison. They demanded she admit to robbery or go away for life on a murder rap.

Following hours of interrogation, Patterson says she falsely confessed that she had ripped the necklace from the victim. "I just wanted to go home," she explained later.

The jury saw that videotaped confession, but Patterson's lawyer never offered testimony about how easily undereducated youngsters can be tricked into making false statements. It frequently happens.

Now, nearly two decades after Patterson was sentenced to 43 years to life (more time than the shooter), the jurors finally got a more complete picture of what happened from Patterson's new lawyers. Six of the 12 jurors have added their voices to Patterson's clemency petition.

One juror wrote: "I voted not guilty initially because my gut told me that Tyra did not rob anyone. ... I changed my vote because other jurors kept bringing up the videotaped statement where Tyra admitted to a robbery." Another said, "The defense did not provide us any reason to believe that Tyra's confession was coerced."

About the 911 call, some jurors said: "She would've never called 911 if she thought she'd done something wrong. ... If I had heard the 911 call at trial, it almost certainly would've given me a reason to follow my instincts and vote not guilty." Another said, "If I had heard that 911 call at trial, I would not have voted to convict."

Juror Nancy Day started an online petition, calling on the Ohio governor to release Patterson immediately. Day has visited Patterson, who is now 38, and says: "I am disturbed that Tyra has been incarcerated for 19 years. We convicted her without a full picture of all the facts. I would have liked to know what I do now back when her future was at stake."

By all accounts, Patterson has made much of her time in prison. She earned her GED, participated in more than 200 self-help groups, earned her boiler engineering license and has learned to love the books she never got to read in school. She says she looks forward to becoming a paralegal once her sentence is up, and giving speeches to youngsters, encouraging them to stay in school and live drug-free lives.

So, did the justice system work well in Tyra Patterson's case? I think it's clear it did not. Is 19 years in prison for stealing a necklace off a sidewalk a fair sentence? Of course not.

Gov. John Kasich of Ohio: Release Tyra Patterson today.

Rembrandts in the Courtroom

July 12, 2014

OK, by a show of hands, how many readers have actually sat in a courtroom and watched a trial? Having been assigned to cover countless high-profile trials over the years, I have to admit I relish it. I love going to courthouses, with their stately facades and imposing corridors. Inside it's like watching a big vat of human soup. We all get stirred up together in a courthouse: the poor, the middle class, the rich. People seeking justice, people in big trouble with the law, people whose families are falling apart. The process is fascinating to watch.

Inside courtrooms, where the most-watched trials take place, there is a group of unsung regulars I have never written about: professional courtroom artists. Whenever I can, I try to get a seat next to one of them. Watching them work is a treat.

Cameras aren't always allowed in court (especially in federal court), so these artists are there as front-row eyewitnesses to capture the scene, those special moments that can be shown on television or in print to give the public a real feel for what it was like in the room.

Elizabeth Williams is one of these artists, and she has just accomplished something remarkable. After a nine-year effort, she has pulled together the artwork of five of the nation's most experienced courtroom artists in the book, "The Illustrated Courtroom: Fifty Years of Court Art." It is a delicious retrospective for court aficionados who can't get enough of headliner trials.

The vast collection of iconic art is punctuated by captivating personal stories from all five artists: Howard Brodie, Richard Tomlinson, Bill Robles, Aggy Kenny and, of course, Williams herself.

The book begins with the late Brodie's intricate render of the courtroom in which Jack Ruby was found guilty of murdering presidential assassin Lee Harvey Oswald in 1964, as well as a sketch of Ruby as he heard the verdict. "Just before the panel brought in a death sentence, Ruby's Adam's apple quivered and he gulped," Brodie wrote on the bottom of the drawing. He recalled that the judge sat on an inflated, rubber doughnut cushion and "decreed that only those within the rail could smoke, denying newsmen and spectators the privilege."

From that time in a Dallas, Texas, courtroom half a century ago, the artwork flows like the pages of a legal history book. Among the pages are many other Brodie accomplishments, his capturing the action at the Watergate cover-up trial, the Patty Hearst case and scores of others.

Richard Tomlinson, also deceased, was there to see the radical Abbie Hoffman on trial for selling cocaine. The artist describes how his long-held philosophy, "to approach each subject as if it is the only chance I'll ever have to draw them, because it just might be," came in handy during the 1973 trial. Hoffman skipped bail, changed his name and appearance and didn't resurface until 1980.

Tomlinson's bold drawings of David Berkowitz (aka the "Son of Sam") are powerful, as is his portrait of Mark David Chapman (John Lennon's killer). He spent two full years drawing participants in the Black Panther 21 case, among many others.

"Now I'm glad the book took nine years," Williams told me on the phone, "because if I'd started it later, Howard and Richard would have been gone and we would have had no recollections from them." Kenny's water-colored sketches are riveting. Among her included works are scenes from the trials of Iran-Contra defendants, including John Poindexter and Oliver North.

"Strange details sometimes stick with you, and I was very aware of Ollie's mother wearing a prim bright-yellow hat," Kenny recalls.

Also in the book are Kenny's drawings from inside the U.S. Supreme Court -- John Chambers, the "Preppie Murderer," Sydney Biddle Barrows aka "The Mayflower Madam" (another who favored prim hats) and Jerry Sandusky. Her 1974 portrait of James Earl Ray is shocking; he displayed nonchalance as he faced charges of assassinating Rev. Martin Luther King Jr.

"Drawing (Ray) in a makeshift courtroom set up in a penitentiary was a first for me," Kenny says. "I felt as if I was drawing an infamous felon in a school cafeteria." Kenny reveals that another courtroom artist there that day married Ray the next year.

Much of the book highlights the work of the talented and prolific Bill Robles, considered to be today's dean of courtroom artists. Based in Los Angeles, California, Robles has covered trials for CBS News for more than 40 years and remembers his first assignment, the 1970 murder case against Charles Manson and his followers, as if it were yesterday. Robles' iconic drawing of Manson showing the jury a newspaper headline reading, "Manson Guilty Nixon Declares," which nearly caused a mistrial, is not to be missed. Robles' rendition of the moment Manson grabbed a pencil and leapt to attack the judge graces the book's front cover.

Robles went on to famously capture the trials of Roman Polanski, John DeLorean, Timothy McVeigh, O.J. Simpson, Michael Jackson and too many others to mention here.

Included in Williams' works are drawings from several dirty-money cases, including the infamous Bernard Madoff case. Williams was the only artist to render the moment Madoff was led away in handcuffs by federal marshals, and it was seen worldwide. Her works from several mob trials are also in the book, along with her personal recollections of each. (John Gotti once stood over her and asked in a menacing tone why he "wasn't smiling" in her drawing of him.) They give the reader a real feel for the pressure placed on a courtroom artist.

As the Martha Stewart trial verdict neared, Williams recalls, "The TV networks had their producers in the courtroom with red and black squares of paper they could hold up (on the courthouse steps) to indicate guilty or not guilty." All correspondents had to do was glance up from their camera position to see the signal and instantly report out the news. The artwork was expected to be finished immediately.

For me, this book was a great trip down memory lane, and it reminded me of the service these special artists do for the rest of us. They take us inside courtrooms, where many have never been.

~~~

CHAPTER 4
Homeland Security

"The last thing the Department of Homeland Security is about is infringing on anybody's constitutionally protected rights." ~ **Janet Napolitano**

When former Department of Homeland Security Secretary Janet Napolitano uttered this quote I had to wonder what planet she lived on! By the time the department was established in 2002, the Transportation Security Administration was already up and running in our nation's airports. TSA was folded into Homeland Security in early 2003.

Who doesn't remember the first flight they took after Sept. 11, 2001, and suddenly having to surrender their personal belongings for a hands-on search at the airport?

I will never forget boarding a flight in Burbank, California, when TSA was new. First, I had to endure the indignity of having to prove who I was and having my carry-on suitcase opened for a public search. Suddenly, a stern-looking TSA officer cupped her hand under my breasts to see if I was wearing an underwire bra!

"What happened to our rights as American citizens. I understand we want to stop terrorists, but this is overkill!" I thought as I was being groped.

I miss the day when Americans could fly off on a carefree vacation without being made to feel violated or like a criminal while traveling. I long for the day when we can drive through states that border Mexico and not be subjected to random highway stops by armed U.S. agents asking for identification. America was founded on the idea of personal freedom, and I often feel mine has been diminished.

Hundreds of billions of taxpayer dollars have been spent on homeland security efforts since the 9/11terrorist attacks . Thankfully, we haven't had another major foreign terrorist attack on American soil. But at what cost to our personal liberty? And when is enough spending on homeland security enough?

When Is Photography a Crime?

Sept. 24, 2011

The scene is repeated across America millions of times each year. Citizens raise their cameras to snap a picture and immortalize what they see. Taking photographs is as much of the American fabric as driving a car.

But since 9/11, that right has begun to erode like so many others -- walking onto an airplane unencumbered, living without the multitude of leering surveillance cameras, gaining entrance to a public building without showing identification.

I get the reason for all the cautious security, I honestly do. I think our country is still under the threat of a terrorist attack. But some of those with badges tasked with monitoring the threat overstep their bounds in the name of national security. I can't get over the feeling that every time they overreact, the terrorists, who are determined to change our freedom-loving way of life, win.

The 2011 extensions of the Patriot Act expanded law enforcement powers to search for evidence of possible terrorist activity. The law says nothing about allowing officers to order us to put down our cameras, cellphones and other recording devices. Yet, in case after case, it is this law that's invoked when a security official wants to get a civilian to stop taking pictures.

I've read about all sorts of horror stories involving the seemingly innocent taking of photographs.

In February, Nancy Geovese stopped her car on a public road outside a public airport and took a picture she thought would be great for her "Support Our Troops" website. After this mother of three snapped photos of a decorative helicopter display, she was arrested by Suffolk County, New York, officers and told she was being charged with terrorism. After a long ordeal, including being put into a straitjacket and a solitary cell, she was charged with criminal trespass. Geovese sued the town and police department for $70 million in a case that is still pending.

Then there was the story of a veteran NASA employee named Walter Miller who was spotted taking pictures of an art exhibit near the Indianapolis City-County building. He was detained and told to stop because "homeland security" prohibited photos of the facility. Just so you understand the nonsensical nature of this, Google that

Indiana building and see how many pictures of the structure are already out there.

If the subject of someone's photograph happens to be a police officer, the photographer can be in serious jeopardy -- even if they take the picture in their own home.

In Houston, a homeowner named Francisco Olvera was having a house party when an officer responded to a noise complaint. When asked for his identification, Olvera went to get his wallet. He did not think the officer had the right to follow him inside, so he snapped a picture with his cellphone. Big mistake. Olvera was charged with illegal photography, public intoxication and loud music. All charges were later dropped.

Anthony Graber, a motorcyclist in Maryland, admits he was speeding on the highway and should have anticipated he might be pulled over by a state trooper. But he failed to turn off his helmet cam during the stop, and after he posted the video on the internet, Graber got the surprise of his life. He was indicted for violating the state's wiretapping laws. He faces up to 16 years in prison.

In Seattle, amateur photographer Bogdan Mohora happened to be an eyewitness to police arresting a man on a public street. By his account, he was 10 feet away when he took a few pictures and began to walk away. The officers followed and demanded his camera. When Mohora asked what he had done wrong, he was handcuffed and taken to the precinct. No charges were filed, but he was told he could have been arrested for provoking a riot or endangering a police officer. Mohora won an $8,000 settlement with the city.

I could go on and on with cases of civilians, and even some members of the accredited media, being harassed for taking a photo or a few minutes of video. But I think you get my drift.

For those who think overvigilant security is better than being lax, the words of security expert Bruce Schneier may be of interest. "Look at the 9/11 attacks, the Moscow and London subway bombings, the Fort Hood shooting -- no photos," he says. "I'm not seeing a whole lot of plots that hinge on photography."

Other security professionals point to the *positive* aspects of a citizenry armed with Canons, Nikons and flip-cams. After the unsuccessful Times Square car-bombing, detectives found clues about the suspect in home movies shot by tourists. Police departments across the country are making arrests by watching videos posted on YouTube by shortsighted shutterbugs.

I don't want to give up any more of my rights as an American citizen. And I don't think we need to if only we would adequately train all security personnel about the specifics of the law in their state.

Citizens have every right to take a picture or video in a public place, as long as they don't disturb the peace or impede police from doing their duty. To think otherwise is downright un-American.

Does the Department of Homeland Security Make You Feel Secure?

May 11, 2013

I've been doing a lot of thinking about the Department of Homeland Security lately. The DHS was formed after the Sept. 11, 2001, attacks, of course, but since then it has grown to mammoth proportions. It now has more than 200,000 employees, and it is the nation's third-largest Cabinet department after the Defense Department and Department of Veterans Affairs.

The taxpayers' bill for DHS is also enormous. If all goes as planned, you and I will send $59 billion more of our hard-earned dollars to the DHS this year to advance its mission to "prevent attacks and protect Americans -- on the land, in the sea and in the air."

Here we are more than a dozen years after 9/11 -- and hundreds of billions of dollars later -- and we still have no foolproof way to sift through our own suspected terrorist watch list.

It's called the Terrorist Identities Datamart Environment, or TIDE, and it current holds a whopping 700,000 suspect names. Something as simple as a misspelled name can gum up the works and render the list next to useless.

After Russian and Saudi intelligence agents labeled Boston bomber Tamerlan Tsarnaev a "follower of radical Islam" and warned us in 2011 to keep an eye on him, neither the FBI nor the CIA found any evidence that he was connected to extremist Muslim groups.

Nonetheless, Tsarnaev's name was entered onto the TIDE list, but, yes, you guessed it, his last name was misspelled. The list should have spit out Tsarnaev's name when he travelled from Massachusetts to Chechnya and Dagestan (known terrorist training grounds) in 2012, but it didn't. Tsarnaev stayed in Russia for six full months and then returned to the United States unhampered and apparently unwatched. It was during that trip, American intelligence believes, the older Tsarnaev brother became radicalized and programmed to do harm to as many Americans as possible.

Tsarnaev's dramatically accusatory mother, who is back in Dagestan (she left the Boston, Massachusetts, area after being charged with shoplifting), has claimed the FBI hounded her son for five years. If that really happened, don't you think the FBI would have discovered the Tsarnaev brothers' bomb plot and acted to stop it?

On the other hand, there seem to be so many holes in our national security safety net I don't know what to think anymore. I'm still unclear as to which agency was actually supposed to watch Tsarnaev. The FBI? DHS? U.S. Immigration and Customs Enforcement? Or some other far-flung governmental body?

I have worked with countless devoted and tireless agents of the FBI, Secret Service, U.S. Customs, and state and local police departments across the country.

I hate to cast aspersions on any law-enforcement agency's dedicated work keeping us safe. But it is clear more than a decade after 9/11 that the U.S. infrastructure needed to ferret out possible terrorists is still blatantly lacking in major ways.

Homeland Security Secretary Janet Napolitano was recently forced to admit a major deficiency. She revealed we still don't have a trustworthy computerized system to figure out which foreign students are in the country legally or on expired student visas. Unbelievable!

That student visa lapse allowed a young man from Kazakhstan to recently re-enter the United States and head back to Boston even though he wasn't enrolled in school anymore. That person is now charged with trying to help the younger Dzhokhar Tsarnaev cover up his Boston Marathon bombing crimes by removing evidence from his dorm room.

Napolitano confirms that since the tragedy in Boston, U.S. Customs and Border Protection agents have been laboriously checking student visa files -- by hand -- to identify which are still valid and which are not. Maybe, Napolitano says, we'll have an automated system by the end of this month. Really? Between Sept. 11, 2001, and now no one thought it was important to keep computerized and organized tabs on foreign-student visas?

It's clear we need to shake up the organization of all our domestic protection efforts to come up with a mandatory and cooperative framework that assures all our government agencies work together and are more responsive to today's security needs.

Now comes word of a new threat that seems to have caught authorities by surprise. While the national debate was focused on new gun control laws, there was a unique kind of gun being added to the American arsenal: plastic guns produced by relatively inexpensive 3-D printers. These new printers do have positive applications. They can produce low-cost medical, automotive and toy parts.

Gun-makers simply load the printers with sheets of thick plastic and program them to follow a computerized blueprint. Plastic gun parts are then formed and snapped together and loaded with traditional ammunition. They are just as deadly as any other firearm.

There is one small piece of metal included, designed to meet some obscure federal law on guns. But this new breed of weapon is thought to be mostly undetectable. That means our traditional screening procedures at airports, schools and government buildings could be useless.

I don't know if Homeland Security should have been on top of this new invention. Maybe it's the Bureau of Alcohol, Tobacco, Firearms and Explosives or the FBI or any other number of government agencies.

I do know that as terror and crime continue to morph into various and scary forms, it is imperative that our bloated and disorganized government agencies get it together. Lives depend on it.

Homeland Security vs. Your Civil Rights

Oct. 5, 2013

The Fourth Amendment of the U.S. Constitution provides "The right of the people to be secure in their persons, houses, papers, and effects, against unreasonable searches and seizures." The amendment assures us that only when law enforcement has "probable cause" to suspect a person of a crime, may their space be violated.

Well, here's a wake-up call, folks. For years now, and especially since Sept. 11, 2001, that fundamental American right has been eroding. All across the nation, every single day armed officers with badges are stopping, interrogating, searching and detaining U.S. citizens with little or no explanation, or probable cause. This isn't my America.

The time has come for law-abiding citizens to rise up and demand that law enforcement give us the courtesy and respect that all human beings should display toward one another. It is time we stopped acting like their unconstitutional activity is OK.

I get that there are terrorists and other criminals out there. I understand that an officer's job is fraught with the potential for danger. But that does not give officers the right to treat all of us like suspects. From the nation's airports, train stations and federal buildings to random spot checks along roads and at public gatherings, checkpoints with scowling, intimidating officers have become the norm.

At the risk of winding up on some Homeland Security watch list, I declare that the bulk of today's violations emanate from a bloated DHS that consistently falls back on the mysterious claim that it is merely (as its mission statement puts it) "Preventing terrorists and terrorists' weapons, including weapons of mass destruction, from entering the United States." The DHS is now the largest uniformed federal law-enforcement agency in the nation, and every day it reaches out to local and state police and even other federal agencies demanding citizen stops with little or no explanation.

Since 2008, Terry Bressi calculates that he has been stopped and interrogated by Customs and Border Patrol officers about 300 times. Each time he is asked to declare his citizenship, and each time he politely declines. Bressi is put off by what he calls the "creeping authoritarianism" that is taking over the country. His work for the University of Arizona's Lunar and Planetary Lab in Tucson requires him to drive 56 miles away to the Kitt Peak National Observatory. Bressi takes an east-west state road that is almost 50 miles north of the Mexican border and never intersects with any other road coming from the border.

"CBP has diverted border patrol agents away from the border -- where actual crimes are known to take place -- and brought them inland to stop, seize, interrogate and search domestic travelers inside the country," Bressi told National Public Radio.

"People who live and commute in the area have to go through this checkpoint and are stopped by armed border agents as they are simply trying to go about their daily lives," he says. The mild-mannered Bressi became so outraged with the frequent stops that he began to videotape them and put them on his website, Checkpointusa.com.

At small general aviation airports private pilots have reported being surrounded by local and federal agents and intimidated into allowing random searches of their airplanes. This has happened, according to the Aircraft Owners and Pilots Association, to at least 40 of their members from New York to California to Colorado to Oklahoma. Most of the pilots were not told why they were stopped, interrogated and searched. None of the stops resulted in charges being filed.

There have been reports that the CBP has routinely boarded Amtrak trains operating between Chicago and New York, questioned passengers about their citizenship and detaining thousands of nonresidents who don't immediately produce the proper papers. Again, answering these officers is voluntary, but at these little-publicized checkpoints, those questioned say, they are never informed of that right, and when confronted by armed agents, they feel intimidated into automatic compliance.

Earlier this summer three carloads of American citizens returning to the states from the same wedding in Toronto, Canada, were detained simultaneously in Detroit, Michigan, and Niagara Falls, New York. They were held incommunicado in a freezing cold room, without explanation, for more than six hours. When Sarah Abdurrahman asked an agent why they were being detained for so long, she says, "He said it was not my right to know." When she asked for the names of the agents who held her family and friends, she was told it was not her right to know. These detainees are sure they were singled out because they are practicing Muslims.

Because so few of us politely stand up for our own civil rights, this idea of an anything-goes policing has seeped down to state and local departments.

After several residents of Albemarle, Virginia, complained about speeding cars in their neighborhood, police responded. They didn't increase patrols or establish a speed trap to catch lawbreakers. No, they put up a checkpoint and demanded every driver present their driver's license and state their destination. This did not set well with Joe Draego, who was simply trying to get home.

Draego told a local TV reporter: "I kept asking, 'Have I committed a crime?' and they kept saying, 'No.' And I said I'm not willing to give you my ID. I've done nothing wrong." A police officer threatened to present him with an arrest warrant the next day. It never arrived.

"This is how it started in Nazi Germany -- police state checkpoints," Draego said.

Jack Furlong is a veteran criminal defense and civil rights lawyer for whom I have great respect. In discussing this decline of our Fourth Amendment rights he summed it up best: "We have become a nation of roadblocks, temporary detention, and stop and frisk, and we have accepted the status quo as sheep. Our Founding Fathers would be appalled."

Think about that.

Big Brother Has Arrived

Nov. 16, 2013

So, George Orwell was off by 29 years.

In 1949, Orwell's masterpiece novel, "1984," wove a tale about a fictitious shadowy world in which government surveillance was ubiquitous, public mind control was an open secret and independent thinking was labeled and prosecuted as a "thought crime." The tyrant in control was the mysterious being called Big Brother.

Orwell's prophecies didn't materialize in the year 1984, of course, but they are on a fast track to reality today.

We're all well aware of the millions of randomly situated video cameras all across the country -- at banks, hotels, state and federal offices, schools, retail stores and other public buildings -- capturing what we do 24/7. Facial recognition systems are in place at airports, casinos, some police departments and other places we can't even fathom.

But what you may not realize is the extent to which other types of taxpayer-funded surveillance capabilities have been put in place. The Department of Homeland Security, which is spearheading much of the covert action, would surely say it is all about staying one step ahead of the terrorists. But what about the rest of us caught up in these surreptitious programs?

Take a stroll through any number of major American cities, and you are likely smack in the middle of a clandestine government-funded observation zone.

Take Seattle, Washington, for example. Earlier this year, that city announced that it had bought what's called a mesh network system, with the roughly $2.7 million it got from the DHS. City officials said the system would be used by first responders as a dedicated wireless communications network in cases of emergency. Residents began to notice foot-long white boxes with stubby vertical antennas being installed at about 160 locations around downtown.

Then it was learned that each of the wireless boxes continually searches for Wi-Fi signals, such as the type emitted by your cellphone or iPad, and stores the information at a centralized location. In other words, if you walk by one of the boxes with your cellphone, it captures your personal information from the phone's Wi-Fi signal. The boxes are so sophisticated they can instantaneously store information about the last 1,000 places you have been with that phone.

Talk about Big Brother! I don't know about you, but I'm not particularly keen on the government keeping tabs on me everywhere I go.

The Seattle Police Department has said little about the system except to explain that it isn't up and running yet. Local reporters were skeptical. When they grabbed their cellphones and passed under the mesh network boxes, their devices alerted them to the fact that the system was already online.

It feels like a real-life version of the CBS drama "Person of Interest," where the disembodied voice says in the opening monologue: "You are being watched. The government has a secret system -- a machine -- that spies on you every hour of every day."

Seattle is hardly the only city taking steps to surreptitiously keep track of its population. Countless U.S. cities have gotten multiple millions of DHS dollars to put toward various covert systems.

The IntelliStreets Lighting System is a system that converts new or existing street lights into Wi-Fi towers that connect to one another to make another kind of mesh network. A promotional video touting the energy efficiency and the "Homeland Security options" of the system makes IntelliStreets sound like the best thing since sliced bread. The company's website mentions that miniature computers inside each light allow for "security ... data harvesting and digital media."

Think about that. As you walk or drive by a location, the poles overhead can eavesdrop on you and then store both audio and video of your conversation. You haven't done anything wrong, you say? No matter. While the system is recording you it can also gobble up your cellsphone's information at the same time.

IntelliStreets is already in place in several locations: Las Vegas, Nevada, the Superdome in New Orleans, Louisiana, the Sony Pictures lot in Culver City, California, and the Navy Pier in Chicago, Illinois.

Get set. It could be coming to your city next.

There is another eavesdropping system in place in some 70 major U.S. cities. Unlike the other systems mentioned, ShotSpotter has obvious and immediate crime-fighting benefits. It uses a network of listening devices that alerts police to locations where gunshots have been detected. It has proven to be highly accurate, and when the microphones are activated, ShotSpotter has also been known to pick up and record conversations. In a shooting case in Massachusetts, the ShotSpotter audio of two men arguing became part of the criminal case. Experts say it doesn't appear that any privacy was breached, as the argument occurred outside in a public setting where there was no legal expectation of privacy.

If the recent National Security Agency scandals -- domestic spying and phone taps on foreign leaders -- have taught us anything, it should be that too much surveillance results in collecting too much data, which can never be adequately analyzed. Can't we stop and take a breath here and figure out if every living, breathing person needs to be subjected to surveillance to keep the country safe?

Yes, we have the technology now to monitor millions and millions of our own citizens, innocent people just going about their lives. The question is: Should we? Where's the line between controlling the technology and the technology controlling us?

If George Orwell were still alive, he would surely be warning us to take care.

When Is the Homeland Secure Enough?

Nov. 30, 2013

Readers of this column know I spend a considerable amount of time dissecting what's wrong with our crime and justice system. But during this season of giving thanks for the positive things in life, let's pause to express thanks for the fact that our No. 1 national worry -- falling victim to another devastating terror attack -- did not come to pass.

Improving national security has been the top priority since Sept. 11, 2001, and the fact that we haven't had another major terror attack on U.S. soil should be a comfort to us all. It has been because, in large part, of our awakened awareness (and acceptance) that there are factions in the world that would like to kill us all and destroy America. We've thrown everything we can at trying to insulate ourselves from the madness.

I was in New York during the 9/11 attacks. I smelled the acrid air in downtown Manhattan still lingering days after the planes obliterated the Twin Towers. I saw the zombie-like stares of citizens going about their routine while trying to absorb the enormity of what had happened. All sense of security was gone after that awful day. I never want to feel that sense of utter helplessness again.

Twelve years later, I'm thankful that America has adopted a whole new way of looking at our nation's safety. Now, when we see something, we say something. We have voluntarily given up portions of our privacy to make sure terrorists trying to navigate among us will be identified before they can do harm. Law enforcement is more attuned now to the extremist's way of thinking and operating. Over the last decade, the Department of Homeland Security has won budgets that topped half a trillion dollars -- $589 billion dollars by my calculation -- money earmarked to help keep us safe.

I'm thankful that as a nation we have that money to spend to make ourselves more secure. But I would not be a good citizen if I failed to ask, do we really have to keep spending upward of $60 billion dollars on homeland security every year? And for how many more years will that level of spending continue?

Let's look at some facts.

The government's Worldwide Incidents Tracking System reports that the total number of global terror attacks has dropped almost 30 percent since 2007 -- according to the latest figures available (from 2011) of the 13,288 people killed in terror attacks, only 17 were U.S. citizens. The year before that there were 15 Americans killed. The WITS report says those numbers are comparable to the annual number of us who are crushed to death by falling televisions or other furniture. (Thanks to reader Daniel Petry for calling my attention to this report.)

"This is not to diminish the real -- albeit shrinking -- threat of terrorism, or to minimize the loss and suffering of the 13,000 killed and over 45,000 injured around the world," the WITS report states, "For Americans, however, it should emphasize that an irrational fear of terrorism is both unwarranted and a poor basis for public policy decisions."

The more recent acts of terror are occurring in places like Afghanistan, Pakistan, Iran and Somalia. Sadly, the overwhelming majority of the causalities -- even when the target is an American-run installation -- are local Muslims, not Americans.

Besides the 2012 tragedy at the U.S. mission in Benghazi, Libya, where four Americans were killed and four others injured, we've done a pretty stellar job at protecting ourselves both at home and at foreign posts.

So, what's the projected year in which we can begin to scale back our homeland security spending? I know it isn't routine to take away money from a government agency, but hasn't the more than half a trillion dollars already built us the security structure we need? It seems that at some time we might be able to consider a maintenance-level budget that keeps the security wheels rolling without adding expensive new accoutrements.

I don't pretend to have all the answers to the questions I pose here, but I fret that no one in Washington, D.C. seems to be asking them. Every year we just throw more money at the DHS and a host of other government agencies and programs without talking about long-term strategies. When is enough enough? I fear the answer is never.

From Washington we continue to hear politically tinged fear-mongering from both sides of the aisle. Republicans have a tough-guy image to uphold, and Democrats don't dare be perceived as being weak on national defense.

No one whose job it is to argue forever-larger Homeland Security budgets acknowledges that we haven't had a terrorist death in America in 12 years. No one mentions that al-Qaida got lucky when we were less prepared in 2001 and that we are more secure today. In hushed, conspiratorial terms, politicians, the DHS and military officials continue to tell us the terror threat is very, very real. And, well, just leave it to them; they'll make sure we're safe.

This is not to say we shouldn't continue to be vigilant here at home (specifically at our border crossings) and, especially, abroad. If terror cells are allowed to flourish over there, they will attempt to export their violence here to the United States, no doubt.

I'm thankful that we have security experts in this country who have gotten us to this much safer and more secure spot. I'd feel better if they'd reach a point where they'd admit we've got a good, strong national security organization in place.

At that point, maybe we could start diverting a few billion dollars to other worthy programs.

Your Nose Could Save Your Life

March 8, 2014

My dear grandma Cora always grew geraniums -- red geraniums, to be specific. Nearly every time I went to went to visit her she had pots of them flowering outside the front door. I would gently stroke the leaves and breathe in that unmistakable geranium smell. To this day I love the smell of geraniums, so much I grow them myself all year-round.

Now I've discovered that retaining the memory of that smell could help save lives. The same holds true for the smell of garlic, horseradish and other common odors. If suddenly detected in the wrong place at the wrong time, it could signal that a chemical weapons attack is underway.

Look, I'm not one of those doomsday planners. I figure when it's my time to go, then I'm ready to see what's next. But after a conversation with a 30-year veteran of law enforcement named Rod Davis of First Responder Prep, a man who applies smell science to public safety, I came to realize how vulnerable we all are.

Our world is full of chemical weapons. Some were manufactured as far back as World War I and still exist today. Newer arsenals have added to the total number and increased the possibility of mass murder. Syria, pressured by the United Nations, says it is currently in the process of getting rid of 1,200 tons of chemical weapons. We know there were all sorts of chemical weapons developed for use during the Iran/Iraq war in the 1980s. In the early 1990s, our Operation Desert Shield/Desert Storm troops discovered massive Iraqi chemical weapons stockpiles. North Korea is suspected of having a stockpile, too.

In this age of random and deadly terrorist attacks here in the U.S., what would stop a determined criminal from using a chemical weapon instead of a gun or a homemade bomb? Law enforcement rushing to the scene would likely not have personal protective equipment with them -- gas masks or rubber suits -- and they would have to rely on all their training and their senses to keep themselves and the public safe.

As Rod Davis puts it, "Science has proven that our sense of smell is the only sense directly hardwired to the brain." So this former police chief and commander of criminal investigations has come up with a set of 8 by 10 reusable training cards embedded with a near-permanent "rub-for-scent" component that helps emergency teams memorize the deadly smells. Teaching first responders those smells ahead of any attack, says Davis, could spell the difference between life and death.

Davis' patent-pending idea has already been marketed to police, fire and public safety offices nationwide.

He says he has had interest from an unidentified Middle Eastern country that wants to use his scent technology expertise to train their military to use all their senses when responding to emergency situations.

Davis says he came up with his idea of a pack of carry-along cards a few years ago while attending an emergency response training session. "The instructor told us that many of the most common chemical weapons give off smells ... like geraniums," he told me on the phone from his home office in Mechanicsville, Virginia. "The officer next to me leaned over and whispered, 'Gee, I don't think I've ever seen a geranium, let alone smelled one!'"

Davis researched the world's stockpiles and came up with the top eight chemical weapons with distinctive odors. Those are the scents embedded in his training cards.

For example, did you know that the lethal chemical cyclosarin smells like peaches? It can cause seizures, paralysis, respiratory failure and death.

The nerve agent soman smells like VapoRub or camphor. When it's heated, it turns into a deadly gas.

The same happens with another nerve agent called tabun, which has a decidedly fruity odor.

Hydrogen cyanide smells like almonds. It is so extremely toxic and immediately fatal to humans that it has been used in gas chamber executions.

As the name indicates, hydrogen sulfide smells like sulfur or rotten eggs. If exposed to high enough levels, it can be immediately lethal.

If you suddenly and inexplicably smell the odor of newly mowed hay, you may be in the vicinity of a release of Phosgene, which was used as a chemical weapon in both World War I and World War II. It still exists in the world. It attacks the respiratory system and is fatal.

The chemical sulfur mustard can smell like either garlic or onions. It doesn't kill people, but it incapacitates them almost immediately and results in the need for prolonged, intensive medical care.

And, finally, the blister agent lewisite. It is an extremely toxic arsenic-based liquid that attacks human tissue, eyes and lungs and smells like grandma Cora's geraniums.

Some readers are surely thinking, "Good grief, don't put the idea of using a chemical weapon in some madman's mind!" But, please, understand, many of those who hate America already have access to these agents. And if you think the distance between our country and theirs will prove to be a deterrent, I suggest you think again.

We need to talk about this stuff. We need to be prepared to respond to all sorts of threats. And chemical-based armaments are the most readily available and most often used weapon of mass destruction in the world. Training with scent technology just makes good sense.

Are first responders in your area ready?

Radical Muslims Want Us Dead

April 28, 2014

Extreme factions of the Muslim religion want us dead -- every American and everyone who embraces a religion different than theirs. We are infidels, heathens and heretics, and they believe it is their mission to wipe us off the face of the Earth.

I know it isn't politically correct to publicly discuss how the most radicalized elements of the Muslim faith have targeted Americans for death. I know it is not acceptable to profile people based on their country of origin or religious traditions -- not even when cold, hard, bloody, murderous facts directly stare us in the face.

What kind of Alice in Wonderland thinking keeps this country from stating the obvious? What is the matter with us, as a people, that we cannot readily see and say who our enemy is?

Now, before I'm waved off as suffering from Islamophobia, let's take a look at the two basic types of terror we face today. The first kind is homegrown, and we've suffered through a lot of it lately. It erupts when deranged people get a hold of a weapon and start destroying lives in our elementary schools, theaters and on college campuses. These are the random mass murders that evolve from the profound mental illness of our fellow citizens. I've written extensively in this space about the need to identify and help treat that group in advance of their deadly sprees.

The second kind of terror is more insidious. It is carefully and meticulously planned. It springs from a fanatical religious place few of us can really understand. It is uniquely anti-American, and while its perpetrators wrap themselves in a cloak of godliness, their actions are a bona fide war, a cherished duty of jihad against people they don't even know: us.

Radicalized offshoot cults of Islam twice attacked the World Trade Center (in 1993 and again in 2001) and forced down packed passenger jets at the Pentagon and a field in Pennsylvania. One enraged Muslim flexing his jihadi muscles used U.S.-military issued weapons at Ft. Hood, Texas, to gun down 13 Americans and wound 32 others. And now, the two profoundly misguided Muslim brother-bombers in Boston, Massachusetts. All were murderous assassins who did not target a particular person. They put a bull's-eye on any and all U.S. citizens -- men, women and children of any age -- and their goal was to kill and spill as much American blood as possible.

In the midst of their rampage around Boston, the Tsarnaev brothers carjacked a luxury SUV and bragged to the Chinese driver about placing pressure-cooker bombs at the marathon's finish line. Later, the victim told police the terrorists allowed him to live because, "(he is) not American." That says it all.

The terror-filled week that played out in Boston grabbed many of us by our collective throat and slammed us against the wall because we had become complacent. We believed it couldn't happen again on American soil. Even in the face of attacks on American embassies overseas (and the still unavenged torture and assassination of U.S. Ambassador Chris Stevens in Benghazi), we have swallowed pronouncements from Washington, D.C. that "al-Qaida is on its heels," that the terrorist organization is nearly "decapitated," to use the president's word.

That, of course, is nonsense given what happened in Massachusetts last week. There is also an unconfirmed report from a British newspaper that the FBI is searching for a 12-member sleeper cell linked to the Boston bombers -- a cell that "has been waiting several years for their day to come," according to a source close to the investigation. And this week, the Royal Canadian Mounted Police announced the arrest of two "al-Qaida inspired" suspects bent on derailing a passenger train as it crossed a suspended trestle bridge in Toronto. According to CBC News, the pair had been under surveillance for more than a year and was getting their marching orders from an al-Qaida operative living on the Afghanistan/Iran border. The RCMP now admits they have been monitoring a broad network of terrorism suspects in their country.

Taken together, it seems clear that radical Muslim elements have a toehold right here in North America. They are not radical Catholics or extremist Methodists or fanatical Quakers. The terrorists who fervently want us dead are a splinter group of Muslims that hate Americans so much they will spend years silently organizing and plotting our demise and not care if they die in the process.

This is not a column to condemn or place under suspicion the millions of compassionate, forgiving and loving Muslims in the world. I know that at the core of their belief is love and a tolerance of all people and ideologies. But honest folk must agree that festering within the peace-loving Muslim religion is a rotten core of murderous terrorists.

It is clear that Muslim leaders are unable to police the flock. It is certain that Muslim-dominated countries that get multiple billions in

U.S. foreign aid -- Afghanistan, Pakistan, Yemen, Iraq -- aren't helping eliminate the threat, either. That leaves it up to us to fight our own battle against terrorism.

How is that supposed to work if we cannot openly discuss the enemy without fear of being branded as prejudiced? It is not an act of discrimination to mention who they are. These violent Muslims have been out to destroy us for decades.

So, cling to your political correctness if you must. I will adhere to the wise old saying, "Those who don't know history are doomed to repeat it."

~~~

CHAPTER 5
Race Relations

"Hating people because of their color is wrong. And it doesn't matter which color does the hating. It's just plain wrong." ~ **Muhammad Ali**

Since the earliest Homo sapiens wandered the Earth tribes of people have mistrusted anyone who looked different or spoke a strange language. It is built in to the human condition to be suspicious of those who are not like us.

In the 21st century, that innate tendency remains, and today we label it prejudice or racism. As I wrote in one column in this chapter, I don't particularly like using the word racism to describe bias against one another because we are all one race: the human race.

That said, we need to acknowledge how suspicion and downright hatred of others is the cause for so much misunderstanding, so many acts of violence and, frankly, so much wasted energy and money in a country that embraces the idea that all men and women are created equal.

There isn't one ethnic group that needs to check its prejudice at the door; it is all ethnic groups. We all need to condemn the crimes that sprout from this bias, condemn that bias until it dies under its own ugly weight.

Time for Tolerance

Aug. 1, 2009

There is still an intolerable amount of racism in America. There are too many people in the U.S. who are bigoted and downright dismissive of those who don't look like they do.

That said, let's all admit something. Some of us see racism behind every act, and that in itself becomes a sort of racism, too.

The catalyst for writing this week's column is, of course, the recent disorderly conduct arrest of Harvard Professor Henry Louis Gates at his home in Cambridge, Massachusetts, following a concerned citizen's report that two men appeared to be trying to break into a home.

There's no need to rehash all the overanalyzed facts of this case, but suffice it to say Professor Gates interpreted the actions of one of the responding officers, Sgt. James Crowley, as racially motivated. Crowley and the other officers (including patrolmen who are both Latino and African-American) say it was Gates who stepped out of line by being belligerent in his responses as they tried to investigate. After showing his identification to prove he was in his own home, Professor Gates balked at the request to step outside. He's said to have loudly proclaimed that no white man would be put through such a humiliation. He declared he was a victim of racial profiling.

Professor Gates, a top scholar on race relations in America, obviously didn't stop to wonder why the police would ask him to step outdoors.

The original 911 report had two men attempting to break into the house and police procedure trains officers to immediately account for everyone involved. They needed to know if there was danger lurking inside and their first instinct was to clear the house and check. Sadly, Professor Gates jumped to the conclusion that it was the color of his skin motivating the officers and not his safety.

Here's what no one has said in all the breathless reporting on this story: When the police tell you to do something, they are under no obligation to tell you why they're asking. When the police make a request, you'd best comply, otherwise, things could go badly for you. It's the advice parents have long given their children as they go out into the world. Do what the police say. If you've got a complaint, register it later.

This is not a blast at Gates. It's a reminder of how things work. Police are there to help us and respond to our emergency needs. It defeats our own best interests to automatically treat them as racist.

This is also a pat on the back for all those members of law enforcement who walk into potentially dangerous situations every single day in every single city in America. It's a tip of the hat to those who keep the peace and allow the rest of us live in a (relatively) lawful society. Are there some bad apples within law enforcement? Of course, and I've written about rogue cops in past columns.

It makes me sad that a man as educated as Professor Gates, an accomplished author and one who was voted among the nation's most influential Americans, would immediately think of himself as a victim and perceive the police as adversaries. Just as disturbing was the knee-jerk comment from our equally well-educated President Obama that the officers acted "stupidly" before he knew the facts.

Among the facts: Sgt. Crowley is a well-respected and respectful officer, the brother of three other cops. And far from being a racist, Crowley is the man who, 16 years ago, as a Brandeis University police officer, got down on a gymnasium floor and tried to breathe life back into Celtics superstar Reggie Lewis after he'd collapsed during practice. Crowley's mother says it still "bothers him terribly" that he couldn't save the African-American athlete's life.

I cannot imagine what it would be like to live in another color skin, the immense indignation I would feel if I were unfairly treated because of it. But the truth is we've made tremendous strides in this country toward a more just society. Is everything completely equal? No. But compared to a hundred years ago we're almost downright harmonious!

Maybe we've been talking about the wrong thing here. Maybe it's a generational thing. The 58-year-old Gates surely remembers past painful discrimination. But he cannot be blind to the fact that bigotry and intolerance is practiced by all sorts of folks -- whites, Latinos, Asians and yes, even African-Americans.

It's a positive thing that we're talking about this now. As we do, let's remember that some of the people who look different from us wear badges. They should automatically get the benefit of the doubt. When we chip away at authority figures, police in particular, we chip away at our own well-being and safety.

How About Getting the Facts First?

Mar. 31, 2012

There are two sides to every story. So, why do the media sometimes run whole-hogged with the most sensational version of events, and why do we eat it up like candy?

It is time for some critical thinking about a widely reported crime story currently in the news.

More than a month ago, a tragic incident occurred in a gated community in Sanford, Florida, when a neighborhood watch volunteer shot and killed a 17-year-old young man. The teen was black; the man with the gun was mixed-race Latino. The teen was walking back from the store; the adult was in his car going to the store.

When I read the first accounts of how young Trayvon Martin died, I was outraged. It seemed as though a 28-year-old gun-toting man named George Zimmerman -- a guy who had called 911 dozens of times over the last year -- was one of those modern day gunslinger types who went around his neighborhood hunting for suspects to bully. Several news accounts called him a "cop wanna-be" who likely targeted the hoodie-wearing teen because of his race.

TV news played a 911 tape on which Zimmerman was heard reporting the suspicious activity of young Martin, and even though the operator clearly told the older man not to leave his car to follow the suspect, Zimmerman did so anyway. The media reported Martin was on his cellphone telling his girlfriend that a man in an SUV was following him, and she told him to run away. Within minutes, the defenseless teenager was inexplicably dead with a bullet in his chest.

Zimmerman was not arrested, and there was much speculation that it was because of Florida's controversial stand-your-ground law, which allows threatened people to defend themselves with their guns.

I was left with so many questions! Common sense told me Zimmerman didn't stand his ground anywhere. He had obviously gotten out of his vehicle and followed the kid, so was there another reason he wasn't arrested for the shooting? And if the stand-your-ground law was the reason there had been no arrest, why was Sanford Police Chief Bill Lee forced to step aside? He didn't pass the law; the state legislature did. Shouldn't the anger have been focused on lawmakers, not police?

Finally, five weeks after the Feb. 26 shooting, I opened the paper to learn that there was more to this story than an overzealous adult stalking and killing a black kid.

The new perspective came from the original police report, which noted Zimmerman had a bloody nose, gashes on the back of his head and grass stains on his back.

Obviously there had been some sort of fight. Zimmerman had told police that as he moved to go back to his vehicle, the teenager asked him if he "had a problem." When he answered "No" and reached for his phone to make another 911 call, Zimmerman said Martin declared, "Well, you do now" and knocked him to the ground.

The young man then bashed his head into the concrete several times, and in the scuffle, Zimmerman claimed, he shot Martin in self-defense. An eyewitness backs up this account, saying the person in the red shirt (Zimmerman) was being beaten by the person in the dark hoodie (Martin). However, ABC News then broadcast video of Zimmerman arriving at the police station in handcuffs, and none of the injuries listed on the report were visible.

Look, I don't know the complete truth of what happened that awful night when Martin died. And neither do the loudmouths who have descended on the scene to demand justice. Revs. Jesse Jackson and Al Sharpton led a protest in Sanford. They had their picture taken with Martin's grief-stricken parents and demanded that the city arrest Zimmerman or risk "going down as the Birmingham and Selma of the 21st century," as Sharpton put it.

The New Black Panther Party said it was mobilizing 10,000 black men to capture Zimmerman, who has been in hiding since the shooting and is reported to be extremely distraught after several death threats. The Panther Party's Hashim Nzinga announced on CNN there was a $10,000 bounty on Zimmerman's head. Another party member, Mikhail Muhammad, said of the shooter: "He should be fearful for his life. You can't keep killing black children."

The Rev. C.L. Bryant, a onetime NAACP official from Texas, said what I was thinking about these self-aggrandizing vigilantes. He called Jackson and Sharpton "race hustlers" and said they are "acting as though they are buzzards circling the carcass of this young boy." The facts show that there is no epidemic of whites killing black children in America. As the conservative Bryant put it, "The greatest danger to the lives of young black men are (other) young black men."

The bottom line to this case and the media's coverage of it is this: None of it feels like it is leading us down the path to true justice. It feels like a mob of uninformed, hot-headed people playing to the cameras is leading the way.

A young man is dead, and his pitiable parents, instead of being allowed to grieve, are being paraded around by opportunists demanding unattainable instant justice. This is not the way our justice system works. It should be slow, deliberate and fair to everyone involved. There are two sides to every story.

Softening the Rhetoric on Race

Aug. 10, 2013

Now that the flaming rhetoric over the Trayvon Martin shooting case has mostly subsided, it seems like a good time to more calmly discuss the issue of racism in America. Does it exist? You bet it does. But intellectually honest people have to admit prejudice is a longstanding exercise practiced by people of all backgrounds. In this instance, blacks and whites.

I got to thinking about this recently after reading a column titled "Profiling Obama," written by Bill Keller of The New York Times, a writer I have much admired. It described our president's dilemma of appearing "too black" to some people and "not black enough" to others. At the end of the column, there was a quote from Benjamin Jealous, president of the NAACP. "There's sort of a persistent misperception that talking about race is black folk's burden," he said. "Ultimately, only men can end sexism, and only white people can end racism."

I almost fell out of my chair! Was Jealous seriously saying that black people are never prejudiced against whites and that it is always the other way around? Had Jealous missed the part of the Zimmerman trial in which a female witness who was on the phone with the black Trayvon Martin right before the shooting quoted the teenager as calling the older man "a creepy-ass white cracker"?

And did it escape Jealous' attention when, just a few weeks later, Rep. Charlie Rangel, an African-American Democrat from New York, opined about the tea party, "It's the same group we faced in the South with those white crackers and the dogs and the police." Sounds like a nasty, prejudiced, anti-white epithet to me.

That Keller allowed the Jealous quote to go unchallenged bothered me. It allowed the misinterpretation to stand that whites are to blame for all the racial tension in America, which of course is absurd. There is enough distrust, prejudice and downright hate to go around.

The sad fact is everyone needs to check their racist attitudes because we all have them. Discrimination and bigotry have been a plague on humanity for thousands of years. For as long as there has been civilization, tribes of similar people have looked upon those who are different skeptically. It is a built-in component of human nature to distrust those who are not like you.

I hesitate to repeat the word racism because I honestly think we are all one race: the human race. What we're really talking about is conflict based on ethnic differences that have been around since long before biblical times.

Today, ethnic struggles simmer worldwide: Arabs and Jews, Turks and Armenians, Greeks and Turks, Sunni Muslims and Shiite Muslims, the Serbs and the Bosnians.

America has had several ethnic conflicts, but the prejudice between blacks and whites has endured the longest. Its roots are steeped, of course, in the horrible history of U.S. slavery. It has been 148 years since Congress passed the 14th Amendment to the U.S. Constitution putting an end to slavery. Nonetheless, for some blacks the ugly past can neither be forgotten nor forgiven.

On the other hand, in the white community there is a widespread belief that a majority of crimes are perpetrated by blacks. Whites probably don't stop to realize that crime often rises from areas of greatest poverty, and since police more often patrol poor black neighborhoods, it's a given that that is where more arrests take place.

What are the cold, hard facts from the Bureau of Justice Statistics? Ethnic groups usually prey on their own. Between 1976 and 2005, for example, 94 percent of black murder victims were killed by other blacks, and 86 percent of murdered whites were killed by other whites. Truth be told, people from both these ethnic groups would feel threatened if walking alone at night and coming face to face with a group of young men of the opposite color.

So, what do we do about this built-in prejudice we all carry around?

May I suggest we take a lesson from a young college student at the University of North Carolina at Wilmington?

Brent Campbell was keeping up his solitary workout schedule for the track team when a pickup truck carrying five young white men began threatening him, screaming profanity and yelling racial slurs. The verbal attack shook Campbell to his core, and then he realized the truck had turned around and was headed his way again. The driver slowed down and angrily stared at the young athlete, letting loose with a torrent of N-word-laced threats. Campbell, the son of a minister, dutifully reported the incident to campus police.

"The real issue is that nobody knows each other," he calmly said during a TV interview. In a letter to school officials, Campbell suggested a punishment for the culprits if and when they are caught. He wants them to be compelled to get to know him.

He said: "I'd want to meet with them over lunch or dinner once a week for a year ... make them do that instead of getting expelled. Let's just talk."

In a comment wise beyond his years, this college junior says it is clear the young men were taught such ugly thoughts. "Hate, bitterness, anger like this grows in the dark," the handsome young man told CNN, "So, the hope is that I get to shed some light on that." And the first thing he would say to his tormentors? "I forgive you," he said. "And I really mean that."

That, my friends, is the only way to begin to wipe out thousands of years of distrust, prejudice and bigotry. We all need to adopt Campbell's attitude and find the strength to understand and embrace the entire human race.

Lopsided Outrage Over Racially Motivated Crimes

Sept. 14, 2013

It keeps happening. Nearly every week there are more brutal crimes that bear all the earmarks of being racially motivated, but because the victims are white, you will probably never hear about them.

We've all seen the rallies around black victims of white-perpetrated violent crime, and that's cool. It's the right of every American citizen to peacefully protest. But when did it become acceptable to ignore the same types of crime when the roles are reversed and the victim is white? Why is it that we hear so little hue-and-cry on behalf of Caucasians who are victimized by blacks?

I know this is a provocative topic, but it is high time America talks about it and embraces the idea that no matter what the color of skin involved, preying on others is not allowed. Ever. Period.

On Sept. 4 in a densely populated park in New York City, a black man named Martin Redrick allegedly went on a rampage. Eyewitnesses say that in broad daylight he suddenly began to shout, "The next white person who walks by I'm going to (expletive)!" The next unlucky white person happened to be a retired train conductor, Jeffrey Babbitt, 62, who was simply taking a stroll near his favorite comic book store.

"His fist went in, and the man's head bobbed, and he hit the ground, and you could hear his skull hitting the ground," one witness said of the attack. Redrick, 40, then turned on the two other white people who stepped forward to help. Babbitt, who was the sole caretaker for his 94-year-old, Alzheimer-afflicted mother, was declared brain-dead, and five days later he died.

There were no public demonstrations for the "quiet and gentle" Babbitt. No one shouted, "No justice, no peace!" and called for immediate police action on his behalf.

Ten days earlier in Pittsburg, Pennsylvania, four black teenage girls set upon Ginger Slepski, who is white. The girls had allegedly thrown a bottle at Slepski's car, and when she stopped to ask, "What is your problem?" she said the girls repeatedly urged each other to "Get that white (expletive)" and "Shut up, white (expletive)" What followed was a savage beating. Slepski, 32, told a reporter: "I thought it was so animalistic, so violent. I thought they were going to kill me." The mother of two suffered bruises to her head, scrapes on her arms, legs and feet and torn ligaments in her shoulder, which left her unable to return to work as an electrician. The teens were charged with robbery and racial intimidation.

Again, no marches or protests on Slepski's behalf; no "community activists" appeared to chant "What do we want? Peace! When do we want it? Now!"; no black leaders spoke out to urge tolerance, unity and good behavior by their flock.

You've likely heard about the random shooting of a white Australian man who moved to Oklahoma to pursue his dream of playing American baseball.

As Christopher Lane, 23, jogged in a quiet Oklahoma neighborhood, he was shot in the back and left to die. One of the two black teens charged with first-degree murder in the case had posted pictures of himself online posing with guns and piles of cash. In April, the 15-year-old tweeted, "90 percent of white ppl (people) are nasty. #HATETHEM." No racial bias charges have been filed, however, as the white teenage driver of the getaway car maintains they killed out of summertime boredom not racism.

Lane's loved ones in Australia were aghast and offered the only public outcry about the murder. America was mostly silent. When was it exactly that we lost permission to openly and honestly talk about those who commit such heinous crimes? We hesitate, of course, because we fear being branded as racist if we turn the hate-crime mirror the other way. I think it's high time we did.

In Spokane, Washington, Police Chief Frank Staub has already declared, "Race was not a factor," in the murder of 88-year-old World War II veteran Delbert "Shorty" Belton. This hero from the battle in Okinawa, who came home with a purple heart, was beaten to death as he sat outside the Eagles Lodge waiting for a friend. In court, the two black teenage suspects tried to claim they beat the elderly Belton over a crack cocaine deal gone bad.

Except for a quick quote from a Belton relative about how preposterous the drug deal claim was, there was little more. The nation displayed no prolonged outrage for the senseless death of an unsteady old white man, a war hero, at the hands of two black thugs. The police chief apparently decided what experience tells me a jury should decide. This might very well have been a racially motivated killing, but the suspects won't be tried for that.

Very different from the case of George Zimmerman, who was charged with killing black teen Trayvon Martin. In that case, where both CNN and The New York Times described Zimmerman as a "white Hispanic" (whatever that is), black activists Revs. Al Sharpton and Jesse Jackson revved up public outcry until the stiffest possible murder charges were filed.

The truth is, Zimmerman, who was acquitted of the murder charge, is actually of Peruvian heritage, and one of his grandfathers was black. See the slippery slope we tread when we try to label one another by race?

I'm telling you. The lesson we should be preaching isn't just racial tolerance. It is that life is precious, to be cherished, and no human has the right to lay hands on another. We should all unify around the idea of peaceful coexistence and a no-excuse defense for predators. Period.

Are We Asking the Right Questions About Police and Race?

Nov. 24, 2014

As the nation continued to watch for the grand jury announcement out of Ferguson, Missouri, this week, USA Today released a disturbing analysis of arrest records from across the country. After pouring over FBI records from more than 3,500 police departments, the newspaper finds that blacks are far more likely to be arrested than people of other races -- and for all sorts of crimes -- from murder to marijuana possession.

USA Today called the racial divide in America's 2011-2012 arrest rates a "staggering disparity" with at least 70 police departments from Connecticut to California arresting blacks at a rate 10 times higher than people of other races.

But before you jump to any conclusions, the paper also quoted experts who said the lopsided nature of arrests didn't necessarily prove racism or racial profiling. Read that sentence again, please.

My worry is that some people will choose to glom on to the arrest numbers alone and ignore the very important questions these statistics raise.

Of course, it was the shooting death of unarmed black teenager Michael Brown by Ferguson's white police officer Darren Wilson that once again re-ignited the discussion about racial tensions and perceived police bias.

So let's look at the FBI's stats on Ferguson. Police there arrested black residents not quite three times more often than whites. But look deeper. More than 67 percent of Ferguson's population is black; only 29 percent is white. It's not difficult to understand, then, why more blacks might be arrested there.

Census Bureau statistics show the largest sector of Ferguson residents are between the ages of 15 and 19 -- prime age for committing crimes.

This is not to say there was no police bias at play in Ferguson or any of the other areas cited in this latest report.

The paper's analysis concluded that at least 1,581 other police departments arrested blacks at rates even higher than in Ferguson, including cop shops in cities as large and diverse as Chicago, Illinois, and San Francisco, California.

It was mindboggling to learn that in 2011 and 2012 in areas around Detroit, Michigan -- the poorest and blackest of America's major cities, according to USA Today -- arrest rates for blacks were up to 26 percent higher than for people of other races.

Yet police there insist no one is targeted for their race.

"Our officers aren't being told to look for any particular demographic," former Dearborn police officer Gregg Algier told the paper. "We come across what we come across."

Police at the Virginia shore were quoted saying, "We're arresting folks based on who's committing the crime," which begs the question: Is the black community doing all it can to produce law-abiding citizens? Does it do enough to help promote education, healthy family-oriented lifestyles and self-discipline? If the complaint is that police officers need to restrain themselves, doesn't that also apply to the citizens they encounter on the job? Tensions can't always be laid at the feet of the police, right?

Statistics can sometimes be startling. But don't be swayed by mere numbers. We need to keep asking questions and seeking answers.

What societal pressures impact today's racial equation? What can be done to help at-risk young people? Why are so many police departments predominantly staffed by whites, even when they are in majority black communities? Why aren't more candidates of color stepping forward to serve? If drug arrests are high, what kind of public resources are earmarked for drug rehab programs? I guarantee the amount will surely be less than the cost of incarcerating those arrested on drug charges.

I cringe when I hear activists calling for their brand of justice on young Brown's behalf. They have no idea what evidence was presented to the secret grand jury, yet they are positive the only just end is to find Officer Wilson guilty. That's not the way the system works. Do we need to revive high school civics courses so people understand that?

There are reasons the arrest rate for blacks is higher than for whites. I want to understand what they are and take steps to fix them. What no one should want is mob rule, fueled by inconsistent and often incorrect media reports, blindly telling us who is guilty and who is not.

After Deadly Disputes, Policing Can Never Be the Same

Dec. 15, 2014

Note to sheriffs and police chiefs: If you aren't actively seeking ideas to foster better relations between your community and your officers, you probably should resign.

If you are still operating under the illusion that social unrest could never come to your town, you better think again.

If you don't realize that a new day has dawned in law enforcement -- a day where a growing number of citizens automatically mistrust cops -- you might want to get back out on the street and walk a beat for a day or two.

There is now a nationwide, colorblind call demanding a change in the way law enforcement interacts with the people they have sworn to protect.

There is no turning back now. The bad apples in the policing barrel have spoiled it for the rest of you.

Most recently, a cop in Cleveland gave a 12-year-old black child -- who was unfortunately playing with a realistic-looking toy gun -- just a few seconds to live before pulling his gun and shooting him dead. Other officers reportedly then restrained his mother, telling her to "calm down," and then tackled, handcuffed and tossed his 14-year-old sister in the back of a squad car.

There was, of course, the headline grabbing Ferguson, Missouri, shooting of unarmed black teenager Michael Brown in August. Before that, in July, the much-publicized death of an unarmed black man named Eric Garner who was selling single cigarettes on a street corner in Staten Island, New York. In March, police in Albuquerque, New Mexico, shot and killed a homeless white man following a more than four-hour standoff over his illegal camping.

Each of these cases has a backstory, of course, but the cold, hard fact is that there have been too many recent cases involving the use of questionable deadly force by police. Their seemingly callous actions after the fact only add to the growing anti-law enforcement feeling.

Across the country, people of all colors are asking: "Isn't there a more humane way for peace officers to respond to tense situations? Can't police be trained to diffuse disputes in a way that does not include fatal gunfire? Why are so many unarmed citizens losing their lives?"

I'm wondering whether it really is all about race. Or might it have something to do with the poverty and sense of hopelessness that traps so many minority Americans in gang-infested neighborhoods? Have those consumed with surviving the desperation simply forgotten to teach their children to respect law enforcement, to acquiesce when an officer tells you to stop an illegal action?

Why did young Brown decide to confront Ferguson Officer Darren Wilson in the street that day? Why hadn't Garner stopped illegally selling cigarettes after police had repeatedly warned him not to? This isn't blaming the victim; it's trying to understand motivations.

Anyone who reads this column regularly knows I am a friend to law enforcement officers and completely understand their daily challenges. To those who wear a badge, I say you've got another challenge on your plate now. A good chunk of the population has come to see your profession as one to automatically fear and mistrust. It is way more than just a public relations problem, and multiple steps are required to fix things.

Police academies have to adopt better ways of weeding out psychologically unsuitable cadets. Instructors need to include more nonconfrontational training and stress the art of street-level problem solving.

Police unions need to stop automatically going before cameras to defend questionable shoots and do more to pressure departments into providing state-of-the-art training and crime-fighting tools, such as Tasers and body cameras. Demand qualified dispatchers who know the full facts of a situation to convey them to officers in the field.

The cop on the beat who displays the uber-macho, bad-guy attitude when dealing with the public needs a slap upside the head and a reminder that the arbitrary enforcement of the law is the mark of tyranny. Citizens will always fight against it.

And finally, back to the sheriffs and chiefs of police. Learn a lesson from what's occurred recently, from the tiny burb of Ferguson to the inner city of Staten Island. You set the tone for your department. Even if you don't think adjustments are necessary, take another look. Citizens of all colors are demanding change.

Stop the Running, Stop the Shooting

May 4, 2015

After watching the situation in Baltimore, Maryland, these past couple of weeks -- yet another American city strangled by violence stemming from the death of yet another unarmed black man -- it suddenly dawned on me. It all starts with one stupid action.

I want to yell advice at the top of my lungs.

Stop running away from police!

But that is only half of the problem.

Stop instinctively shooting or manhandling suspects!

It is clear that both sides in these deadly clashes are to blame for inviting and escalating their situations. President Obama calls it a "Slow-Rolling Crisis" and reminds us, "We shouldn't pretend that it's new." I agree. Baltimore, Albuquerque, Philadelphia, Nashville, Los Angeles -- these are among the many American cities with a history of police brutality allegations.

More advice.

Stop assuming every cop is out to get you for something.

Stop assuming every young minority male is guilty of something.

Stop engaging in suspicious or criminal activity that you know will likely attract the police.

Stop giving handcuffed suspects with no seat belt protection retaliatory "rough rides" in the back of police transport vans.

Some young men of color do not respect or trust the police. They often don't obey commands to stop, show identification or answer questions. These young men only make it worse for themselves.

At the same time, some officers lack respect as well. They see a young man of color and automatically go to extremes. They approach aggressively; they speak to them in a tone that goes against their status as a protector of all citizens. A few officers reach for their guns first and think later, in my opinion.

When these two forces converge, they can create a deadly encounter.

The senseless death of Freddy Gray, 25, of Baltimore touched off this latest spasm of violence. On the morning of April 12, police on bicycles locked eyes with Gray (likely known to them as a man with a serious drug-dealing record dating back to 2007) on a Baltimore street corner. Gray suddenly began to run. Police followed, caught him and took him into custody on unknown charges. He was tossed into a police transport van for the ride to booking.

Gray's family says he died after his neck was broken, his upper spine was smashed and his voice box was crushed.

They believe the injuries happened after he was arrested and given one of those "rough rides." There is no official confirmation of this, but something happened in that van.

Less than an hour later, Gray was admitted to a hospital, where he went into a coma and died.

Peaceful protests were organized in Baltimore, but they morphed into what can only be called bloody riots. Stores were looted; cars were set on fire; police officers were attacked and sent to the hospital. Dozens of protesters were arrested. Firefighters were outnumbered by rioters -- their fire hoses cut by thugs. The governor declared a state of emergency and called in the National Guard. The mayor decreed a week-long curfew. Police Commissioner Anthony Batts revealed much of the damage was done by rampaging high school kids.

"You had one mother who grabbed their child who had a hood on his head, and she started smacking him on the head because she was so embarrassed," Batts said during a news conference. "I wish I had more parents that took charge of their kids out there tonight," he said.

That mother's name was Toya Graham, and video of her pulling her 16-year-old son Michael away from a group of young thugs -- smacking him all the way home -- brought hope to my heart.

I am a friend to good police officers, and they are mortified by all the recent deaths of unarmed black citizens.

In Cleveland, Tamir Rice, just 12 years old, was shot dead on the sidewalk after he failed to drop his toy gun fast enough. Walter Scott, 50, of South Carolina, was shot in the back multiple times as he ran away from a traffic stop, apparently afraid his unpaid child support would catch up with him. Other unarmed black men like Eric Garner in New York and Ezell Ford, a mentally challenged unarmed black man in Los Angeles, also died at the hands of police.

So let me ask you this. How do we stop this awful cycle? Which side finds respect for the other first -- or does neither?

How about starting with a call to all mothers of young men to do what Toya Graham did? Take responsibility for their own progeny and teach them to respect the law whether they are young minorities or police officers with a badge. Stop running. Stop shooting.

Reactions to Police Killings
Reveal Twisted Values

May 18, 2015

The right to freedom of speech in America gives every citizen almost absolute permission to say whatever they think about a given topic. Even if the comments are offensive to the majority, citizens have a right to express their opinion.

So go ahead -- say what you want. But realize the law does not necessarily protect you from others' reactions to your comments. And sometimes what people say is so damnably stupid they deserve some blowback.

Such was the case with 19-year-old Sierra McCurdy. After two Hattiesburg, Mississippi, police officers were executed during a routine stop, this thoughtless teenager gleefully wrote on Facebook, "GOT 'EM," followed by three handgun emoticons. It wasn't her only mean-spirited message. McCurdy, using the slang spelling so often seen on the internet, followed up saying, "We can turn this bxtch into Baltimore real quick" and "Police take away innocent people lives everyday now & get away w/it. F--- them...(no mercy)."

Officer Benjamin Deen, a white man, was 34 and left two children behind. Liquori Tate was 25, unmarried and black -- just like McCurdy. Did she know the color of either of these patrolman when she made her hateful comments? Were they knee-jerk statements against authority that she thought her peers would applaud or were her posts racial in nature, made after assuming both officers were white?

Either way, it's an unconscionable opinion. And she made it worse for herself by including a smiling selfie, taken while wearing her Subway sandwich shop uniform. After McCurdy's offensive messages were spread far and wide, she was fired.

I can just hear the excuses now: McCurdy is only 19, and, well, teens post the darnedest things. But you know what? That's old enough to know you don't celebrate the meaningless assassination of two human beings.

Four suspects have been arrested in conjunction with the officer's murders: two brothers and two others. All are black, if that even matters. It could just as well have been four white punks arrested. Race is not the point here.

It is the callousness so many display for human life these days. When did so many of us decide physical confrontation is the answer to conflict? And why do so many, like that young girl in Mississippi, react with delight when someone dies in a tragic street battle?

No, it's not just race. It is the erosion of respect for human life. It is the idea that vengeance matters more than life. When that destructive attitude prevails, there aren't enough laws in the land to control things.

Yes, there has been a spate of seemingly senseless (and highly publicized) deaths of minority men at the hands of police lately. And some officers, in Baltimore and South Charleston, South Carolina, for example, now face serious charges for their actions. The system will judge them.

But in my opinion, the media overhypes and badly reports on a handful of police-related incidents in a land where more than 1 million sworn law enforcement officers go to work every day. Rumors are reported as facts, and as the untruths are repeated, bands of uninformed protesters cry out for immediate justice. They would rather scream "racism!" than stop to understand what prompted the incidents.

Fact: Those young men in Mississippi were stopped for speeding and reportedly reacted by murdering two officers. Fact: Investigations in Ferguson, Missouri, proved that a young man decided to attack an officer in his car and fight with him in the street rather than stop walking down the middle of the road as instructed. Fact: A teenager in Madison, Wisconsin, hopped up on a mix of hallucinogenic mushrooms, marijuana and Xanax delivered a concussive blow to an officer responding to a 911 call. Fearing for his life, the cop lawfully used his gun, and the young man was killed.

That biracial victim's mother was quoted commenting on the police, saying: "They could have done a lot. What they didn't do was give my son any respect."

Really? How much respect did her son give the responding officer? Respect is a two-way street. Until we all walk down that path, we'll continue to read about more of these senseless deaths.

~~~

CHAPTER 6
Mass Media, Social Media and Crime

"If people in the media cannot decide whether they are in the business of reporting news or manufacturing propaganda, it is all the more important that the public understand that difference, and choose their news sources accordingly." ~ **Thomas Sowell, columnist**

Since the early 1930s, back in the days of the Lindbergh kidnapping and the murderous spree of a couple named Bonnie and Clyde, the media has determined the public's perception of guilt and innocence.

The media has helped influenced presidential elections, set the tone of social discourse and made crime-watching a national pastime.

As a working journalist for decades I've had a front row seat on how the craft has developed in this 24/7 internet world. Anyone with a computer can call themselves a journalist. And these days journalism consumed via the internet may hold the most powerful sway since it commands more daily, hourly eyeballs than any other.

The unrelenting competition for audiences has caused many a reporter to embrace the quick and dirty angle rather than the contemplative or investigative treatment of a story. In addition, newsroom budgets often can't afford the luxury of much editorial oversight. Assumptions are made, mistakes are often not acknowledged and public opinion polls now put the trustworthiness of journalists down alongside that of used car salesmen and politicians.

In short, never take what you read as gospel. Always apply your own common sense.

Rest in Peace, Patsy

July 12, 2008

The media, not charged, but guilty in Ramsey case...

Patsy Ramsey is looking down from the heavens she always prayed to with her trademark beauty pageant smile. Standing next to her is her beautiful daughter, Jon Benet Ramsey. They are benevolent but still wagging a finger of "I-told-you-so" at all of us.

The letter of exoneration was stunning in what it revealed. A new form of forensic testing found DNA from two distinct males on the clothing Ramsey was wearing when she was killed. And that DNA matches the sample taken from her underwear back in 1997.

In other words, the killer left three separate spots of evidence to help track him down. None of the DNA matches any member of the Ramsey family.

Mary Lacy, the current district attorney of Boulder, Colorado, says she wishes she could have delivered the news before Patsy Ramsey died in 2006. Lacy's declaration that her office will now "treat you as the victims of this crime, with the sympathy due you" may have come as a relief to patriarch John Ramsey, but I doubt it.

"We became entertainment for the country," Ramsey once said long after he'd lost both his daughter and his wife. His implication was that the media made sure everyone thought they were guilty of murdering their child.

I agree. I was part of the media pact that descended on Boulder right after Christmas 1996. For months, my colleagues and I tramped around town trying to find the truth. Tabloid headlines read, "Did Daddy Do It?" and "Cops: Mom Confesses!"

There was a frenzy of media to get something -- anything -- and for months the story was top of the news. My boss at the now-defunct TV program "Hard Copy" sent me on a one-way ticket to Boulder, and when I couldn't develop any new angle she ordered me to follow Jon Benet Ramsey's brother, Burke, to and from his elementary school.

I refused to shadow a little kid, especially one who just lost his little sister. I left the TV program about a month later.

The media was brutal. Extensive handwriting tests concluded that Patsy Ramsey did not pen the ransom note left at the scene, but there were leaks from investigators that she might have used her left hand to write it. John Ramsey's computers were seized, and another police leak revealed they had reason to look for child pornography. Ed Gelb, a highly regarded polygraph expert, conducted five different tests with John and Patsy and concluded that they "passed with flying colors -- no deception."

And the most remarkable underreported news, to my mind, was the revelation that at the time of Jon Benet's death, 38 of her neighbors were listed as registered sex offenders, and there had been over 100 burglaries in the immediate area. To my knowledge, the police did not pursue those leads, even though the victim had been paraded around as a mini-beauty queen.

Just nine months after the 6-year-old's murder there was a very similar intruder/sexual attack in the neighborhood. While a family was out of their home, a man broke in and hid in the house until they were all asleep. He then attacked their 12-year-old daughter and got away when the parents responded to her screams.

Yet, the media, the public and so many Americans still continued to point at the parents. Shame on us.

The Ramsey family survived the death of a child, public humiliation, living "under an umbrella of suspicion," repeated handwriting tests and lie detector tests, false leads and hopes, several recurrences of Patsy's cancer and the maniacal rantings of a sexually confused kook.

In the spring of 2006, Patsy Ramsey was fighting what would be her last bout with ovarian cancer. And suddenly, from out of the woodwork, they began to get emails from halfway around the world. A slight, fragile-looking man named John Mark Karr was taken into custody in the Philippines and paraded in front of the predictable gaggle of media, where he confessed.

"I was with Jon Benet when she died," he said and demurely batted his eyelashes. When asked to explain the details, Karr simply said, "Her death was an accident." He was brought back to Colorado to face charges, but the authorities instead determined Karr was one of those inexplicable characters who confess to crimes they did not commit. By this time Patsy had died and was spared the spectacle.

In 2000, I was assigned to cover a lecture given by the Ramseys to a group of young journalists in Washington, D.C. I learned that day that Patsy had studied journalism and was passionate about its ethics. Their message to the students that day was simple. Don't print it or say it unless you can prove it. And in a twist on the golden rule, Patsy said, "Don't go forward and do to others what has been done to us."

That's good advice for all of us.

Helicopter Lawyers

Oct. 11, 2008

Ahem, I'd like to get the attention of the American Bar Association, please. While I'm at it, I'd like the attention of each of the state chapters of the ABA, too.

Are you there? Good. Listen, at the risk of making some of my lawyer friends mad at me, I want to register a complaint about some of your members.

They are the lawyers who go on television to pontificate about court cases they have no connection to and have never sat in on.

As a veteran courthouse reporter, I know how the game is played. The TV host needs someone to interview about a high-profile legal case, and who better than a lawyer, right? No problem so far. We can all certainly benefit from a good and thoughtful lawyer's legal perspective.

My complaint is about those attorneys who appear on television not to enlighten, but to perform and promote themselves. Often they are in a New York studio offering up very specific pronouncements about what's happening in, say, the Las Vegas courtroom where OJ Simpson was on trial. They're not even there! They shouldn't be telling me, as I heard one say the other day, about how the Simpson jury members are digesting the evidence.

I covered the headline-grabbing criminal case of entertainer Michael Jackson in 2005. All the major television outlets had cameras there, including many from foreign countries. It was a lawyer magnet.

During breaks reporters would stretch their legs in a small courtyard and the helicopter lawyers would descend. They'd hover about under the guise of helping us really understand what was going on, yet some hadn't bothered to step inside the courtroom before pontificating! A few would literally fly in from other cities and states and immediately hit media row to comment. Still, others, we came to find out, were friends of the court-gagged attorneys inside, there to act as mouthpieces to hammer home a particular viewpoint.

It happened at the Scott Peterson murder trial in Northern California and the Robert Blake murder trial in Southern California. It happened at the Martha Stewart perjury and conspiracy trial in

Manhattan, New York. It happens during any trial where television cameras turn up. Lawyers get invited -- or just show up -- to get their mug on TV. Almost invariably they can't resist the typical reporter question, "Who's winning so far?" and the bogus scorecarding begins.

Should reporters be more careful in choosing who they actually put on the air? You bet they should. But back to my main complaint -- lawyers -- who flock to cameras like moths to lights.

I guess it's the recklessness of their comments that bugs me most. During ongoing trials I've heard experienced attorneys call a prosecutor's case "full of laughable evidence," and I've heard the witnesses labeled as "lying weirdoes." Mere suspects in a case are labeled "obviously guilty as sin" or worse a "candidate for the electric chair."

Aren't there rules against this?

The ABA has the set of Model Rules for members. It's not binding, but 47 states have adopted them in whole or in part. Among other things, the rules bar "conduct that is prejudicial to the administration of justice" and "conduct involving dishonesty...or misrepresentation." Recklessly saying things on TV that could affect the outcome of a trial would seem to fly in the face of those rules. What good are rules if members ignore them?

In this 24/7 news atmosphere, sitting jurors could easily have a spouse blurt out one of these irresponsible comments or inadvertently see it on the internet or television. It's known that many jurors ignore the judge's admonition not to discuss, watch TV or read anything about the case on which they are sitting. It is human nature to sneak a peek at something that's been banned.

Set aside the jurors for a moment. The general public is listening too. When they hear one lawyer bashing another's case it can't possibly help the legal profession as a whole. While there are exemplary attorneys explaining legal issues in the media, it is the ones who rant and rave we remember most.

Doug O'Brien is a rare bird, both a lawyer and national broadcast journalist. He worries that the public may reach opinions based on bad punditry. He says:

"Because no media outlet has the time or space for complete explanations, people who actually listen to what a lawyer pundit says can go away with the wrong impression of the law ... Then, surprise!

(If) the outcome is different than expected ... they think a lawyer or judge is pulling a fast one. That hurts the legal profession."

I wonder why the ABA hasn't done something to reign in these careless self-promoters.

Dying to Be Entertaining

Oct. 18, 2008

Exactly when did murder become so entertaining?

Death has been the center of classic literature throughout history. Think Cain and Abel, Romeo and Juliet, Julius Caesar and Cleopatra. But there's something very different about reading the great books and watching what passes for entertainment these days.

Take television, for example, where murder is served up as a nightly ritual on "Law & Order," "CSI," "Cold Case," "N.C.I.S." and other shows. Some have become so popular that spinoff shows were spawned.

But none take murder to the level Showtime's Sunday-night showpiece "Dexter" does. The cable network has just announced that the program broke a ratings record, with total viewers jumping 21 percent over last year.

When Showtime first began airing "Dexter" and its parent company, CBS, aired episodes on the network during the writers' strike, some church groups spoke out about its storyline.

Now, it's my turn.

"Dexter" is a about a crime-lab forensic tech who helps investigate serial killers, all the while struggling against his own serial killer urges. As the story goes, Dexter Morgan was adopted as a toddler by a police officer who, after recognizing the boy's sociopathic personality, trained him to exercise his murderous tendencies only on those who truly deserve it. Naturally, Dexter (played by Michael C. Hall) doesn't emerge from the darkness into light. Oh, no. Of course not! What would be the fun in that? Instead, Dexter kills off serial killers and mysteriously dodges detection from his law enforcement colleagues, including his own police-officer sister.

I've watched the program because, well, who doesn't like a good mystery? But in the end, I come away wondering the same thing I wondered after watching old episodes of "Superman": Why didn't all those smart people around Clark Kent figure him out? Why did none of them realize what he was really up to? More disturbingly, with "Dexter" I'm left wondering whether Showtime is somehow glorifying the taking of life, as if it's OK for Dexter to resort to the very tactic the show's various serial killers employ: cold-blooded murder.

And frankly, it bothers me that the program is shown on Sunday nights. That was always family TV night in our house, the final opportunity for all of us to be together before the work week. Sunday nights were special when I was a kid because after a big family meal my cousins, Sandy and Terry, and I were allowed to snuggle up and watch Ed Sullivan or "Bonanza."

Somehow I think Sullivan and Little Joe (not to mention Hoss) would be horrified by Dexter's antics. Yet "TV Guide" calls the program "bloody good stuff." Showtime promotes it with the phrase "A killer show at a killer deal!" It's murder as a magnet to sell cable-TV programming. Amazing.

The "Dexter" website features a screen that becomes slowly spattered with blood. It invites visitors to "Dexter-ize" the website of their choice. You can also play the Body Bag Toss Game in which you help Dexter get rid of the evidence. Then there's the Scramble Slay Game and the Dexter Marketplace, where you can buy a set of coasters with the chalk outline of a dissected body or a set of blood-spattered pillowcases.

What has happened to us?

Look, I love a good crime story. And I don't mean to preach here. But I've dedicated a big part of my career to covering crime and justice, and it is with firsthand certainty that I tell you real murder is never entertaining. The smell of it hits you the moment you arrive at a scene. The amount of blood can literally make you gag, and most of the time seeking justice for the dead is a pretty ugly experience. While it takes the characters on "Law & Order" an hour to move through discovery, trial and verdict, it often takes years in real-life -- if it happens at all. None of the steps after murder are fun.

Ask homicide detectives, staffers in the district attorney's office or the people who clean up crime scenes whether murder is entertaining to them. Like me, they probably watch many programs that highlight what they do. But unlike you, they may come away with a heavy heart, thinking, "That's not really the way it is."

I don't want to curb television writers' creativity or abridge free speech. But I would like it if we could all take a step back once in a while and judge things on an ethical and moral plane.

It is one thing to read a book or see a program about solving murder, the world's most heinous crime. It's quite another for an entertainment vehicle to choose murder as a method of payback. Murder is murder. Can't they figure out another way to entertain us?

CSI Don't Think So!

Jan. 3, 2009

Emmy Award-winning TV producer Jerry Bruckheimer has let me down. He's let all of us down.

For years we've been riveted by his prime-time programs: The "CSI" franchise based in Miami, Las Vegas and New York, "Cold Case," "Without a Trace" and others. I am one of Bruckheimer's biggest fans.

But on a recent episode of "CSI Miami," Bruckheimer's quality control broke down. He allowed his writers to get away with poetic license that could seriously damage law enforcement efforts.

In an episode called "The Tipping Point," a thug declares of his 'hood, "God gave up on this neighborhood a long time ago." And, indeed, we learn that the population has been scared into silence by the violent actions of the local gang. But then a do-gooder named Reverend Mike is murdered. Investigators are stymied until one brave young person calls Crime Stoppers with vital information.

This is a wonderful message for those urban numbskulls who still think cooperating with police is "snitching."

But what do Bruckheimer's writers have the authorities say when they learn there is a Crime Stoppers tip? Are they thankful? No.

"Those people are just trying to make a buck off the county," one ignorant character says to another. "Can we trust them?"

Within minutes we see the tipster, a worried young woman named Yolanda, exiting an elevator at police headquarters asking, "So, you can guarantee no one will know I'm the one who called?" And she is reassured by the lead detective that all tips are confidential. Later, as the officer scrolls through a computer list of other Crime Stopper calls (and we clearly see a roster of names and address) another

"CSI" dumbbell dismissively questions the detective's action, saying: "The tip line? I thought it was mostly crackpots!"

Now, if any of the program's writers bothered to check facts they would have found that Crime Stoppers is nothing like they described. First, the reward fund is 100 percent donated from civilian sources, and no county, state or federal money is accepted. Doing so would require a paper trail no one wants. Why? Because all tips are strictly confidential! No one would ever ask for a caller's name or address, and that information is never stored on some computerized master list. When someone with a tip phones Crime Stoppers they are given a unique tipster ID number and told to keep calling back to see if they are due a reward check.

For "CSI Miami" to show tipster Yolanda being outed and brought into a public cop shop is impossible. It would never happen.

And so, what occurs next in the episode is completely inconceivable. Somehow the street gang finds out Yolanda has been talking to police. She's hog-tied and left inside a building that's about to be obliterated by a massive bomb. She's saved at the last minute because the lead character, Horatio Caine, pulls a Dudley Do-Right.

The lesson left from this "CSI Miami" episode is that if you snitch, you're in danger. If you talk to the police about a crime, the bad guy will find out and get you. If you're lame enough to call Crime Stoppers, you must be a "crackpot."

How many young people saw that episode and got that lesson in their brain? And I'll bet it's not just Crime Stopper personnel who cringed at the program. Good detectives everywhere welcome anonymous tips, especially in murder cases. They've already got to fight the rap-music message that "snitchin' ain't cool." They don't need a popular primetime TV show (dedicated to crime fighting, no less!) helping spread that self-destructive line.

Look, I'm a writer. I value the First Amendment, character development and all that. What I don't value is lazy writing that leaves the wrong impression when the real facts are so compelling.

As I coincidentally wrote in this space recently, Crime Stoppers has been in existence for more than 30 years. Its success is directly attributed to good citizens who do the right thing. In the U.S., more than 800,000 cases like murder, rape, armed robbery and child molestation have been cleared thanks to Crime Stopper tipsters.

More than a $1 billion in property has been recovered, $4 billion worth of illegal drugs.

At the end of the "CSI" episode the bad guys are busted because Yolanda picked up a phone. She got a $1,000 reward after her information led to arrests. That's a scenario "CSI" got right. It happens every day in our 50 states and 24 other countries where Crime Stoppers operates.

Come on, Hollywood. You don't have to make it up. Just follow the facts, especially when you're dealing with something as crucial as Crime Stoppers. And please, Jerry Bruckheimer, don't rerun that episode.

Killer Classifieds

May 2, 2009

Jim Buckmaster must think we're stupid. He's the CEO of Craigslist, the popular and controversial internet classified ad site. Faced with another major public relations disaster, this time the murder of a young woman who reportedly hooked up with her killer via Craigslist, all Buckmaster had to say was, "I would not describe any section of our site as 'sex related.'" He admits Craigslist does feature an "erotic services" section, but he says it was not designed to offer more than "legitimate escort services, sensual massages or exotic dancers."

What does he think "erotic service" leads to, a game of patty-cake?

In case you've been on a different planet lately, Craigslist is a worldwide internet site featuring millions of ads on everything from "Jobs, housing, goods, services, romance, local activities, advice -- just about anything, really."

The most recent story has to do with the brutal beating and shooting death of 25-year-old Julissa Brisman in a luxury Boston, Massachusetts, hotel room. That's where police say she met medical school student Philip Markoff, now dubbed the Craigslist killer. At this writing, Markoff is charged with Brisman's murder and is suspected in the kidnapping and assault of at least two other women he met through the same site.

Let me set the record straight. Craigslist includes ads for sex -- lots of them. So Buckmaster either doesn't know his own product or he's parsing words to an extent that would put Bill Clinton to shame. Besides the erotic services section, there's a whole "personals" section with subtitles such as "women seeking men," "women seeking women," "men seeking men." Just what does Buckmaster think these people are seeking? A ping-pong partner?

Suzy Spencer, a best-selling author who's researching a book on sexual trends in America, tells me that the Craigslist "Casual Encounters" section is also sexually oriented. She says: "It's where men and women go specifically to find partners for spur-of-the-moment, no-strings-attached sex, not a date for dinner and a movie. I know; it's where I've found many of my (book's) sources, and they've told me in minute detail about the sex they had with partners they found via Craigslist."

Look, I'm not blaming Craigslist for this young woman's murder. But you'd think its corporate culture might include the acceptance of some responsibility, maybe even a public admission, that their site has been a facilitator for predators on the prowl.

Supporters of the site have said it's actually a good thing Markoff turned to Craigslist because police were able to follow the computer clues right to his doorstep. I say there's never much good news when someone has been murdered.

The complaints about Craigslist and sex ads aren't new. Last year 40 state attorneys general put pressure on the company and forced it to take steps to tone down its salacious postings. In March 2008 Craigslist began requiring all those who placed erotic ads to supply a telephone number, thinking that would be a deterrent. It wasn't. In Nov. 2008 the company agreed to charge erotic service advertisers a small credit card fee, which could go to identify them. Craigslist, then put in the uncomfortable position of both running and profiting from the erotic ads, declared that the money would go to charities fighting human trafficking and child exploitation. That was nice.

Not much changed, however, as thousands of the scandalous ads continued to crop up on the site. Just last month, Tom Dart, sheriff of Cook County, Illinois, filed a federal lawsuit against Craigslist, or as he called it, "the largest source of prostitution in America."

A veteran social worker source of mine in Oakland, California, agrees with the sheriff. She says Craigslist continues to be a major path of income for young girls she works with. Some of them brag that they were as young as 12 when they began to tap Craigslist classifieds whenever they needed to make some cold, hard cash. For the men who responded, that was felony statutory rape.

Buckmaster insists that most of his site's classifieds are for furniture, appliances, jobs and legitimate services. Only about "one percent of ads posted on Craigslist are in the erotic services section," he says. So here's a question: If they constitute that small a contribution to Craigslist and the site makes no money from them, why not take the high road and refuse to run them? Who among us wouldn't applaud that course of action? Wouldn't that be a better public relations move than insisting Craigslist is not culpable in any way?

I wonder what Craig himself thinks about all this. Yes, the site's founder, Craig Newman, still works there as its iconic head and customer service representative. I wonder if he's totally proud of what his corporate creation has become.

Update: In the fall of 2010 Craigslist quietly removed its "adult services" category. The move came after the attorneys general from 17 states were preparing legal actions against Craigslist for what they alleged were "rampant" ads for prostitution and child sex trafficking.

When Does Internet Fantasy Become Actual Crime?

Mar. 16, 2013

It was a bizarre criminal case sensationalized by both the media and the defense team. Slogans and spins were tossed about so fast and so furiously that the real facts of the case were hard to determine. At the core of the federal case was a very important issue: When do thoughts expressed in internet chatrooms become fodder for criminal prosecution? Could something you write online be used against you in a court of law?

From the get-go reporters branded the defendant in this case, New York Police Officer Gilberto Valle, "The Cannibal Cop" - a man who used the internet to feed his vile fantasies and conspire with others to kidnap, cook and eat female victims.

Attorneys for Valle maintained that federal prosecutors were trying to convict their client "for his thoughts (and) his (written) fantasies," not for any bona fide criminal activity.

I was ready to be outraged at the idea that the feds were trying to convict someone based solely on rambling cyber-writings no matter how despicable they might have been. I latched onto a line in the closing argument of defense attorney Julia Gatto when she said: "This prosecution rests on the ugliness of Gil's thoughts. We don't convict human beings because of ugly thoughts."

It turns out neither characterization was accurate. The Cannibal Cop hadn't cannibalized anyone. No human being was physically hurt, although Valle's wife was emotionally destroyed when she stumbled across graphic and incriminating information on her new husband's computer. (She immediately left home, taking their baby daughter with her, and contacted the FBI to report what she had found.)

And the evidence in court revealed that it wasn't just "fantasy role-playing," as Valle's defense team would have had the jury believe. There was plenty of evidence gathered by federal investigators that revealed overt acts committed by Valle in furtherance of the crimes of kidnapping and maybe even attempted murder. An FBI agent who spoke with Valle after his arrest testified that the defendant had admitted that his cyber-fantasy life was "bleeding" over into his real life.

To summarize the prosecutor's court case: Officer Valle -- married just three months -- had long corresponded with other "death fetishists" worldwide about his potential kidnap victims, torturous forms of cooking prey and elaborate dining plans with the head of the female victim used as a centerpiece. He listed among his intended victims his wife, two of his college friends and a local high school softball star.

Valle's explicit emails to fellow fetishists outlined in gruesome and sick detail his plans for the targeted women once he had captured and trussed them.

He wrote of cooking rotisseries, of wanting to hear his victims scream and cry out in pain. He wrote of how he drooled over one of his potential victims during a weekend brunch date with his wife.

He wrote that he longed for "the day I cram a chloroform-soaked rag in her face." The prosecution described Valle as a "sexual sadist" and said that the brunch date was Valle's way of conducting surveillance of an intended victim.

Officer Valle's email correspondence with a New Jersey man revealed he had agreed to take $5,000 in exchange for kidnapping a specific victim for him. And there was testimony that Officer Valle had been seen on that woman's block, conducting surveillance of her home. (That New Jersey man has also been arrested and is currently awaiting trial.)

There was also evidence presented to the six-man, six-woman jury that Officer Valle had illegally accessed both the NYPD and a federal databases to gather personal information about his intended female targets. Records of his internet searches were there for all to see, with specific dates and times attached.

When the defense described this case with the snappy description of being a "thought prosecution," and when other defense attorneys jumped in to warn that all of us should worry that anything we write online could be used against us, I had to hope that discerning consumers of news could see through the bluster. What was the defense team really saying, that prosecutors had no right to act unless Valle had actually killed and cannibalized some poor, unsuspecting woman? To my mind, that is some kind of tortured thinking all on its own.

The fact? Valle faced no "thought charges." There were only two counts: conspiring to kidnap and accessing a federal database without authorization. Neither charge was based solely on his inner thoughts or his disgusting writings. And the jury obviously felt there was enough evidence that he had taken concrete actions toward committing a crime to find him guilty on both counts.

After the verdict, attorney Preet Bharara said in a statement: "A unanimous jury found that Gilberto Valle's detailed and specific plans to abduct women for the purpose of committing grotesque crimes were very real. ... The internet is a forum for the free exchange of ideas, but it does not confer immunity for plotting crimes and taking steps to carry out those crimes."

The defense team has announced it will appeal Valle's conviction, and so you will likely hear more about how the government is out to violate your rights or to turn your internet chats against you. Don't be fooled. I'm confident that our freedoms of speech, writing and thought are safe and sound.

UPDATE: In June 2014, a federal court judge overturned Valle's conspiracy conviction, saying evidence supported the claim that

Valle was only "fantasy role-playing." The conviction on illegally accessing a government database stood, but Valle was released after serving 21 months in prison. At this writing the government is appealing dismissal of the conspiracy charge.

Media Misstep: All Victims Count

May 24, 2014

An open letter to the editor at Time magazine:

It was with great anticipation that I picked up your May 14, 2014, edition with the big, red college pennant on the cover emblazoned with the word "RAPE."

"Great," I thought, "The mainstream media is finally going to report about the sexual crimes committed against our young people."

It didn't take me long to realize that your reporters and editors completely ignored half of the equation. Not one mention was made of male sexual abuse victims. Why is that? Don't male victims count?

Don't you see that this kind of reporting sends exactly that message? If the media only talks about the female victims of these horrible crimes, the male victims will continue to stay silent, and the predators will remain free!

Sincerely yours,

Diane Dimond

Last week, I wrote about the latest National Crime Victimization Survey's stunning statistic that 38 percent of sexual violence victims are male. They are set upon in all sorts of places like private homes, athletic venues, sleep-away camps and college campuses, especially during fraternity hazing rituals. I also wrote about the mental and emotional dynamics behind so many victimized young males who choose to suffer in silence and not report their abuse. When survivors do reveal, they often wait decades to speak the truth and seek support for their emotional scars.

I am confounded that the mainstream media doesn't report on this as fervently as they report sex crimes against females. This kind of journalism makes it enormously more difficult for male victims. You can't wipe away the moldy stigma of something unless you shine a light on it.

Recently, a survivor of convicted child molester Jerry Sandusky made headlines when he spoke of the public reaction to his charge of childhood sex abuse by the popular Penn State football coach. Aaron Fisher made it clear people just didn't understand how difficult it was for him to finally come forward, to be Victim No. 1 and the youngest of the 10 victims mentioned at trial. Fisher said the very worst part of the process came after he reported his abuse to police.

Fisher's victimization started when he was 11 years old, and at 14 he finally mustered up the courage to tell. Then he waited years while the police conducted a sparsely staffed investigation of Sandusky. Fisher told The Spokesman-Review newspaper in Spokane, Washington, that he felt police "broke promises" and dragged their feet. And once word leaked out about his allegations, neighbors made him feel like the villain.

"Because of who he was and what he created and what he did in his lifetime, pretty much Sandusky was a god on earth for people," Fisher said.

When he finally testified at trial, Fisher was 18. Those four years of silence from the justice system and the cold shoulder from others were the "worst thing ever - the worst altogether of anything," he said.

Silence never solves anything.

The story of FBI Special Agent Jim Clemente, a man who spent a career specializing in Child Sex Crimes investigations, makes my point. It is Clemente's personal story of falling prey to a sexual predator and living for years with the near-crippling fear of exposure.

At 15, Clemente was a scrawny teen, seeking independence and just coming to grips with his sexuality. A counselor at Catholic wilderness camp took him under his wing. The boy thought of him as a real "man's man" and was honored when asked to stay on at the end of the camp season to help close up the compound.

This trusted church employee took young Clemente to a bar, let him drive his car, gave him beer, spoke to him about masturbation and pornography and then did the unthinkable. The abuse had a profound effect. Clemente told me he suffered guilt, sorrow, loneliness, shame and depression. Unable to trust anyone, he pushed away his family and friends. Recurring nightmares haunted him.

Clemente had always dreamed of a profession in law enforcement and felt if he revealed what had happened to him or if he sought therapy his career would be jeopardized. So Clemente stayed silent for a decade. The FBI calls this delayed disclosure. It is not unusual, and it occurs whether the perpetrator is male or female.

Clemente's brother finally told him about lewd Polaroids of other boy campers he had once seen in the counselor's office, pictures taken through a peephole. Clemente, then a prosecutor for the City of New York, realized he had to track down this predator and stop him.

The man was eventually convicted, but there's no telling how many boys he had violated over the years. Clemente discovered he had taught and coached at 13 different schools and had been accused of sexual abuse against boys numerous times. But no one ever reported the suspect to police, and he simply moved on to new hunting grounds. There was more silence, which obviously only compounded the problem and exposed more boys to harm.

The CDC's 2010 Sexual Violence Survey reports that over 25 million American males will suffer sexual violence in their lifetimes. Yet the bulk of the money spent to help victims goes to women-only services. The media rarely mentions male survivors of sexual abuse. And many of us ignorantly believe if a victim doesn't tell right away, they are suspect.

"I find it hard to believe that after cases like Sandusky ... people still don't understand the fact that boys who are sexually abused typically take 20, 30 or more years to come forward," Clemente said. It's a shame, he wrote in an email, that, "The public seems to more readily accept that men will make false allegations that they were victimized, rather than understand that it takes a great deal of time to overcome the stigma of victimization, the fears of being seen as damaged goods, as not being a man, as being gay or being a potential offender."

I submit that the public will never fully understand until the media starts reporting the full and complete story of sexual abuse survivors. Hey, Time magazine, how about a follow-up cover story?

Revenge on Purveyors of Revenge Porn

April 13, 2015

Can I get a high-five and a hallelujah for the California judge who recently sentenced cyber-criminal Kevin Bollaert to 18 years behind bars? Finally, some of the smarmy creatures who psychopathically roam the dark corners of the internet are being brought to justice.

Every indication is that laws and punishments are slowly but surely catching up with these creeps.

Bollaert, age 27, is one of those repulsive human beings who made money off the pain of others by posting so-called "revenge porn," sexually suggestive photographs previously exchanged between lovers and now used to humiliate them after the relationship soured.

From his home base in San Diego, California, Bollaert solicited jilted lovers to send in nude and embarrassing photos, mostly of young women, and then posted thousands of them online. When he was finally caught and charged with identity theft and extortion, Bollaert was asked by an investigator why he started such an awful cyber-exploitation business.

"I don't know, dude. Like, it was just fun," he said.

At the now-defunct UGotPosted website, Bollaert uploaded more than 10,000 intimate images in just 10 months. To further shame the victims, Bollaert included their name, location, age and Facebook profile.

But according to court documents, he didn't stop there. After women begged him via email to remove their private pictures, Bollaert steered them to his second website, ChangeMyReputation. There he extorted hundreds of dollars from each victim before agreeing to take down the offending photos.

Testimony from tearful victims revealed the human damage. One woman said that after reading some 400 vulgar messages on her social media sites, her shaky emotional state forced her to quit college and seek help at a mental hospital. Another, quoted in the criminal complaint, said that after her family found out about her nude photos she was disowned and thrown out of the house. A third victim who got her intimate pictures removed, only to see them reposted, said she nearly killed herself when police said they could do nothing to help.

Before announcing Bollaert's sentence, Superior Court Judge David Gill made it clear that probation was "clearly off the table" and that offenders like the one who stood before him deserve "a large dose of punishment."

I bet that sent a shiver up the spine of Hunter Moore, 28, who Rolling Stone magazine once called "The most hated man on the internet." Moore operated a similar site, also in California, called IsAnyoneUp. He has pleaded guilty to federal cyber-crime charges. He admits that in addition to accepting private revenge photos, he and an accomplice hacked nude photos from other sites and reposted them. Moore faces up to seven years in prison when he's sentenced in June.

Yep. It seems the laws are finally catching up with the ugliest realities of the internet.

In Texas last year, a woman won a $500,000 settlement from an ex-boyfriend who had promised he would erase provocative photos and videos she sent him over the years. Instead, after they broke up he plastered them across the internet and then cruelly taunted her with statistics about how many people had seen them.

In Tampa, Florida, last October, a young woman was horrified to learn that her ex had not only posted her sexually suggestive photos online but had also emailed them to her mother. She won a $600,000 award.

Those two men are unlikely to be able to pay the hefty awards, but pending appeals, the court judgements could dog them for the rest of their lives.

As it stands now, 17 states have passed laws regulating revenge porn in one way or another: Alaska, Arizona, California, Colorado, Delaware, Georgia, Hawaii, Idaho, Illinois, Maryland, New Mexico, New Jersey, Idaho, Pennsylvania, Utah, Virginia and Wisconsin. (Texas is also poised to pass such a law.) If you don't see your state on the list, you might want to ask your lawmakers, "What are we waiting for?"

More and more victims have begun to fight back, with or without state laws to back up their civil court claims. So here's a warning for anyone bent on some kind of internet-based revenge: If your victim challenges you in court, you may be found liable -- for the rest of your life.

~~~

CHAPTER 7
Prisons

"Under a government which imprisons any unjustly, the true place for a just man is also a prison." ~ **Henry David Thoreau**

Oh, what a terrible mess we've made of our prison system in America! Under the guise of altering behavior with the threat of hefty, mandatory prison sentences, we have overstuffed our nation's prisons past the bursting point. We hold the dubious distinction of incarcerating a larger percentage of our population than any other civilized country in the world.

Some might call it racially motivated. I call it the road to hell paved with good intentions.

We lump the mentally ill in with the most hardcore criminals, we lump in drug addicts with career killers and rapists as if there is no distinction. And, I'm ashamed to say that our prison system condemns more inmates (including juveniles) to debilitating and soul-stripping solitary confinement than Nazi Germany ever thought about, sometimes years and even decades of torturous solitary confinement.

Why do we allow it? Because our "leaders" told us it was the only way to keep the rest of us safe.

At the same time, some prisons go overboard allowing inmates perks they could never afford on the outside -- degrees in higher education and sex change operations for example -- all paid for by you and me, the taxpayers.

As I say, our prison system is a terrible mess.

A Look Inside Gitmo --
From Someone Who Lived There

Feb. 5, 2009

President Barack Obama has fast-tracked closing the multimillion dollar American-constructed-and-controlled detention center at Guantanamo Bay, Cuba.

OK, so now where do all the bad guys go after Gitmo shuts its doors?

It's a question that's long plagued Brig. Gen. Greg Zanetti, who from January 2008 to January 2009 was the deputy commander of Gitmo.

"These are bad men," Zanetti told me after his recent return to his native Albuquerque, New Mexico. In a slow, emphatic voice, he said: "There is an edge to these guys Americans just don't understand. They want us dead."

And without quite saying it, I got the feeling Zanetti meant the new president is among those who don't get it.

Gen. Zanetti, a West Point graduate with a mile-long military resume, knows all about the Gitmo gang. He has walked among them and read their background files, and he knows them by name. He gave me a quick history lesson full of perspective.

Right after the Sept. 11 attacks "we were an angry nation," he says. We went to the battlefield and scooped up hundreds of enemy combatants. Some were thought to be so valuable they were taken to secret places in secret countries, and lifesaving intelligence was reportedly extracted. Does the general think we used torture to get it? He won't go there. But he says that nearly every man picked up by U.S. forces praised the 9/11 terrorists and would have gleefully killed more Americans to earn their spots on the martyr list.

"There have been a total of about 770 enemy combatants arrive at Gitmo," Zanetti told me. Over the years, some were determined to be low-level threats and released; others were sent back to their home countries for further imprisonment or into the welcoming arms of their old terror buddies, who declared them to be "The Heroes of Guantanamo!" Recent reports conclude more than 60 ex-Gitmo residents have returned to their terrorist ways.

Today, Gitmo holds just 250 enemy combatants. They are the 250 no American prison wants and no foreign country will claim.

They are the worst of the worst, according to the general, who watched as they bit, kicked, elbowed or threw their feces and vomit on the New Mexico National Guardsmen, who went to Cuba with him for the one-year tour of duty.

"Most Americans don't understand that the mistreatment at Gitmo is prisoner on guard," not the other way around, says Zanetti.

The detainees enjoy what Zanetti called a "'Hogan's Heroes'-type camp ... like an old-age home for terrorists," he said.

They aren't locked away in cells 24/7. They have communal rooms, where they mingle and enjoy their native periodicals. There are ocean views and flat-screen televisions, and some prisoners are allowed to grow their own food. Their Qurans and Muslim prayer rugs are brought out five times a day, and a cultural adviser is on hand to guide the menu for the several feast days they mark each month, complete with traditional dishes of lamb and cucumber sauces.

While they mingle, they continue to scheme against the U.S., according to the general. They've learned, sometimes from their own American-appointed lawyers, that the most effective way to continue the revolution is to turn our system against us.

They engage in a strategic legal and media war, designed to paint themselves as victims. We saw it during the disruptive trial of Zacarias Moussaoui, and we will surely see it again if there are more civilian trials here. And what would happen if a trial technicality actually set a terrorist free?

But the undeniable and unpleasant fact is that the United States has held these men for years without charges and without trials, and that is most certainly not the American way.

"I am bothered by the prolonged detentions," the general said. But he explained that Gitmo has hosted scores of foreign delegations, from the International Red Cross, Russia, Middle East and several European countries. Only Saudi Arabia took its prisoners back and repatriated them, giving them homes and cars if they behaved themselves. In fact, the general told me, when the delegation from Yemen arrived, several of the majority Yemeni prisoners pointed at the representatives and declared, "That's the person who recruited me to fight!" None were taken home.

President Obama seems certain some countries will step forward, but I don't see a line forming at Gitmo's door.

There is still the possibility of holding military trials, but what happens if the defendant is found guilty? He'll have to be jailed somewhere and the community N.I.M.B.Y. (Not In My Backyard) protests are in full swing at the most-often mentioned U.S. locations: Leavenworth, Colorado's supermax penitentiary, and the Naval Brig in South Carolina.

Gee, maybe Gitmo isn't so bad after all.

Is Rape OK With You?

Sept. 7, 2009

Is there anyone out there reading this who condones rape?

No, of course not.

Who in civilized society would believe that the violent sexual assault of another person is OK?

Why do we allow the brutal, repeated rape of our prisoners?

We've known about the problem for decades. We read about the sexual victimization of inmates in books and newspapers, we see it depicted on TV and in the movies. Yet somehow it's been allowed to continue. These attacks are both prisoner-on-prisoner and guard-on-prisoner, and a majority of the time the perpetrator goes unpunished. Why is that?

Do we think that once a person is convicted of a crime he or she loses all constitutional rights? Do you personally believe prisoners should be allowed to pursue justice if they're victimized behind bars? If your answer is no, would you change your mind if the sexual attack happened to a prisoner who is a juvenile?

These are heavy questions, and the answers go to define who we are as a people.

Back in 2003, the Prison Rape Elimination Act was passed, and a special body was created to study the problem. Think about that for a minute. We had to have a special act of Congress before we, as human beings, stood up and said, "You know, prison rape just isn't right."

Even with the presidential act, it took until 2006 for the state of Vermont to take steps to actually criminalize prison staffers' sexual attacks on inmates. It was the last state in the union to do so. And it wasn't until 2007 that Texas finally agreed to investigate hundreds of complaints of sexual victimization of juvenile offenders at Texas Youth Commission facilities.

Look, I'm for prisoners doing hard time if the crime commands it, but we've been demanding better treatment for caged animals lately (think the Michael Vick dogfighting case) than we have for caged humans.

A 2007 study by the Bureau of Justice Statistics found that more than 60,000 inmates are sexually attacked every year, more often by a guard than another prisoner. In fact, there were a surprising number of cases of male staff assaulting male inmates.

The most frequent victims are inmates who are short, young, gay or female. The study also found a real lack of any meaningful punishment for this very obvious crime.

Think about the toll of broken human lives we then put back on the street.

There are cases from states all across America. Here are three examples.

In Colorado last year, a prison guard accused of raping a female inmate was allowed to plead guilty to a mere misdemeanor, and he got just 60 days in jail. This year, a federal judge hearing the victim's civil suit was so disgusted with the leniency of the sentence he imposed $1.3 million in damages for the inmate. Three other female inmates in Colorado have pending civil lawsuits alleging they, too, were forced by state Department of Corrections employees to perform sexual acts. Each prisoner seeks $150 million in damages.

The state of Michigan determined that male employees of its Department of Corrections had acted so egregiously over the years that it established a $100 million fund for victimized inmates to draw from. So far more than 900 prisoners have come forward seeking money for alleged sexual misconduct inside Michigan prisons.

In Oregon, the state is facing a multimillion dollar lawsuit filed by five female prisoners who claim they endured years of sexual abuse by a guard and other Corrections Department employees at the Coffee Creek Correctional Facility in Wilsonville. If the state loses the case, it's a safe bet that prisoners in other Oregon facilities will feel empowered to file their own suits.

Some of these allegations may not be true, of course, but even if half or a third of the 60,000 reports per year are viable, that's too many sexual assaults being perpetrated against too many people. Prisoners have to serve their sentences, but those sentences do not come with rape attached.

The problem should not be viewed as an economic one, although states could save millions if they more closely monitored their prison guards' behavior. It should be seen through a moral and ethical lens.

Six years after the Prison Rape Elimination Act was passed, its commission has finally released an official report. Among the recommendations: better training for staff in recognizing assaults, addressing prison overcrowding, providing proper medical and mental health care for victims, and harsher penalties for staff who engage in assault or allow it to happen.

Gee, it took us all this time to figure that out? Did we believe prisoners are just throw-away citizens, people without civil rights? That's not the American way.

Tax Fraud From Behind Bars

Mar. 5, 2011

At prisons across the country, all incoming mail is opened and checked for contraband before the prisoner ever receives it. What would be considered mail tampering on the outside is standard operating procedure in a prison.

Amazingly, however, outgoing prison mail is mostly just bundled up and shipped out via the U.S. Postal Service with no inspection. The only exception is if a particular prisoner is under suspicion for some sort of criminal activity.

That's a shame because this failure to monitor mail is the first weak link in a chain of inmate tax fraud that's been going on for years, according to government investigators. In just the 2009 tax year, for example, prisoner-inspired IRS fraud cost you, me and every other taxpaying American at least $39 million.

How could this happen? How could a prisoner fake an income tax return from behind bars and have it go unnoticed? Many times, an outsider's bank account is used to launder the money. But many times, sizeable refund checks are deposited directly into prison bank accounts. Don't any officials notice?

While the rest of us sweat to scrape up every W-9 or 1099 form, every receipt and all the corresponding documentation the IRS requires by the annual mid-April deadline, these incarcerated mooks are blatantly committing another criminal act right under their guards' noses.

A recent inspector general's audit of the problem revealed how state prisoners have been getting away with it. First, often using the prison library computer, the inmate steals a Social Security number. While surfing online, it's also pretty easy to locate a list of bankrupted businesses. The prisoner takes the name of one of them and lists it as their former employer on a 1040 form. Oh, and the form is also readily available online and simple for the prisoner to print out and fill out.

In this era of record business failures, it is nearly impossible for the IRS to track the truthfulness of every 1040 form that lists a bankrupted employer.

The federal audit also disclosed just how gutsy these inmates get. More than two dozen of them asked for and got $50,000 worth of federal tax credits for electric cars and other alternative fuel cars. Never mind that they couldn't drive a car if they wanted to! And the report concluded that the $39 million fraud from 2009 was likely even larger because some 10,000 returns from prisoners were never scrutinized.

If the first weak link is the state prison system, which allows the fake tax forms to be mailed out unchallenged, the second overlooked failsafe has to be the IRS itself. The agency is sending out millions of dollars in undeserved tax refunds to convicts without so much as a double check of Social Security numbers or a second thought as to why a check would be going to a prison address in the first place. Apparently there's no built-in filter at the IRS to flag checks going to state prisons.

That's got to change!

In 2008, Congress finally got around to passing a law that allows the IRS to share information about suspicious tax returns with the federal Bureau of Prisons. To date, there's no law that allows the IRS to share with state prison officials. That's got to change, too, especially for the states of California, Florida, Georgia and others with the largest prison populations.

Some prisoners are very smart. Not smart enough to have stayed out of jail, mind you, but intelligent enough to use their abundance of free time to come up with all sorts of scams and launch them from their prison cells. Just because this IRS scam is getting some publicity now doesn't mean it's going to stop. With no way for the IRS and the state to legally communicate, I can just hear the sarcastic titters of the cons now. They'll say: "What? I'm gonna get in trouble? What? Are they gonna put me in jail?"

It ticks me off that at a time when my family and so many others strain to cut corners and watch every penny, this fraud continues year after year with no apparent shift in government procedures to stop it.

Not long ago, I wrote here about how the Government Accountability Office had identified 30 areas of Congress in which multiple billions of dollars could be saved if they acted. Crooks bilking our Medicare and Medicaid systems, unnecessary military spending and people who simply haven't paid their taxes could be more enthusiastically pursued. So far, no action has been taken.

How's this for an idea? From this point forward, and for the rest of the year, how about Congress agrees to expeditiously take up each and every one of those 30 areas outlined by the independent GAO? And once those billions of dollars are saved, can someone please offer a law that lets the IRS share information with state prison officials to stop prison IRS fraud?

Is anybody out there with me?

Meaningful Prison Labor

April 9, 2011

Who doesn't remember the history class lesson about chain-gang, rock-busting punishments for prisoners? Or the Academy Award-winning movie with Paul Newman, "Cool Hand Luke," where prisoners were forced to dig meaningless trenches as their daily chore?

That is not what I'm advocating when I say we should return to full-scale prison labor in this country.

I'm talking about prisoner labor that supplies a real service to the community or that goes to support the prisoner's incarceration - such as growing their own food or building new facilities on prison grounds ... labor projects that go beyond making license plates and picking up litter.

As U.S. Sen. John Ensign, Republican of Nevada, was quoted recently saying, "Do we want them just sitting in prison, lifting weights, becoming violent and thinking about their next crime?"

Of course, the answer is no. And I also don't want them whiling away their time watching television, playing around with e-mail or conducting their gang business on my dime. And by the way, on average it costs roughly $29,000 a year to keep an inmate locked up.

Ensign, long a supporter of the Federal Prison Industries government program - now called Unicor and established by Congress in 1934 to help rehabilitate and train inmates - would like to see the idea expanded. He's offered a bill that would make it mandatory for all low-security prisoners to work 50 hours a week.

Currently, the FPI includes only about 15,000 federal prisoners. They produce products like furniture, electronic components, clothing and fencing. While they don't earn much money - $1.15 an hour tops - they are acquiring marketable skills. Also, companies that manufacture their goods with inmate labor cover a significant portion of prison staff salaries. In these strained economic times it is a win-win situation.

Some critics say forcing prisoners to work for less than minimum wage and in situations without the built-in health and safety guidelines the rest of us enjoy is akin to slavery and, at the very least, is taking advantage of a captive group.

I say we need to remember these are people convicted of preying on innocent fellow citizens who lost some of their rights by the very criminal deeds they perpetrated. One dollar and 15 cents an hour is better than earning nothing while these criminals pay off their debt to society.

In New York, the state is saving about $3.5 million each year by having inmates man the call center phones for the Department of Motor Vehicles.

In California, prisoners are learning to repair leaky public water tanks and are coming away with valuable underwater welding skills. In Florida, inmates have partnered with an agricultural center at the University of Florida and have not only helped the center survive, they are also growing a sizable portion of their own healthy food. After it was shown that inmate farming saved the Florida system nearly $2.5 million, the governor expanded the program.

Ohio prisoners are given buckets and brushes and paint their own cells. In New Jersey, a serious overpopulation of deer has created the constant need to clear carcasses off highways, and prisoners are called to that duty. In Georgia, convicts clean up the grounds of public cemeteries and various open spaces.

In other states, convicts learn the skill of auto body work and painting, as they fix up the municipal motor pool. And those assignments once performed by private contractors or government employees - cleaning courthouses and campsites or cutting the lawn at the governor's mansion, for example - are now the job of carefully supervised prisoners.

That's the key to success for all these inmate work programs - adequate supervision - and the realization that there is a dual positive at work here. The inmates find purpose, and the states save money.

There have been some mishaps along the way of this movement to increase the number of prisoners assigned to work. A small number of convicts who felt exploited in Georgia staged a brief strike. In Ohio, inmates performing various tasks at the governor's home were found drinking on the job and bringing contraband tobacco back to the prison. In New Mexico, what used to be a viable inmate work program has dwindled now to almost nothing, as bad past management and the nation's poor economy joined forces to flummox a once thriving program. In Wisconsin, prisoners used to cut the grass at municipal buildings angered a union leader who realized the program diminished the number of city worker seasonal jobs by about 40 positions.

Overall, however, requiring offenders to work seems like a no-brainer. When the inmate earns money, the burden on their oftentimes cash-strapped families to contribute to their prison bank account is eased. And studies have shown an increase in prisoner's morale, self esteem and hope for their future on the outside.

Besides what it does for the inmates, this idea saves all of us taxpayers multiple millions of dollars every year.

Here's hoping Ensign's proposed bill passes. The sooner the better.

Do Prisoners Deserve Free Medical Treatments?

Sept. 3, 2011

They are charged with breaking laws or victimizing fellow citizens. We respond by making sure they get a lawyer - often on the taxpayer's dime. If they plead "not guilty," we stage expensive trials so they can provide evidence to a judge or jury. If convicted, they are imprisoned.

So, after all that we do, we also have an obligation to provide prisoners with any and all medicines they might need to keep them healthy?

While so many Americans are struggling to meet health insurance and prescription costs, services for prisoners constantly increase. And make no mistake about it: America has so many incarcerated people that we're spending boatloads of money on convicts' medical care. Their services cannot be cut. But health care programs for the general public have been cut back time and time again.

Let's take the state of Ohio as a general example of what it means to maintain the health of convicts. The Ohio prison system has about 51,000 prisoners, and it spends nearly $223 million a year for their medical care. About $28 million of the Ohio total is spent on inmates' prescriptions.

In Oregon, the latest annual figures show that it took $100 million to take care of some 14,000 prisoners. That's seven times more than the state spends on education.

Texas, like every other state, has seen a spike in the number of elderly inmates who often require even more expensive medical treatments. That phenomenon - on top of Texas' regular medical care costs for prisoners - caused expenses to balloon to a staggering $545 million dollars last fiscal year. This, at a time when other crucial state programs are facing mandatory budget cuts.

Every year, the price of tending to old and dying prisoners skyrockets. Realize these inmates must often be transported to hospitals or nursing homes, where they are treated with the latest lifesaving methods and, yes, even though they are incapacitated from their illnesses, the law says they must be provided with security guards around the clock.

Wrap your head around this set of facts, if you can: In California, a state drowning in red ink, the prison system recently identified 21 inmates whose annual health care bill is just under $2 million - each. There are another 1,300 guests of the California penal system who require medical attention amounting to $100,000 apiece.

In the face of those cold, hard facts, California adopted a bill last year granting medical paroles so the sickest inmates could get out of prison and into federally funded health care facilities.

That, of course, only shifted the burden on paper - from the state to the federal level.

So, armed with these staggering statistics, ask yourself: Do prisoners deserve all this free health care, when so many of us struggle to pay for health insurance or, sadly, go without? The answer in a humane society is yes.

But yes to a point.

Are you sitting down? If not, please do. In Massachusetts, a cross-dressing inmate who murdered his wife in 1990 has been suing the state for health care costs related to his desire to have a sex-change operation. Robert Kosilek (who has changed his name to Michelle) has already received hormone injections, electrolysis hair removal and, most recently, a mammogram - all at taxpayer expense. Kosilek remains housed in an all-male prison, and her standard issue prison wardrobe has been augmented with several bras and "some make-up," according to corrections officials.

Still, after a costly 10-year court battle, Kosilek says these steps have not been enough to ease her depression, and the fight continues for the state to pay for a full-on gender reassignment surgery. The case is still pending in Massachusetts' U.S. District Court.

Earlier this year in upstate New York, 55-year-old Kenneth Pike, convicted of raping a 12-year-old family member and sentenced to up to 40 years in prison, desperately needed a heart transplant. He had already undergone triple heart-bypass surgery and had a pacemaker implanted while incarcerated.

After the media reported that the public might have to pay for an $800,000 transplant surgery for a convicted child predator, the outcry was immediate. The Department of Corrections explained that it was "constitutionally obligated to provide health care services to inmates," and Pike's family argued he should be treated like any other patient in need.

In the end, the controversy was so red-hot that Kenneth Pike declined the surgery. At last report, he is still alive.

In 1976, the U.S. Supreme Court ruled that prisoners were entitled to the same medical and dental treatment as everyone else in their communities. Since then, countless state courts have upheld that ruling and repeated that prisons withholding treatment may be held liable for violating the U.S. Constitution's ban on cruel and unusual punishment.

Well, I know lots of folks in my community who can't afford to go to doctor when they feel ill, and they may go to the dentist only when they have a raging toothache.

Whether our politicians want to admit it or not, health care has become a luxury for millions of Americans. Excluding, of course, those convicted of a crime.

Life in a Box

Feb. 25, 2012

Americans were once riveted by the horrific news of U.S. soldiers' and military contractors' treatment of enemy combatants at the Abu Ghraib prison in Baghdad. Media reports beginning in 2004 made us cringe with shame when we realized Americans had humiliated, raped and even killed prisoners of war - and casually taken snapshots of their own crimes.

Today, I believe there is another atrocity taking place inside our own American prison system. Oh, it doesn't involve naked inmates being paraded around on dog collars, as happened in Baghdad, but the end result is just as appalling - if not more so.

In a groundbreaking work by journalist Susan Greene titled "The Gray Box," it is revealed that tens of thousands of American prisoners are being held in prolonged states of solitary confinement in prisons across the country.

Now, before you say, "Well, they were convicted criminals - that's what they get!" let's delve into Greene's award-winning essay.

After years of corresponding with inmates, Greene paints a chilling picture of what our penal system is doing to those labeled as "security risks."

She writes, "Among the misperceptions about solitary confinement is that it's used only on the most violent inmates, and only for a few weeks or months. In fact, an estimated 80,000 Americans - many with no record of violence either inside or outside prison - are living in seclusion. They stay there for years, even decades."

Trying to escape, fighting or being affiliated with a gang can get an inmate tossed into solitary. So can cussing at a guard, filing a lawsuit against prison conditions or simply being a juvenile whose safety might be at risk in the general population.

Make no mistake, I believe prison guards should feel safe at work and that prisons are for punishment. If an inmate breaks the rules, then a few days in the box is standard operation procedure. But aren't prisons also supposed to try to rehabilitate inmates who will someday be released? What good does it do keep a convict secluded for so long that he either emerges in a state of vengeful rage or as a broken, unfixable person?

Greene's article quotes letters and personal interviews with longtime residents of solitary confinement. Their stories of struggling to maintain their minds while in the box reveal disturbing details. So many years go by for some that they have no idea what they look like or what year it is.

Clocks, calendars and mirrors are often not provided.

Alone, they walk in endless circles in cells as small as two queen sized mattresses. They create art out of the few items they are allowed, they count ceiling tiles over and over, some go on hunger strikes. Some inmates take insects as pets so they have something to talk to. A few of the isolated have televisions or cells with a window, but most do not. They get one shower a week, and meals are slipped through a slot in the door. There are no computers and few telephone calls, and many residents of solitary have been there so long their family doesn't even write anymore.

Greene recounts several cases of the mental deterioration caused by prolonged solitary confinement.

Take the case of Anthony Gay of Illinois. He ran afoul of the law after punching another kid and stealing his hat and a dollar. After Gay violated his parole, he ultimately landed in the Tamms super-max prison. He now displays all the classic signs of profound mental illness. He regularly cuts his genitals and eats his flesh. He flings his own waste through the food slot and has earned a 97-year sentence in the box. He wrote to Greene: "I've been trapped for approximately nine years. The trap, like a fly on sticky paper, aggravates and agitates me. America, can you hear me? ... Please speak out and stand up against solitary confinement."

Osiel Rodriguez has lived in total isolation for eight years after trying to escape from a federal penitentiary in Florida, sent there for armed robbery at 22 years old.

"I got it in my head to destroy all my photographs," he wrote to Greene from his solitary cell in Colorado. "I spent some five hours ripping each one to pieces. No one was safe. I did not save one of my mother, father, sisters. My parents will be dust if/when I ever get out of prison." In his mind, life on the outside is just too painful to remember anymore.

Sometimes inmates are isolated for no legitimate reason. After a drunk driving arrest in Las Cruces, N.M., Stephen Slevin was tossed into a solitary cell and forgotten. Nearly two years later - without ever seeing a judge - charges were dropped, and a disheveled, delusional Slevin was released. He thought he had been incarcerated for two months. A jury awarded him 22 million dollars.

Greene writes: "This is what our prisons are doing to people in the name of safety. This is how deeply we're burying them."

I am as ashamed of this as I was hearing the news about Abu Ghraib. America is supposed to be a compassionate country. This sounds like state-sponsored torture to me.

Cruel and Unusual Prisoner Punishment

Aug. 25, 2012

If you are reading this anywhere in America, you know firsthand that this summer has been a record-breaking sizzler. We could be living through the hottest summer season ever.

Think about what you've done to keep cool. You've turned on your air conditioner, or (if you don't have one) maybe you've gone to the movies to cool off. You probably drink lots of ice-cold beverages or jump into a swimming pool or cool shower. Perhaps, like my friend Lester, you drench a kitchen towel, twist it into a U shape and plop it in the freezer to hang around your neck when working outside.

Well, imagine you couldn't do any of those things. Imagine you were isolated in a 10-foot-by-12-foot space with no windows to open up to catch a cooling breeze. You had no fan, no relief and no escape.

That's what countless prisoners in America have had to endure this long, hot summer. In the past, their situation has proven deadly. In Texas, a lawsuit was filed after 10 inmates died from heat-related causes last summer. All were held in cell blocks without air-conditioning. The suit, filed by the Texas Civil Rights Project, focuses on what was called the "wrongful death" of inmate Larry McCollum.

Even though the federal courts have ruled that temperatures over 90 degrees violate the constitutional rights of an inmate, the Hutchins State Jail in Dallas where McCollum died of heat stroke registered an indoor heat index of almost 130 degrees. After he collapsed last July and was taken to the hospital, doctors found McCollum's body temperature still registered over 109 degrees!

The autopsy on the 58-year-old prisoner listed his cause of death as living "in a hot environment without air conditioning." One unnamed Texas corrections official was quoted saying about his prisoners: "I'm supposed to be watching them. I'm not supposed to be boiling them in their cells."

It's not just Texas where inmates are suffering and, in my opinion, being subjected to cruel and unusual punishment. In sunny Florida, only 10 of the 140 state-run prisons have air conditioning. But in those facilities with air, the cool sections are limited to just a few. It is somehow ironic that in a state where they have prison classes to teach inmates how to install and maintain air conditioners there aren't any in the vast majority of their oppressively hot cellblocks.

In Chicago, this summer's life-threatening heat is the worst they've seen in more than a century. In the lockups that do have air conditioners, the units are reported to be breaking down from almost constant use.

Add to that an outbreak of bedbugs within the system this year, and both inmates and prison personnel are left to face a dual threat - unsanitary conditions and heat exhaustion.

The union representing prison guards says the situation has created, "extreme fatigue and dangerous conditions ... a recipe for disaster." It's a reminder that it is not just prisoners who are affected by the extreme heat, it's also prison personnel. (At a prison near Rosharon, Texas, earlier this summer, a 58-year-old corrections official fainted, and the hospital ruled it was from heat exhaustion.)

In Iowa, cooling systems have kept many of the 8,300 inmates comfortable this scorching summer. But taken together the Mount Pleasant and Clarinda Correctional Facilities and the Anamosa State Prison have close to 1,900 inmates who have no air conditioning at all. In the prison at Mitchellville, where another 547 inmates live, there is no cool air in any of the older sections of the complex.

Imagine having to endure this summer trapped in a small, confined, almost airless space. We have strict laws against leaving a child or an animal in a hot, enclosed car. Put aside for a moment the crime committed that caused the prisoner to be incarcerated, and ask yourself: Shouldn't we also care about human beings confined in stifling, life-threatening conditions? Of course we should.

Officials in states across the nation say there simply isn't enough money in their budgets to retrofit all prisons with central air conditioning. So for now, they combat the threat of possible death by heat by catering, first, to those inmates with health problems (like diabetes and high blood pressure) and, second, to those locked up in the hottest sections of the prison. Electric fans, ice and water are being handed out to prisoners across the nation much more frequently than in years gone by.

I couldn't find a reported death of an inmate from heat exhaustion so far this summer. But that doesn't mean some prisoners aren't still being held in inhumane conditions. Who is out there taking the temperature inside every prison and making sure it doesn't go over the court-mandated 90 degrees? Nobody, that's who.

Look, I understand there are some people who think that once a criminal is convicted they should lose all their constitutional rights. In other words, if life is tough on the inside, so be it. But it's never been the American tradition to treat our own people worse than we would treat an animal. If climate change means every summer will be increasingly brutal, we better figure out a way to fix this - or there could be a flood of wrongful death suits to pay.

Guantanamo Bay -- What Have We Wrought?

July 20, 2013

We like to think of ourselves as a great nation, a compassionate country that puts human rights at the forefront of everything we do. Then, how in the world can we defend what the United States continues to do at Guantanamo Bay, Cuba?

The American prison for enemy combatants was established in January 2002 by then-President George W. Bush as a place to park detainees that were connected with the radical Muslim movement waging war against America. A total of 779 prisoners have been sent to Gitmo, and today - 11 years later - we still hold 166 of them. No charges have been filed against most of these men. Years ago about half of them were cleared for return to their home countries (or a willing third-party country), yet they still sit at Gitmo.

President Barack Obama made an election promise to close Guantanamo Bay back in 2007, but he was blocked by Congress, which passed restrictions on what could be done to transfer the prisoners. In April, the president promised again to pressure Congress, saying, "The idea that we would still maintain forever a group of individuals who have not been tried - that is contrary to who we are, it is contrary to our interests, and it needs to stop." The reality, however, is that it is unlikely our fractious Congress will do anything.

So, the 166 men at Gitmo remain in a protracted state of imprisoned limbo, and more than half of them have been on a prolonged hunger strike. Over the years, their health has become so perilous at times that the U.S. military made the decision to strap them down in chairs and force-feed them through tubes inserted in their noses.

What have we wrought? Are human rights activists correct when they say America's policies have left the detainees so completely hopeless and suicidal that they are driven to starve themselves to death? Or are U.S. military officials right when they say the prisoners denying themselves food is just another weapon in their arsenal to paint America as the Great Satan?

I don't know the answer. Likely it is a combination of the two. But the U.S. practice of forcible feeding has been roundly condemned by the World Medical Association, the United Nations High Commissioner for Human Rights and the American Medical Association, which declared the forced feeding violates "core ethical values of the medical profession."

Two Democratic senators - Dianne Feinstein of California and Richard Durbin of Illinois - have written to the president, asking him to order an immediate stop to the "painful, humiliating and degrading process." In a most unusual step, a federal court judge named Gladys Kessler, ruling on a Gitmo prisoner's request for an injunction against his forced-feeding, made a direct appeal to the president to take action on the issue that has been going on for so long.

I wonder if the average American knows about the detainees' individual stories and what has happened to them since they've been in U.S. custody. Their cases are shocking.

The longest continuous hunger-striker appears to be Abdul Rahman Shalabi, 35, a Saudi man who reportedly has been largely tube-fed since 2005. Mohammed Bawazir, 33, a Yemeni, had a lawyer who went to U.S. federal court to try to stop the forced-feeding of his client and lost. That was back in 2006. Another detainee, Tariq Ba Awdah, originally from Yemen, has apparently been on an uninterrupted hunger strike since February 2007. According to the Miami Herald, the 35-year-old wrote to his lawyer, "I haven't tasted food for over six years." Today, a total of 45 Gitmo prisoners are being given nourishment through forcibly inserted gastric tubes.

Think of that in real life terms. Every single day American soldiers are under orders to scoop up these malnourished and skeletal prisoners, strap them down and insert tubes into their noses so nutrients can be administered. I am positive that not one of those soldiers looks forward to that duty.

There are recent reports that some of the other hunger-strikers have begun to eat again, but military doctors told The New York Times they must be on hand to guard against "refeeding syndrome," which can be fatal when "undernourished people suddenly consume food."

Again, what have we wrought? Are you sure that America - the great and benevolent superpower that we think we are - couldn't have come up with a better solution for handling these prisoners? There is a part of me that is ashamed that it has come to this.

No right-thinking person advocates opening up the gates of Gitmo and simply waving goodbye to these 166 prisoners. Some likely still pose a threat to the United States. But let's redouble our efforts to do the right thing. A good first step would be to seriously concentrate on getting those low-risk prisoners who have already been cleared for release out of Gitmo.

Let's face it, at this point Gitmo has imprisoned all of us - imprisoned us in our own braggadocio that we are a country based on human rights. Guantanamo Bay prison is living proof that we are not, and what has already happened there will be a historic stain on our human rights record.

Congress needs to get off its duff and agree to lift the restrictions that keep the cleared prisoners behind bars. They need to agree to transfer the high-risk group to the United States so we can close that hellhole called Gitmo. Giving speeches about the issue isn't action, and it won't solve this humiliating human rights problem. The president needs to step up and truly lead - pound the table if he has to. The world is watching.

UPDATE: As of January 2016 only about 90 prisoners remained at Guantanamo Bay. In total, nearly 780 prisoners were held there by

American forces.Most were released without charge but the U.S. continues to label many of them as "enemy combatants."

The U.S. Prison System Needs a Total Makeover

April 12, 2014

It is way past time to overhaul the U.S. prison system. I'm not talking about a little tweak here and there. I'm talking about throwing a massive metaphorical hand grenade into the entire system and starting over from scratch. We should be ashamed of ourselves for allowing the system to have morphed into what it has.

Why should you care about this? Well, because you're paying for it. Between states and the federal government, the U.S. spends about $74 billion a year housing, feeding, providing health care (such as it is in prison) for inmates and supervising the newly released.

The Bureau of Justice Statistics reported in 2012 there were nearly 7 million Americans under the supervision of adult correctional systems. Translated: One in every 108 adults in the United States was incarcerated, a per-capita world record.

The problem, as I see it, centers on who we are locking up. The Washington Post reports that only one percent of them are in for murder. Four percent are serving time for robbery. The most serious charge against 51 percent of them is a drug offense.

But here is the most startling, heart-wrenching statistic of them all. According to a Justice Department study, more than half of the prisoners in the U.S. suffer from a bona fide mental illness. Among female inmates, about three-quarters have a diagnosable mental disorder.

Why in the world are we locking up the mentally ill in the same place we house violent and predatory criminals? The answer is simple. Because there is nowhere else to put the "crazy people," so we put them in jail after they act out. Many times, their families have spent years begging for mental health care for their disturbed loved one to no avail. And sometimes, the "crazy people" deliberately commit crimes knowing they will be housed, fed and minimally medicated in lockup.

Back in the mid-'50s, psychotropic drugs such as Thorazine were found to be so successful in quelling mental patients' delusions and agitation that within a decade, society decided it was cruel to continue to institutionalize them. The abuse of patients and unsanitary conditions found at some mental hospitals were ascribed to all such institutions, so we closed them down. Patients were given a prescription for their meds and told they were "free." No one seemed to notice that the planned community mental health centers never materialized, and when one of these former patients had a problem, there were very few places they could go for help.

The pattern continues to this day. There are simply not enough mental health beds to service everyone who needs help. Today, commitment is difficult and, sadly, we have to wait for the mentally ill to actually commit a crime before the state steps in. In the last few years, many of America's mass murders were committed by untreated mentally ill people who should have been in a mental health care facility for their protection and for ours.

It's ironic, isn't it? The very society that once agreed it was unjust to lock people up in mental hospitals now allows the mentally disturbed to be locked up in much more dangerous jails and prisons.

We have turned our backs on these folks, and our prisons have become de facto psychiatric facilities. We have decided that these are throwaway human beings and we embrace the idea that being mentally sick is a crime. Our children and grandchildren are going to look back and wonder what was wrong with us.

I could fill this entire page with quotes from wardens describing the horror of what happens to sufferers of schizophrenia, bipolar disorders and other mental illnesses once they enter prison. But the ugly truth is that some of those same wardens employ practices that create even more disturbed individuals.

The widespread use of solitary confinement in prisons has been shown to have a tremendously negative effect. Mostly because inmates - be they habitually violent, in danger from other prisoners or simply a rule breaker - are often held for months and even years in isolation. Do you know what being locked up, alone, for years at a time does to the human mind?

According to Dr. Stuart Grassian, a veteran psychiatrist from Harvard who is considered an expert on the effects of solitary confinement, prolonged seclusion only leads inmates to exhibit more impulsive and violent behavior.

"Ninety-five percent of these people will get out and be released back on the streets," Grassian said on a National Geographic documentary. "All isolation will have done is make them as violent, crazy and dangerous as possible when they get out."

So how long does the system continue doing what we know doesn't work? When do the priorities shift away from warehousing chronic drug addicts with the hope that they will somehow cure themselves by their release date? When do we stop thinking it is morally defensible to house the mentally ill alongside career gang-bangers, rapists and killers? And, what will it take to convince prison administrators to reject the rage-filling practice of prolonged solitary confinement?

Look, I'm not advocating letting anyone out of prison. I'm suggesting it's way past time to take a fresh look at revolutionary new ways to spend that $74 billion every year.

How about we start with a plan that separates the hard-core, habitual criminals from the mentally sick and persistently addicted? Keep the first group in a standard prison setting. Then, turn some of our prisons into psychiatric centers to help the more fragile inmates. The past confirms that an overwhelming majority of those who suffer from mental illness and addiction are not violent. They are lost souls who could possibly get their lives set straight if exposed to the right therapies and medications.

I'm embarrassed that we have adopted a toss-and-forget attitude about so many of our weakest citizens. Prison is not where they belong and it certainly isn't where they will ever learn to become contributing members of society again. By continuing our current policies we ensure only one thing: America's per-capita standing as the world's No. 1 jailer.

The Presidential Clemency Push – But Are We Ready?

July 13, 2015

Seems like Washington is enjoying a rare political Kumbaya moment these days. Both Democrats and Republicans now agree that our justice system ran off the rails with overly burdensome, mandatory sentencing for non-violent drug offenders.

These convicts include Antwon Rogers of Cleveland, Ohio, who was sentenced to life in prison for conspiracy to possess and distribute cocaine - less than 5 ounces of the drug. But because

Rogers had two previous drug convictions, the mandatory federal three-strikes law kicked in and, at the age of 22, he was sentenced to spend the rest of his life in prison. He's been there more than 20 years.

Francis Hayden of Loretto, Kentucky, also got life after his conviction for possessing more than 1,000 marijuana plants that were growing on a farm he managed. Hayden also had two previous drug convictions and that third one sealed his fate.

If space permitted I could cite thousands of these over-sentenced, non-violent drug cases.

Today, there appears to be unified political resolve to fix the problem and, thereby, help ease the prison overcrowding that plagues both the federal prison system and lock-ups in nearly every state. There also seems to be agreement to repair a system that has handed out much harsher sentences to black and brown defendants than to white ones.

The Obama administration started the ball rolling during the president's first term when he signed a law reducing the sentencing gap between those caught with cheaper crack cocaine and those who dealt in powder cocaine - the former being much more prevalent in inner-city, minority neighborhoods, the latter often consumed by wealthier, white clientele.

In 2013, the president's attorney general issued new sentencing guidelines instructing prosecutors to steer clear of charges against non-violent drug defendants that would result in over-the-top sentences.

And now, Obama is reportedly poised to commute the sentences of more and more low-level drug convicts who, if they were sentenced today, would never have gotten the draconian punishments they got years ago.

The plan is already in motion.

Last December, the president commuted the sentences of eight drug offenders. This March he awarded commutations to 22 more (eight of them were serving life sentences) and they will all leave prison at the end of this month. They were chosen out of the thousands who had applied for the new clemency program because, as the president put it, they had, "demonstrated the ability to turn their lives around."

But how many of these released prisoners will be headed for the straight-and-narrow as Theresa Brown of Pompano Beach, Florida, seems to be? She was serving life after being connected to a cocaine conspiracy. Her attorney said she was a "very, very small time street-level dealer," whose own addiction led her to fall prey to a big-time drug dealer who was both mentally and sexually abusive. Brown had broken away from him and was in rehab when she was arrested.

During Brown's more than 20 years in prison she has been a model prisoner and in a letter to her sentencing judge she wrote, "I am rehabilitated ... allow me to help society with the programs that are out there for the youth of today. ... How would they know there's a better way? How would they know unless someone is sent to tell them?"

But can we all just take a breath here? One thing never mentioned as this drive to right the wrongs of the past rolls on: What happened to these prisoners while they were locked up?

Federal prison is not an instructive or nurturing place. It is crude, ugly and full of danger and sometimes forces inmates to act in non-civilized ways just to survive. Will those whose sentences are commuted to time served leave prison better citizens? Did the prison in which they were held provide continuing education or job training? During their years (and sometimes decades) of imprisonment, did they receive instruction on how to live a constructive life on the outside? And what's been done to help those whose addictive personalities got them in trouble in the first place? Federal prisons are not known for stellar rehabilitation efforts.

I really don't want to rain on this feel-good campaign. Many convicts who received these harsh sentences deserve some relief. They are certainly ready to get out of prison. But are we ready to help them create better lives for themselves? I don't think so.

~~~

CHAPTER 8
The Death Penalty

"Many that live deserve death. And some that die deserve life. Can you give it to them? Then do not be too eager to deal out death in judgment." ~ J.R.R. Tolkien, "The Fellowship of the Ring"

Enforcement of the death penalty is one of those issues about which most people have already formed an opinion. Nothing I -- or anyone else -- writes will likely change any minds.

Unless the reader happens to be like me. As I wrote in one of the columns that follows, "I'm against the death penalty ... until I'm not."

In the world of crime of which I write, where so little shocks me anymore, I sometimes read about an incident that so infuriates and sickens me that I believe putting the perpetrator to death is the only logical conclusion. Then again, I don't really want to live in a world where well- meaning people intentionally take the lives of others. And don't get me started on wrongfully convicted people who may have been executed for crimes they did not commit!

The only way for me to sort out my see-saw feelings on the topic of the death penalty is to write about it.

Justice For Junny -- Watching an Execution

Nov. 29, 2008

Sometimes I meet people on this crime and justice beat who just take my breath away. I want to tell you about one. Where she found the courage to go through what she did is beyond me.

Her name is Vicki Rios-Martinez. She's a mother of six, a grandmother to 12 and the survivor of a murder so heinous you may never forget the details. From that unspeakable crime Rios-Martinez found the courage to fight for a change in the law.

In short, her young son, Junny Rios-Martinez Jr, was kidnapped, sexually molested and murdered 17 years ago. It was only recently that Vicki and her husband watched their son's killer be put to death at the Starke, Florida, state prison.

Now, I've stood inside a death chamber, but I've never witnessed an execution. I don't think I'd have the stomach for it. But Vicki Rios-Martinez and her family did.

Seventeen years after the most horrible day of her life, there she was, sitting in the gallery of the execution chamber, wearing a T-shirt with Junny's picture on it, hoping the death of a monster named Mark Dean Schwab would somehow bring her a long-sought conclusion.

Instead, she found herself contrasting how her 11-year-old son died with how Schwab passed.

"The procedure was very, very peaceful," she told me. "His eyes shut, his jaw went slack and he never woke up again. There was no suffering for Mark Schwab."

In other words, Schawb's death was nothing like her little Junny's.

Junny Rios-Martinez was everybody's buddy. He was outgoing, athletic, handsome. He was 5 feet tall and weighed just 76 pounds. His picture appeared in a local Florida newspaper after he won a kite-flying contest, and that's all it took to arouse Schwab. He posed as a reporter who wanted to do a follow-up interview with Rios-Martinez, and within weeks he'd cunningly groomed both the boy and the parents to trust him.

Here's the part that's so unbelievable. Schwab had been out of prison for just one month when he first contacted the Rios-Martinez family. He had a history of violent child sexual attacks, and both his previous victims were about Junny's age. Schwab had faced the possibility of life in prison, but he was sentenced to serve only eight years for viciously raping a 13-year-old boy. He served less than half that time, getting out in just three years. He got no psychological treatment or rehab in prison. He was enrolled in a sex-offender treatment program at the time he began to openly stalk Junny. A lot of good that did.

After they found little Junny's naked body in a footlocker, carelessly thrown into a drainage ditch, there was a trial. Schwab was found guilty and sentenced to death. And then the penalty phase was drawn out by appeal after appeal for a decade and a half. During that time, Vicki Rios-Martinez and her family grieved, prayed for justice and tried to heal.

"We discovered there is only one page in all the law books for victim's families," Vicki said. "All the rest of that law book stuff is for protection of the criminals."

So she took it upon herself to add some pages to the Florida law books. She and her family won passage of the Junny Rios-Martinez,

Jr. Act, which prohibits those convicted of sexual battery from receiving early release.

Theirs is a large loving clan, and they worked hard to achieve the American Dream. Vicki Rios-Martinez and her husband run a popular hair salon. He also works at the Parks Department and plays in a band. Vicki, who says that she was always against the death penalty until Junny's murder, now gives victim-impact speeches to law enforcement groups.

So why, after 17 years and finally getting into a happy routine again, did they want to watch the execution of their son's murderer?

"For closure," Vicki says. But she admits she came away feeling short-changed.

"We give a convict this peaceful passage. It wasn't scary. ... He didn't have to face us," she said, because when the curtain opened between the death chamber and the gallery, Schwab was already sedated and strapped to the gurney. The whole thing was over in less than 15 minutes.

She told me: "If you were the victim (of that man) you would face him and look into his eyes at the very last moment. You know, the eyes are the soul. They robbed us of looking into his soul. ... Maybe he would have wanted to say something to us." Her voice trailed off.

Vicki Rios-Martinez just recently lost her beloved aunt and her father. And she wishes, without a hint of bitterness in her voice, that they would have had such a peaceful way to leave this Earth.

"We give it to the criminal," she says again. "But not to the suffering." Nothing for the victim.

Death Penalty Debate Renewed

March 12, 2011

I'm against the death penalty. Until I'm not.

Mention a criminal who has sexually abused or murdered a child and I waver. Show me a terrorist who wants to kill Americans because we don't share his religion and I vacillate. Catch a stone-cold cop killer and I think if we don't punish the murderer to the fullest we allow the very fabric of our nation's security to unravel.

Yet, with all that said, there seems to be a built-in contradiction to killing a killer, don't you think?

The governor of Illinois took a bold step this week when he signed a bill that abolishes the death penalty in his state. Gov. Pat Quinn said he took the step because in the past the system in Illinois found at least 20 men guilty of capital offenses and condemned them to death only to have evidence crop up later that exonerated them.

"If the system cannot be guaranteed 100 percent error free, then we cannot have the system," said Quinn. "It just is not right."

Illinois is a perfect microcosm of our decades long national debate and flip-flop on the issue. We had capital punishment. Then we banned it. And in 1976 the U.S. Supreme court reinstated a state's right to apply the death penalty.

In the 1990s, after Illinois figured out it had at least 13 innocent people on death row (the figure rose to 20 later), former Gov. George Ryan made news worldwide when he issued a suspension of all executions. Right before he left office in 2003 Ryan literally cleared out death row and commuted the sentences of 167 convicts, leaving them to serve life in prison with no parole.

In making his pronouncement Gov. Quinn commuted the sentences of 15 more condemned convicts, and now they will serve life with no hope of parole.

I know many of the loved ones seeking to avenge the innocent dead will not be pleased, but you know, in the scheme of things a life sentence is pretty horrible to contemplate. Instead of being released from this Earth via a lethal injection, these prisoners will be forced to think about the terrible acts that put them there every single day. They will grow old and infirm behind bars within a foul society. Instead of dreaming about someday being free, they know they will have to spend every single minute of every single day locked up like an animal. There is no escape. That daily suffering seems like vengeance enough.

Interestingly, many victims' families are against the death penalty, believing it serves no purpose in bringing back their loved ones.

Illinois now joins 15 other states and the District of Columbia in doing away with the death penalty. However, as if to underscore how frequently the winds change on the issue, New Mexico's newly elected governor, Susana Martinez, wants to bring it back to the Land of Enchantment.

It is a question from biblical times, what to do with those who take the lives of others. The Book of Deuteronomy waves off pity and speaks of "an eye for an eye." But as spiritual leader Mahatma Gandhi put it, "An eye for an eye makes the whole world blind."

So, after Gov. Quinn's recent stand on the issue, maybe this is a good time for all of us to rethink what we believe about capital punishment. Should the United States be in the business of killing killers? Is it the best way to keep the rest of us safe? And here's a question for those who focus on the cost of prisons. Is it fair to focus on money when we're talking about life and death?

Ask yourself honestly. Could you perform an execution?

Maybe we could mitigate the number of executions by limiting them to those who have committed the worst crimes. But who decides that the killer of a child or police officer deserves death, while the murderer of an elderly person gets life in prison?

As you ponder the issue, realize that since 1976 states have executed about 1,240 convicts. There are currently at least 3,254 more waiting for their lethal injection, or whatever other mode of death they chose, as some states allow the inmates to pick their destinies -- electrocution, lethal gas, shooting or hanging. It seems odd to think that we still carry out firing squads in America. But Utah staged one as recently as June 2010. And Delaware had a hanging in 1996.

I've stood inside the death chamber of a prison and had the door close behind me. Everything in the room was white -- white, the color of innocence and purity -- except for the two thick, brown leather straps at the foot of the deathbed, which buckle in the feet of the condemned, and those in the middle that hold down the hands and chest.

There seems to be nothing innocent or pure about taking the life of another human being. Not even an evil one. But I've interviewed enough victims' family members to know that their need for retribution is sincere, that it comes from deep within, and that oftentimes it can't be quenched until the killer is killed. I understand.

Executing the Retarded?

July 22, 2012

When I saw the headlines my stomach lurched. The state of Georgia has issued an execution warrant for a retarded man? Oh, good grief, I thought. Has America come to this?

Despite a U.S. Supreme Court ruling more than a decade ago banning the execution of retarded citizens, Georgia officials were going to go ahead and send Warren Lee Hill Jr. to the death chamber anyway?

Multiple news stories told me that plans to execute Hill were moving forward because he couldn't prove he was mentally retarded "beyond a reasonable doubt." Why would the state of Georgia put that kind of caveat on retardation? I wondered. How could they possibly want to put to death a man who didn't have the capacity to know right from wrong?

Then I did some research and remembered why it's so important to look past the headlines. I came to realize that lawyers for two-time convicted murderer Warren Lee Hill may have been trying to game the system.

Look, anyone who reads this column regularly knows that I struggle mightily with my opinion of the death penalty. I'm not for it, but then again, if the criminal has committed multiple crimes (like a serial killer) or crimes against a child, well, then my anti-execution resolution gets shaky.

The saga of 52-year-old Hill is a long one. It starts in 1986 when he murdered his 18-year-old girlfriend by shooting her 11 times. He was convicted and sent to the Lee Correctional Institution to serve life in prison. There he murdered again, by beating to death another inmate as he slept in his bed. According to the case file, "Hill removed a 2-by-6 (foot) board that served as a sink leg in the prison bathroom and forcefully beat the victim numerous times with the board about the head and chest as on-looking prisoners pleaded with him to stop." The board was studded with nails, and Hill reportedly mocked the man as he beat the life out of him.

The injuries sustained by victim Joseph Handspike were brutal. Several of his teeth were knocked out, his left eye was detached from the socket, and he was unable to speak to guards because of the blood pouring from his mouth and nose. He died in a hospital emergency room 90 minutes later from blunt force trauma.

It may be grisly to read such details, but I think it is important to include in any discussion about clemency for criminals the damage they inflicted on their victims.

That must be central to any conversation.

During Hill's second murder trial in 1991, his own attorney called a clinical psychologist who testified that Hill had an IQ of 77 (mild retardation is designated by an IQ between 59 and 69). While below normal intelligence, Dr. William Dickinson testified, Hill was able to fully understand right from wrong and the ramifications of his actions. A high school friend called Hill "bright, sharp and mature." After graduating high school, evidence showed, Hill joined the Navy and rose to the rank of seaman second class. The jury unanimously convicted Hill of malice murder, and he received a death sentence.

In 1993, Hill's attorney appealed his conviction to the Georgia Supreme Court and again did not claim mental retardation as a defense. The state's high court rejected the appeal.

In 1996, more than five years after the inmate's murder, suddenly lawyers for Hill claimed that he could not be put to death because he was clinically retarded. They pegged his IQ at 70, which is still a point above mild retardation.

There has been a lot of legal back and forth in this case since that declaration of retardation, but the bottom line is Warren Lee Hill is set to be executed at 7 p.m. on July 18, 2012. This makes me uncomfortable. I don't like the idea of state-sanctioned killing, but I certainly understand the case better now that I took the time to dig into it.

None of the battery of psychological tests Hill took before his lawyers professed he was mentally deficient. Yet Hill's attorney, Brian Kammer, maintains, "It is morally wrong to execute someone who has been found more likely than not to be mentally retarded." He says that his client has a mental capacity of a sixth-grader.

Georgia is no backward state when it comes to this issue. In 1988, Georgia became the first in the nation to abolish capital punishment for mentally retarded convicts, as long as they could prove their handicap beyond a reasonable doubt. And therein lies the rub for Hill. There is, on the very face of this case, a reasonable doubt about his claim.

But there is no doubt that Hill has murdered twice, and that his 18-year-old girlfriend, Myra Wright, and inmate Joseph Handspike, ripped apart by bullets and a board, were never given the option of losing their life via a quiet lethal injection.

Bring Back Firing Squads

May 3, 2014

It's clearly time to bring back firing squads.

If we're going to keep carrying out the death penalty in this country, and if we are going to continue to grandly insist that such deaths are "humane executions," then only a return to a firing squad will insure a speedy and relatively pain-free death for the condemned.

You might think I'm kidding, but I'm not. I say line up six to eight sharp shooters, employ the old practice of giving one of them a blank instead of a bullet, and instruct them to aim for the prisoner's heart. I guarantee the convicts will be dead before they hit the ground.

Compare that to what we've been led to believe is the least barbaric option of taking a life: lethal injection.

As we recently saw in the bungled execution of Clayton Lockett at the Oklahoma State Penitentiary, things can go wrong -- very wrong -- using a lethal injection.

The problem is critical now because European manufacturers of lethal drugs have decided they will no longer supply the U.S. because we are the only Western country that still has the death penalty. So, penitentiaries across America are scrambling to find alternative "cocktails" of drugs to kill those whose death row appeals have run out.

Lockett, 38, became Oklahoma's first prisoner to receive a new three-drug concoction designed to do three things: First, render him unconscious and unable to feel pain. Second, make him unable to breathe. And finally, stop his heart.

It soon became clear that this convicted kidnapper, rapist and murderer of an 18-year-old girl never fell into unconsciousness even though a doctor declared he had. Four minutes later, Lockett's body twitched, and he rose up from the gurney muttering, "Oh, man." A prison official quickly pulled the curtain on the spectator's window, declared "vein failure," and the execution was interrupted. According to prison officials, Lockett died of a heart attack 45 minutes later.

Lockett's case is not unique. Three months ago, an Ohio man convicted of rape and aggravated murder became that state's first guinea pig of an untried lethal cocktail. Witnesses to Dennis McGuire's execution said that after the injection he clenched his fists, gasped loudly for air and made choking sounds for 15 minutes before he was declared dead.

Who thinks that is more humane than a quick hail of bullets to the heart?

I can cite several more cases of bungled lethal injections -- including that of a 265-pound man whose execution took nearly 10 needle sticks over two hours because technicians couldn't find a proper vein -- but I don't want to be accused of overlooking the victims' frightening final minutes.

Certainly the victims of all condemned killers faced much more brutal and undeserved ends, and we should never forget the crimes against them.

That goes without saying. But that's not the point of this column.

The Boston Globe recently took a look back at executions in the U.S. from 1890 to 2010 and found that botched attempts have happened regularly no matter the mode of death. A reminder as you read on: The U.S. Constitution guarantees that none of us is to be subjected to cruel and unusual punishment.

The Globe found that at hangings there were some convicts who "had to be dropped and hanged more than once when the initial fall did not kill them." In addition, there was the problem of unwanted decapitations. Those condemned to the electric chair sometimes had to be repeatedly shocked before they died. Some caught on fire, and executioners reported smelling burnt flesh. Death row inmates sent to the gas chamber "often struggled, convulsed, gasped for breath and were asphyxiated for extended periods of time before they succumbed." None of these manners of death is nearly as quick or reliable as a firing squad.

Today, 32 states, the U.S. military and the federal government all have death penalty by lethal injection statutes on the books. (Only New Mexico, Connecticut and Maryland have voted to abolish capital punishment.) According to the latest Gallup poll on the death penalty, a full 60 percent of Americans still support this punishment for convicted murderers. And so, my point is that if this really is the path we want to take, there is no more failproof way to carry out an execution than a firing squad. Period. End of discussion.

Like many Americans, I struggle with being both against the death penalty and for it in certain cases. For example, another Oklahoma man was set to be executed right after Clayton Lockett, but Charles Warner's date with death has been postponed, pending an investigation into the state's practices. Warner does not dispute that he raped and killed an 11-month-old baby girl, and for fiends like that I'm hard pressed to suggest he should live another day. Am I a gung-ho advocate for the death penalty? No. Am I vehemently against it? Well, I guess not. That's my constitutionally protected opinion (as fluid as it is), so please, no hate mail.

At this juncture, when U.S. prisons are hard pressed to even get the chemicals for a lethal injection, maybe it's time for each of us to search our souls and ask what we think is right. There are evil people in the world who do horrid things. If the justice system finds they should be eliminated, how do we want to achieve that?

Only two states currently authorize firing squads, and one, Utah, is phasing out the practice. Ironically, Oklahoma, the state that botched an execution and sparked a social conversation, would allow firing squads, but only if the courts first find both lethal injection and electrocution to be unconstitutional.

That's not on the horizon anytime soon. So, what's the bottom line? The flawed system of lethal injection is here to stay unless and until we tell lawmakers we want something different. Do you?

Getting Our Act Together on the Death Penalty

Feb. 2, 2015

If we as a nation are going to allow the execution of convicted murderers, rapists and traitors, can't we get our act together about how to take their lives?

Back in 2010, European countries began a movement to abolish the death penalty around the world. European pharmaceutical companies began to refuse to sell any anesthetics to the U.S. that could be used to facilitate an execution. And that left prisons in the more than 30 states that carry out the death penalty without easy access to the medications needed to kill the condemned.

Since then, these states have used a mish-mash of drugs to carry out executions. Some have used a two-drug or three-drug cocktail, administered in stages. The first stage is designed to render the convict unconscious so they feel no pain as other heart-stopping drugs are introduced. Other states use just one drug, such as pentobarbital, but that has also begun to be difficult to procure. One state, Missouri, announced it would use propofol -- the anesthetic cited in the death of entertainer Michael Jackson -- but then revised its lethal injection procedure before doing so.

Midazolam, hydromorphone, sodium thiopental, the barbiturate anesthetic Brevital...they're all part of the grand experiment our penal institutions have used in this modern-day quest to carry out "humane executions." Sounds like an oxymoron to me.

This is not the place to argue about the pros or cons of the death penalty. According to the latest Gallup poll, 63 percent of Americans are in favor of capital punishment (although it should be noted that that number has tumbled since the mid-'90s, when 80 percent favored the idea.)

So it goes, majority rules. So, when do we get our collective act together and figure out a single best way to do this that is beyond reproach? Why have we dithered and experimented with it for so long? If we truly support the idea of the death penalty we should certainly agree on an acceptable process.

The U.S. Supreme Court now says it will hear a challenge to Oklahoma's lethal injection practices.

And the justices stayed the pending execution of the three Oklahoma convicts whose names appear on the case. That state employs a commonly used three-drug protocol that relies on Midazolam as the first drug. Lawyers for the condemned will argue that the drug is unreliable and has the potential to cause terrible suffering. They'll say that the procedure violates a citizen's constitutional right to be protected from cruel and unusual punishment.

I know, I know, those facing the executioner have made others suffer in oftentimes incomprehensible ways. Why should we care if they suffer a bit as they die? Why do we hear so much about a convict's rights at the time of execution, and so little about the grisly crime for which they were convicted?

Again, this is not the place to argue the penalty. Rather, we should discuss a unified process for carrying out the law.

The high court will decide on Oklahoma's procedure, but it will do nothing concrete that guides the nation toward a unified way to execute its worst criminals. I guess we have to demand that.

In the past, I've suggested a return to the firing squad, although I'm no ardent supporter of the death penalty. A firing squad would be fast and efficient -- no fuss or muss. But if we're determined to painlessly put to sleep our convicts with a lethal injection, how about using a massive dose of heroin? Heaven knows every state and the federal government has an ample supply of the confiscated drug that brings death so quickly. Addicts are often found with the needle still in their arm (actor Phillip Seymour Hoffman to name just one.)

Anesthesiologists successfully put thousands of people into states of unconsciousness every day, so why can't executioners? We euthanize our ailing pets, but would the drug cocktail a veterinarian uses even work on humans? Is anyone studying this?

As one vet wrote to the editor of The New York Times, "If we MUST persist in executing people, how about we convene a panel of MD's, get some good options, and then pass a law making it illegal for drug companies to refuse to provide the drugs?"

I'm not sure such a law could be passed, but I know it's way past time for this discussion to take place.

If we can't discuss it, maybe we should stop doing it.

Who Are We and What Do We Believe?

June 1, 2015

We live in a world of confounding contradictions.

We call ourselves a peace-loving people, yet we continue to engage in far-flung wars. Gangs, guns and drug deals proliferate domestically. This is not a recipe for peace by any measure.

Nearly half of us say that we are morally against the death penalty. Yet a jury in Boston, Massachusettes -- a decidedly anti-capital punishment region of the country -- sentenced to death the surviving Boston marathon bomber, 21-year-old Dzhokhar Tsarnaev.

Another jury in Aurora, Colorado, is currently considering the death penalty for an admitted killer who, in July of 2012, shot to death a dozen moviegoers and wounded at least 70 others at a midnight showing of the Batman movie "The Dark Knight Rises." This defendant also outfitted his apartment with an elaborate and deadly booby-trap, hoping to kill those who arrived to investigate.

We earnestly say that we feel for families struggling to help a relative with mental illness. But society has done little to help establish institutions to treat these unfortunate people. We seem blind to the idea that if we help the most tortured souls among us they can't or won't harm themselves or others.

We automatically expect that when we call 911 police will instantly and heroically come to our rescue. Yet many fail to understand that officers are constantly confronted with situations that require snap decisions, and the daily deadly dangers they face can cause their very human instinct of survival to kick in -- even when it's not really a life-or-death situation.

We preach personal responsibility and then think nothing of suing over an accident, hoping someone or some entity with deep pockets will make us rich.

Many cry for "income equality" across the land. But stop and think about that. A nation where everyone makes the same money, regardless of work product, is a socialist nation. Is that really what we want? Forced equality is not fair.

Many condemn Big Business and corporations as evil and want them abolished. Yet they have never run a business or provided job opportunities for their fellow Americans. They fail to realize where jobs that can lift people out of poverty come from. Conversely, corporate leaders who advertise their good deeds but pay no taxes are an abomination.

We claim we are for good government, yet continue to re-elect politicians who lack the integrity and foresight to do what's right for the country. We know Washington is a mess, but our busy lives keep us from demanding ways to fix it. We repeatedly fall prey to huckster politicians who promise everything and only deliver to their own political party. Even worse, a majority of us don't even bother to vote.

Some law-abiding Americans make pleas for amnesty for all those who have entered our country illegally. They extol the virtues and good intentions of the alien working class, while ignoring the very real problems that come with opening our borders -- overtaxed hospitals, schools and welfare programs, for example. Giving away resources comes with a price.

Contradictions abound, yet few seem to notice. It seems we've just stopped thinking through today's issues.

Who among us doesn't say that they want an exemplary, competitive, affordable education system for our youth? But can you honestly say we have one? No.

When will we stop saying we're for something and then fail to act to make it happen? That's more than a contradiction, I fear. It is self-destructive.

We claim to be an enlightened group of parents who protect our young like no generation before us, but check the growing number of missing, exploited and sexually abused children. We may brag that we are "helicopter parents" who perpetually hover to swat away danger, but sadly, the statistics prove there aren't enough good parents to go around.

We distract ourselves and argue about things that mean so little. Like whether the word "thug" is racist. Criminal thugs live in crime-ridden inner-city neighborhoods, and they commit multiple murders in Waco, Texas, over something as silly as a motorcycle gang rivalry. Thugs are white, black, Hispanic, Asian and lots of colors in between.

A wise man once told me that when confronted with a myriad of problems, there is really only one main problem. So what's this nation's one problem? It is us.

We have failed to install the leadership this country deserves. It is way past time to change that. I wonder if we will see that change in our lifetimes.

Update: In August 2015, James Holmes, the so-called Colorado theater shooter, was sentenced to 12 life sentences plus 3,318 years.

~~~

CHAPTER 9
Families and the System

"When I see the '10 Most Wanted' lists ... I always have this thought: If we'd made them feel wanted earlier, they wouldn't be wanted now." ~ **Eddie Cantor, comedian**

I'm with Eddie Cantor! I always wonder what kind of childhood criminals had. Not that it's any excuse for their bad acts -- not at all. But following the details of how they were raised often provides a straight line to their criminal act. The kid who was regularly beaten or humiliated at home becomes the school bully. The child who lost a parent at a young age grows up acting out, seeking thrills and attention -- even if it's negative attention.

It is a documented fact that young people ages 12 to 25 are the most at-risk group of citizens -- at risk to become victims, at risk to commit criminal acts. A study of the so-called "age-crime curve" also shows that juveniles who begin to offend before the age of 12 are more likely to continue their criminal behavior into adulthood.

So, since we know this to be true, why don't we concentrate more attention and resources on our young?

And while we're at it, let's also try to understand and give attention to the abandoned, the abused, the disabled and the elderly. No matter the station in life, all citizens have inalienable rights under the U.S. Constitution.

I often explore these themes in my columns.

Today's Bullies, Tomorrow's Criminals?

Aug. 7, 2010

Have you ever been the victim of a bully? Have you ever stood silent and let a bully pick on someone?

Most people wouldn't consider bullying a crime, but it could be creating criminals right before our very eyes.

A study from a group called Fight Crime: Invest in Kids concluded that nearly 60 percent of boys who researchers classified as bullies in grades six through nine were convicted of at least one crime by the age of 24. And get this: Forty percent of those same boys grew up to have three or more criminal convictions.

In other words, today's bully could be tomorrow's criminal.

So, what can we do about it?

I'm a big believer in families taking responsibility for the actions of their children. But boys and girls reserve their bullying for when they are away from Mom and Dad. That means other adults have to step up at schools, camps, sporting events and youth activity centers. We need to tell parents when their children are being bullies. And we should teach all kids to refuse to join in the taunting. It is abuse, pure and simple. Children can be scarred for life by a bully. And, once robbed of their self-esteem, they can suffer from mental and physical problems, drop out of school and even commit suicide.

I'm not being dramatic here. It happens too often.

Case in point: In 2006, a 13-year-old Missouri girl was the victim of cyberbullying by a former friend's mother, and she ultimately took her life. Thirteen-year-old Megan Meier hanged herself in her bedroom after believing a MySpace boyfriend had dumped her. In reality, there was no boy. A neighbor, 49-year-old Lori Drew, had concocted the online persona after Megan and Drew's daughter fought. Drew faces criminal charges.

Newsweek magazine recently featured a cover story on a gay teen named Larry King who was bullied for years and fought back by being flamboyant in his homosexuality. He was murdered by a 14-year-old classmate, shot in the head in an Oxnard, California, computer class, in front of a teacher and a room full of students.

Many mature adults still get teary when recalling their humiliating days at the hands of the class bully, mainly because bullies don't operate alone. They pick up sycophantic disciples along the way, and that multiplies the victim's pain.

I don't usually recommend books in this space, but I do now. It's called "Letters to a Bullied Girl: Messages of Healing and Hope," and it is dramatic in its simplicity. I recommend every parent buy it and read it with their children.

The real-life backstory centers on Olivia Gardner, a teenager from Novato, California. After suffering an epileptic attack at school, she became the brunt of a horrific series of bully-fueled events. Her tormentors taunted her with hurtful names and dragged her backpack through the mud. After they created an "Olivia Haters" website on MySpace, a group of bullies took to wearing bracelets declaring "Olivia Shall Die." The internet ugliness followed Olivia to three different schools over more than two years. She wanted to kill herself until a newspaper story about her plight appeared in the San Francisco Chronicle and her life changed forever.

Two sisters in a neighboring community read the front-page story about Olivia and were compelled to action. Teenagers Emily and Sarah Buder asked friends to write letters of support to Olivia. More than 4,000 poured in.

The book borne of this Samaritan effort features the letters from males and females who were mercilessly teased for being short, tall, fat, skinny or smart, or fo having buck teeth, eyeglasses, bad skin or a large nose. Some letter writers revealed they had taken grief for being poor, having an alcoholic parent or because they were from a minority group. Many admitted they wept when they read about what happened to Olivia.

Some who wrote were contrite former bullies who admitted they did what they did because their own lives were out of their control. They told Olivia, and through her the rest of us, that bullies seek to humiliate to make others feel as insignificant as they feel.

Many of the letters in the book offered words of wisdom for the young girl. One of the most touching is from "Joshua," who wrote to Olivia: "Please love yourself in the same way your family loves you. As you go through life, you will realize that there are a lot more of 'us' holding you up than 'them' putting you down."

Simple advice for those suffering at the hands of a bully. All adults should pass it forward and step up when we see behavior that could be creating criminals right before our very eyes.

Update: Lori Drew was criminally charged under the Federal Computer Fraud and Abuse Act, and a jury found her guilty of three misdemeanor charges. In July 2009, a judge overturned her convictions.

Is Evil Born or Made?

March 1, 2009

Remember the chilling movie "The Bad Seed," starring the blond pigtailed Patty McCormack? She was a beautiful child but so devoid of feeling that she randomly killed people she didn't like.

Could that be what authorities in Arizona are facing with the 8-year-old boy who confessed to killing his father and a family friend?

We've watched this story play out for about a month now, and I've hesitated to write about it because I thought that any day now we'd learn the awful truth behind what motivated this child. How does a young boy pick up a .22-caliber single-action rifle and pump four bullets into his own father, and then six more bullets into a man who rents a room in the family home?

Two dead and a little boy left squirming in a police interrogation room with no familiar face to guide him on how to answer the officer's kind but relentless questions. Police say that the boy's stepmother gave them permission to question the child alone.

Everyone who's even peripherally involved in law enforcement knows you don't question a defenseless suspect without a lawyer present or at the very least, in the case of a child, without a parent in the room. It will only come back to bite you in the end. But let's put aside the shortsightedness of those well-meaning officers who were just trying to get at the truth.

The boy first told a story of finding both men nearly dead inside the house when he came home from school. Then he admitted he had shot them to "end their suffering," and as a child who had been taught the finer points of hunting by his dad, this seemed plausible. But something made the officers keep pushing, and in less than an hour the tiny suspect in the chair began to crumble and he admitted the unthinkable.

The boy's birth mother lives in Mississippi and immediately after the deaths the child, who was not considered a suspect, was allowed to spend that awful night with his grandparents. Upon learning of his confession later in the week, his grandmother was quoted in a court document as saying: "I knew this would happen! They were too hard on him" -- a reference to the boy's father and stepmother.

Indeed, the boy had told police he got in trouble "most of the time" and had been spanked "five times by his stepmother" the night before the fatal shooting.

And there are reports that the boy told Child Protective Services he'd kept a written tally of every single time he had been spanked. He reportedly decided that 1,000 spankings would be his limit and after that, he vowed to do something. Interestingly, The Arizona Republic reports that the list of items taken from the boy's home did not include any such tally page of spankings.

One thousand whacks might explain the boy's explosive response, I suppose. But something tells me there's more to the back story. Was the other man in the house -- the boarder -- responsible for some of the boy's angst? Was there some sort of sexual activity going on in the home that prompted this deadly reaction? Might it have been a horrible attempt to get attention from his absentee mother?

Or maybe the kid is one of those "bad seeds" we've heard about? A forensic psychiatrist pal of mine says, "No way."

Dr. Keith Ablow has evaluated many killers and has testified as an expert witness countless times. He reminds us that other children of this young age have inexplicably confessed to murders they did not commit and the system should proceed carefully with this child. (It seems the system is. Multiple mental evaluations have been ordered for the boy before the courts decide exactly how to proceed.)

If the child is guilty, Ablow says, there could be physical reasons for what he did. Maybe he has a brain tumor or another medical problem, such as reaction to medication or an infection of the cerebrospinal fluid that coats the brain. But chances are, says Ablow, the trigger for the murders will be found somewhere in the boy's emotional pathology:

"In 16 years practicing psychiatry, I have never met a murderer who was born evil. In every case, I eventually learned the circumstances that extinguished that person's empathy."

So we are left wondering what could have happened to a boy in just eight short years that would cause him to lose all empathy, become detached enough and desperate enough to pick up a rifle and pump 10 bullets into two people.

I think it's really important we learn the why of these murders -- if only to help other hopeless children who see no other way out but violence.

The Maliciously Missing

July 11, 2009

How many times have you heard about a missing persons case? To be sure, there are hundreds of thousands of Americans reported missing every year. Some come right back home. But too often, families of the missing either get the horrible news that their loved one's body has been found or they continue to suffer with the quiet torment of no news at all.

Then there is the group of missing people who aren't really missing at all. They are hiding. They're called "the maliciously missing" by a woman who knows the subject all too well.

Her name is Maureen Reintjes. On May 19, 2005, she kissed goodbye her husband of 24 years at their new home in Las Vegas, Nevada, and he disappeared. No warning, no reason; he was just gone. Jon Van Dyke, a retired Marine master sergeant, knew about responsibility. He seemed happy with their new life and his new job at the CitiGroup Command Center. They'd worked hard getting their home in shape for a pending family reunion.

"He would never just leave me," Reintjes thought.

For the next four years, her anguish over what terrible event must have happened to her husband was compounded by her financial realities. She lost their home and then another one. She was homeless for a while, struggling mightily to make sense of it all. She spent her days working, her nights on the computer setting up an internet presence to help locate Van Dyke, getting military friends and family to help disseminate the news that he was missing. Late into the night, Reintjes scoured the websites of coroners across America looking for information on unidentified bodies -- not wanting to find him among the dead but desperately looking for the truth.

Then, on Reintjes' birthday, May 11, 2009, one week shy of four years after he chose to walk away, he walked back into her life. He offered no real information on why he left or where he'd been. He wanted a divorce. Fresh with this new hurt, she is still dumbfounded. "I don't know how to feel," she told me. "I have lots of different emotions -- but my emotion is nameless." After her brief contact with him and court officers, she came away thinking that maybe he'd had a mental breakdown or a stroke.

"I was looking at my husband's body, but the man speaking -- it was not his personality."

The harsh reality is, it is not against the law to do what Jon Van Dyke did.

Others share Reintjes' anguish. Just recently, a man named David Rockey resurfaced in Bartlesville, Oklahoma, after having been gone seven years. He went off to what he told his family was a job interview in a nearby town one day and never came back. His wife, Peggy, and the family battled the pain of loss and uncertainty over Rockey's fate. Police continued to work his missing persons case whenever there was a tip. Rockey's disappearing act unraveled when he presented his expired driver's license to the South Dakota Department of Public Safety so he could get a new one. He now explains that his reason for leaving was "personal" and that he survived doing odd off-the-books jobs in Kansas, Nebraska and South Dakota. Peggy Rockey has filed for divorce.

Since there is no specific law to stop someone who decides they want to erase the old and start anew, there is no relief for the tortured families they leave behind. With the economy as bad as it is, authorities fear increasing financial pressures will cause a rise in the number of these maliciously missing cases.

No one has the right to simply walk away from mortgage payments, utility bills, child support and other court-mandated payments. The problem comes, of course, in locating and bringing to justice those who deliberately disappear to escape the obligations of life.

No telling how many people are in Maureen Reintjes' shoes now, combing through coroners' websites and news reports looking for any clue. Imagine their task. There are now estimated to be up to 60,000 unidentified bodies in the U.S., and there's no fully functioning one-stop location to check whether one of those bodies is that of their missing loved one.

A seed of hope has been planted at a publicly searchable repository called the National Missing and Unidentified Persons System, or NamUs. It's the first-ever registry to combine information on both missing persons and found bodies. Sadly, it relies entirely on those in law enforcement who have the time and inclination to enter pertinent information. Not many do.

It's a good first step, but we've got many more steps to go to help ease the heartache so many American families endure every day.

Beware a New Breed of Children

Feb. 6, 2010

Every human being needs to feel connected -- attached -- to other human beings around them. It's an innate craving we all have and cannot fight. The hunger for attachment begins with infants who bond with their mother's soothing voices, tender caresses and nurturing care. It's through this kind of attention the child comes to know the feelings of being safe and protected. The quality of the bonds children form with adults in their world early on will affect every relationship they'll have for the rest of their lives.

Sadly, some children never get the love they need to grow into healthy, empathetic, trusting people. As they grow, they form their own protective shield to keep out the rest of the world. They have no trust in others, and their behavior often turns self-destructive, and even criminal.

What ails this unfortunate group now has a name: reactive attachment disorder. It's a fairly new addition to the American Psychiatric Association book of every recognized psychiatric disorder known to man -- The Diagnostic and Statistical Manual of Mental Disorders.

The professionals say that RAD, as it's called, isn't just a trendy or a diagnosis du jour. They've discovered that young children who fail to form meaningful bonds, those who display early aggression and antisocial behaviors, often grow up to be sociopaths and turn to lives of crime.

In other words, RAD kids are the potential criminals of tomorrow. If we would only dedicate time and money to serve the needs of these children today, we might all be spared their wrath and their potentially deadly deeds in the future.

"If you see a serial killer, chances are very strong they were a RAD kid," says Jay Pullen, executive director of The Attachment Healing Center in Albuquerque, New Mexico. He mentions convicted Oklahoma City bomber Timothy McVeigh as likely being a RAD sufferer. I mention serial killer and cannibal Jeffery Dahmer.

Pullen says that it's fairly easy to diagnose RAD children, as they often display a wide range of similar behaviors -- setting fires, making violent threats, smearing feces, killing animals or stealing food -- as a way to combat their early memories of being left hungry in some way. All these behaviors are designed to repel other people so they can more comfortably retreat into their solitary shell.

Pullen is quick to say that RAD is not a lifetime curse, that there are successful ways to treat these kids. All it takes is time, money and the determination to help.

Various states, from New Mexico to Missouri to California to New York, are desperately searching for ways to lessen the plight of neglected children. The motivation is perfectly captured in this quote from former Chief Justice Kathleen Blatz of Minnesota's Supreme Court: "The difference between that poor child and a felon is about eight years."

There may be no other time in history when so many children are separated, ignored or neglected by the very people who are supposed to love them the most. According to the Children's Defense Fund, a record number of kids are shuffled between foster homes these days or reported to be victims of emotional and sexual abuse. If a parent is depressed or angry or addicted, it's likely their children aren't getting the nurturing they need.

You may think you're not affected by reactive attachment disorder, but Pullen says that nothing could be further from the truth. Your tax dollars go to deal with RAD kids once they enter the justice or adoption system. Whether you see graffiti on the side of a building, a neighbor's home damaged by an arson fire or your child's classroom repeatedly disrupted by the disordered child, reactive attachment disorder does affect you and yours.

Pioneer in-house treatments have been devised to help willing parents learn the most effective way to deal with these self-sabotaging children. One mother of a RAD child had to learn to ignore her daughter's chilling notes. One note, which the girl taped to the foot of her bed, read, "I'm going to slash your throat with a butcher knife."

Instead of reacting negatively to that, as she tucked in the child, the mother learned to say instead: "Yes, I see that. Now, hop into bed. We have to get you off to school in the morning." That kind of statement acknowledges the youngster's message but reinforces trust by presenting the idea that parent and child are part of a team.

The experts on RAD say that it all comes down to neurologically rewiring these kids to break their bad behavior cycles. In cases where parents are at the crux of the problem, RAD therapists recommend moving the children to a more nurturing environment. Foster parents and adoptive parents are often these kids' best hope.

We ignore these troubled children at our own peril. If we don't help them assimilate now, they could come back to grab our attention in much more serious and dangerous ways.

Inspired Justice in a World of Tight Budgets

Nov. 5, 2011

A golden retriever named Lily sits patiently at the glass entryway of a red brick building tucked behind Good Samaritan Hospital in Rockland County, New York.

Lily is a specially trained therapy dog, and she instinctively knows just what to do when the next troubled person arrives. She gives comfort to the physically and sexually abused, and it doesn't matter whether they are young or old, male or female. Lily, and the new Spirit of Rockland Special Victims Unit in which she works, is a godsend to everyone who walks in the door.

This isn't like the special victims units you see on television. There are no officers with guns bustling about, no metal desks or low-hanging fluorescent lights. There is nothing gritty about this SVU.

Veteran detective Lt. Mary Murphy greets you at the door. She arrives for work dressed like your friendly next-door neighbor with Lily in the back seat. Patricia Gunning, a senior sex crimes prosecutor with the district attorney's office, is also there to gently walk victims through the system and gather the evidence needed to get a conviction.

Doctors, victim advocates and Child Protective Services personnel also have space in this building.

The interior of this SVU includes walls painted in various shades of soothing pastels. There is comfortable padded furniture. Cheerful artwork featuring flowers and waterfalls dots the walls, and many rooms down the hallway are outfitted with child-sized tables and chairs. Other rooms are designed to make adult victims comfortable. Some visitors are battered women -- mentally or physically disabled, or victims of human trafficking or sex trafficking -- and others are abused elders.

There is a medical exam room, and next to it is a beautiful bathroom, complete with a private shower for victims who may need it. A sophisticated closed-circuit TV system links the interview rooms to a large conference room, where detectives can discreetly listen in to traumatized victim's answers without intimidating them. The system is also hooked up to nearby courtrooms, which helps spare frightened children a trip to court.

The Spirit of Rockland is a one-stop victim shop. The feeling you get here is that of care, safety and new beginnings.

When victims relive their nightmare for officers, Lily is always nearby. When tears flow, she gently places her chin on the victim's lap. She's there for solace, warmth and cuddles.

Now, here's the best part: None of this cost taxpayers a dime.

Rockland County District Attorney Tom Zugibe realized what his county lacked in terms of services for the most desperate, so he rolled up his sleeves and went out into the community. His mission was to build the county's first special victims unit.

First, Zugibe got Sister Fran Gorsuch, the director of community initiatives with Bon Secours Charity at Good Samaritan Hospital, to donate an underused 3,200-square-foot building. Sister Fran did one better. She got the board to sign off on a long-term no-rent agreement, plus free utilities.

"This is an extension of our mission," she said. "We are so proud to be a part of this and have it on our campus."

Zugibe then approached the daughter of a legislator who had just graduated with a degree in architecture. She was thrilled to volunteer to design her first project. A local decorator pitched in with a professional layout and color scheme.

To get demolition and rebuilding going, the D.A. and his chief detective, Peter Modafferi, met with the local Joint Trades Council and presented their idea to several union leaders.

"The toughest contractors melted when they heard what we wanted to do," Zugibe told me. Soon, painters, plumbers, electricians, tile setters and lots of others showed up and offered help. Many were unemployed and eager to use their skills again.

They all arrived with donated supplies -- toilets, wiring and lighting fixtures. A local paint store contributed; a carpet company provided flooring; the Home Depot down the street pitched in with drywall. Others contributed toys, books and child-sized furniture.

The artwork that caught my eye when I visited was donated by volunteer artists at DiDi's Art Angels, a group with the mission to "wipe out white drab walls." Office furniture was scrounged from the county's stash of stored items.

"We did it all for no money," Zugibe said proudly. "And what was so rewarding? Nobody said no. Everyone we approached agreed to help."

Visiting the Spirit of Rockland inspired me and made me remember that America is a great country, filled with caring and generous people.

Right now, we're suffering through a period of "can't do." Our economy is in tatters, unemployment is debilitating us, and there's no great spark of hope at the end of the tunnel.

But we are the spark. We light our own way. We are famous for making something big out of nothing. Tom Zugibe and all those who donated their time, goods and elbow grease proved it by creating the Rockland County, New York, Special Victims Unit.

Now, what can we do to get America rolling again?

Felony Murder Laws Need Wiggle Room

Aug. 18, 2012

Any parent would agree that young people can do impulsive and thoughtless things. But what if one of their stupidly spontaneous acts accidently turns deadly? Should society give that young person special consideration? Should it depend on the kid's character in the past? Should the justice system treat him or her the same as a career criminal?

The case that caused these questions to pop into my mind comes from Greensboro, North Carolina, and involves a young woman named Janet Danahey. It doesn't take much imagination to see that what happened to Danahey could happen to any one of our kids.

It was Valentine's Day 2002, and since Danahey and her boyfriend, Thad, had recently (and amicably) broken up, the then-23-year-old got together with two girlfriends that night to play cards and drink some wine. Their circle of friends was always playing pranks on one another, and this night the three girls -- Janet, Nicole and Adrianne -- schemed about what kind of trick they could pull on Thad.

They decided to sabotage his car and visited a grocery store looking for fish oil or something smelly to pour into the young man's fresh air vent. They bought a bottle of clam juice and headed to Thad's apartment building. When they discovered his car wasn't there, Janet grabbed charcoal lighter fluid and set a small fire atop an old futon outside Thad's door. They could hear people inside the apartment, and the idea was to knock and run, leaving Thad's roommates to stamp out the flames.

The night was windy, and the fire soon engulfed the apartment building. Four people were killed: sisters Rachel and Donna Llewellyn, ages 21 and 24; 25-year-old Ryan Bek; and 20-year-old Elizabeth Harris.

Danahey never stopped to think what heartache would result from that childish and senseless act.

She admitted to police and the father of Elizabeth Harris that she had set the fire, and she begged for forgiveness. But she was soon faced with the cold reality of North Carolina's felony murder statute, which dozens of other states also have. Under the felony murder rule, if anyone is killed during the commission of a felony (in this case arson) the perpetrator can be charged with murder and sentenced to death. It holds even if the victim's death was an accident.

Danahey had to choose between pleading guilty and receiving life in prison with no chance of parole or going to trial where, if found guilty, she would automatically get the death penalty. She pleaded guilty.

(The felony murder rule is applied differently depending on the jurisdiction, but generally speaking, the underlying felony must present a "foreseeable danger to life." In some cases, accomplices can face the ultimate penalty, too -- if they exhibited "extreme indifference to human life" -- but in Danahey's case, her two girlfriends never spoke to her again and were not charged. Danahey assumed full responsibility.)

As you ponder this tragedy, realize that before this happened, Danahey had been an exemplary child. As a high school student, she was described as "sweet, responsible and very respectful." Danahey had won the top Girl Scouts award and was active in several clubs, including the Young Christian Society. She played the viola, carried the Olympic torch during part of the run to Atlanta's 1996 Summer Olympic Games and made the dean's list in college. None of this, of course, absolves her of blame. But the record shows that Danahey made one awful decision on one horrific night.

On the other hand, as prosecutors rightfully pointed out in court, Danahey was an intelligent college graduate, a woman who should have known that using an accelerant and starting a fire on a windy night could result in catastrophic damage. And the state maintained that Danahey and her friends exhibited complete indifference by leaving the scene without making sure the fire was actually put out.

Now, 10 years later, Danahey's lawyers note that she has been a model prisoner and have filed a petition for clemency with the outgoing governor to have her sentence reduced to time served.

The attorneys call what happened on that February night: a "joke...a foolish prank...a thoughtless act but with no malicious intent." They have asked for an adjustment "to a sentence that is out of all proportion to the conduct involved." And one of Danahey's most visible supporters is Elizabeth Harris' father, Robert, who said he forgave Danahey years ago. His words are part of the clemency petition:

"I still picture Janet, standing with outreached hands, handcuffed, trembling, shaking almost violently, crying intensely, speaking almost incoherently, 'These are the hands that are responsible for Beth's death.' My reactions were instinctive. I went over to her, held her tightly ... (and) whispered ... 'I forgive you, Janet,' several times."

At this writing, there have been no comments from other victims' family members, so there is no way to know whether they will challenge the clemency request.

One North Carolina newspaper pal wrote me recently saying, "Two-and-a-half years per life doesn't seem like much punishment for a deliberate act of arson that went bad."

I guess I agree with that, but I have this nagging feeling that our felony murder laws should be adjusted for people like Danahey. I think that only career criminals should get life in prison with no chance at parole.

UPDATE: In April 2013, Danahay's attorney withdrew her clemency request and is now asking for her sentence to be adjusted to time served. She remains in prison.

Boy Scouts Promise -- Too Little Too Late?

Sept. 6, 2012

I'd like to take this opportunity to express my thanks to the Boy Scouts of America - NOT.

The national organization has just announced it will reveal to police the names of men it has suspected in the past of stalking young Boy Scouts for sexual purposes.

Well, finally! When you look at the history of this, you see it is long past due.

This oftentimes revered organization was founded in 1910 and almost immediately officials started to keep secret files on sexual predators who hovered around, attempting to prey on young boys. Commendable of them to try to keep some sort of record, but unfortunately the Boy Scouts' hierarchy never reported the suspected child molesters to law enforcement. Back then, such perversions were not a topic fit for public discussion, so the BSA's so-called "perversion files" (officially called the "ineligible volunteer list") were kept secret. The child molesters were left to roam free.

Decades went by, and the number of secret files grew and grew and grew. The New York Times has reported that by 1935 the Scouts had 2,910 "cards" on men who were not suitable to be around young boys.

In more modern times, BSA officials came to their senses - sometimes - and the police were notified about some of the most egregious cases. In the early 1990s, a handful of the perversion files were released to the public through the courts. They revealed that from 1971 to 1991, BSA officials had repeatedly failed to contact authorities about suspected pedophiles operating within their organization - even in cases where they had a confession! Shameful. Just shameful. Again, child molesters were left to roam free.

After that stunning revelation, the Boy Scouts of America vowed to do better. Whether it did is subject to interpretation. I think the BSA did not do nearly what it should have to make sure its Scouts and its communities were safe.

In 2010, a lawsuit was filed by a former Boy Scout in Portland, Ore., who claimed that in the '80s the organization failed to protect him from Timur Dykes, an assistant scout master who had already admitted he had molested Scouts but was allowed to work with boys anyway.

After seeing some of the perversion files, the jury awarded the former Scout $18.5 million dollars. The once secret files shown during the Dykes trial have now been ordered to be released to the public. They are expected to be available later this month - after victims' and accusers' names have been redacted.

And, now, suddenly in advance of the release of those bombshell files - kept between the years 1965 and 1985 - the Boy Scouts of America steps up to make its seemingly altruistic announcement. It apparently plans to scour its perversion files to find the names of suspected pedophiles who have slipped through the cracks and turn the names over to law enforcement agencies around the country. They've hired a former police detective named Mike Johnson to lead the review.

This, after the Boy Scouts of America spent multiple decades caring more about its reputation than making sure child predators were locked up and Scouts were kept safe? Color me not very impressed. It sounds like an awfully familiar modus operandi, doesn't it?

I believe that in this post-Catholic Church/Jerry Sandusky era, all thinking people realize that covering up child molestation has terrible and lasting consequences. One, it lets the predator-monster loose to prey on more children. Two, it leaves behind damaged souls who never got justice for what was done to them as children. Our prisons are full of convicts who report they were childhood victims of sex abuse and that in their psychological confusion and pent-up shame they turned to drugs, violence and crime.

By waiting this long to do the right thing, the Boy Scouts of America has committed another sin in the eyes of childhood molestation victims everywhere. The group's prolonged silence and inaction boils down to this: It is too damn late in some states for victims to ever get justice. The statute of limitations on such crimes has run out.

Yes, release of the perversion files may result in new criminal prosecutions, but even a suspect's confession is not enough. Any prosecutor will tell you they also need a complaining victim to come forward to testify, and that will not be an easy task. After all these years, these now-grown men might very well want to keep their nightmare a secret.

So, thanks, Boy Scouts of America. I've heard the BSA's claim that the organization has been doing all it could to prevent sex abuse within the ranks. But you earn no merit badge from me for your assertion that you spent a century tracking known pedophiles to keep them away from young Scouts. It was simply not enough, and the BSA should have known that years ago.

Congratulations. You've earned your place in the Hall of Shame right behind the Catholic Church, Penn State University and every other group that has chosen its reputation over justice.

You've got a long way to go to untarnish the Boy Scout image.

Hey, Steubenville -- Where Was Everyone?

March 23, 2013

"There are crimes very similar to this that occur every Friday night and every Saturday night in communities across this country." - Ohio Attorney General Mike DeWine

Many of us watched with interest the rape case that recently played out in Steubenville, Ohio. The two defendants - Trent Mays, 17, and Ma'Lik Richmond, 16 - were star members of the local high school's football team, and many in the community felt they had been maliciously targeted for prosecution because of their popularity.

The evidence was overwhelming, however, and both teens were convicted of sexually assaulting a female classmate. There was a video, still pictures and dozens of contemporaneous text and Twitter messages flying back and forth discussing details of the assault. The victim, a 16-year-old girl, was so drunk (or perhaps drugged) that she was unconscious during much of the prolonged assault. Included in the torrent of more than 3,000 tawdry messages read aloud to the court were those from eyewitnesses and classmates joking about the "dead-looking" victim and saying, "Some people deserve" to be urinated upon.

One text sent the day after the attack from defendant Mays begged a friend to delete the video of the incident that had been posted on YouTube and added: "Coach Sac knows about it. Seriously, delete it!" During the trial, it was learned that football coach Reno Saccoccia knew about the sexual assault and refused to suspend the defendants or other players who had knowledge of the incident until the season was nearly over.

As I watched the case unfold - and read the unvarnished blog by former Steubenville resident Alexandra Goddard, who had immediately captured the offending texts, video and pictures before they were deleted - I couldn't stop thinking: Where was everyone else as this crime was happening?

As this young girl was being humiliated and brutalized, stripped of her clothing and carried around like a rag doll, what were her classmates doing? Why didn't anyone step in to say, "Stop!" Didn't other girls at the event feel her shame and move to help cover up her nakedness? Where was the homeowner of the house where the party was being held? What had the parents of these teenagers taught their children about coming to the aid of a fellow human being in trouble?

None of my questions were part of the court proceedings, of course, but as Attorney General DeWine said upon the conviction, "I'll guarantee that there are crimes very similar to this that occur every Friday night and every Saturday night in communities across this country, where you have people, particularly young people, who are drinking too much and a girl is taken advantage of, and a girl is raped." DeWine is right.

It is surely happening in your community and mine, too.

Yet DeWine believes that justice may not have been completely served in the Steubenville case. His investigators interviewed 56 witnesses - from teenagers who attended the party to assistant football coaches and the high school principal - yet there were still 16 people with knowledge of the crime who have refused to talk. So, DeWine will convene a grand jury next month to determine whether other people should be charged in this case.

Leave it alone, you say? The conviction of Mays and Richmond is enough? I don't think so.

Consider that even after the guilty verdicts, some in that football crazed town were still not convinced the pair had done anything wrong, and they turned their wrath on the victim. After the guilty verdicts were announced, two teenage girls were taken into custody for allegedly using Twitter and Facebook posts to threaten her with a "beating" and "homicide." They now face felony counts of witness tampering, among other charges. After the girls' arrest, DeWine announced: "Let me be clear. Threatening a teenage rape victim will not be tolerated. If anyone makes a threat ... we will take it seriously, we will find you, and we will arrest you."

Blogger Goddard reports she and her family continued to be harassed and maligned. She also had to fight back a defamation lawsuit filed against her and two dozen people who left comments on the case at her website. "Perhaps most ridiculously," she wrote, "I was accused of 'complicating' the case because I posted the screen captures of content that these kids willingly posted themselves." Clearly, not all of Steubenville has learned the obvious lesson of this case.

In the meantime, the victim's mother told CNN, "We hope that from this something good can arise ... (to) possibly change the mentality of a youth or help a parent to have more of an awareness (as) to where their children are and what they are doing. The adults need to take responsibility and guide these children."

Yep. This is one of those teachable moments, the perfect time for folks to sit down with their kids and have a serious talk about the issues this case raised. Drinking and drugs, athlete adoration, teenage sex and doing unto others as we would need them to do for us if we were in trouble. It is also a good time for parents to re-examine where the circle of accountability begins and ends when one of our children is so publicly victimized.

A Spooky House, the Law and You

June 10, 2013

Anyone out there live in a haunted house? It might seem like a silly question, but as home sales pick up, you should know that there are laws against selling a house without full disclosure.

Sellers are required to reveal a number of things about their home, like the condition of roof shingles or whether they have had issues with termites, persistent leaks or radon gas. Now, in a growing number of states, the seller must also report suspected poltergeist problems.

Think you've seen ghosts in the hallway? Do objects in the home mysteriously move from place to place? Or have you seen furniture levitating off the floor? How about hearing odd and spooky noises in the dead of night?

I know, who wants to admit to total strangers (let alone a real estate agent) that they think their house is haunted? But there is case law on the books about the issue, and if the buyer suddenly gets freaked out about spirit shenanigans in their newly purchased home, they could decide to go to court to try to get their money back.

The professionals in real estate call these houses "stigmatized properties," and about half of all states have laws regulating their sales, according to the National Association of Realtors. The history of these places can include murders and suicides to people with certain diseases who died in the home. Worrisome histories can cause buyers to shy away for fear the place might be haunted. And the Association of Realtors says it happens more often than you'd think.

The most documented case of buyer's remorse occurred in 1990 in the village of Nyack, New York. Jeffrey and Patrice Stambovsky decided to buy a big, beautiful $650,000 Victorian home nestled near the Hudson River. They plunked down $32,500 as a deposit. Helen Ackley, the owner of the four-bedroom, two-bathroom property had decided to retire to Florida, and when she put up the house for sale she failed to inform the buyers about her ghostly tenants. Neither did her real estate agent.

To be fair, Ackley had openly talked about the benevolent spirits who had occupied space with her family over the years. The information was out there. The elderly woman had described her ghost's activities in detail -- how they left gifts around the house, once helped her decide what color to paint a room and shook her bed each morning to awaken her -- to the local newspaper. In fact, Ackley's story of poltergeists appeared three times in the paper between 1977 and 1989. She had also given a detailed interview for an article in Reader's Digest. The home was even featured as part of a walking tour of "haunted houses" in Nyack.

After a local resident met the visiting Stambovskys and said, "Oh, you're buying the haunted house?" the couple wanted to back out of the deal. They lived 30 miles south in New York City and had no knowledge of the folklore about the house. The couple did not appear at the signing, which meant they forfeited their down payment, but they were no longer obligated to buy the house. Ackley, in no hurry to get to Florida, would not cancel the sale or return the buyer's money, so they all headed to court.

The case took awhile to resolve. The Stambovskys lost the first round after a lower court ruled it was their obligation to research the history of the home before committing to buy. But the New York Appellate Court ultimately ruled in the couple's favor. The point of the story is, of course, that it is far better to be upfront about suspected paranormal activity in your home than to keep it a secret. You could be tied up in court for years!

Some states have a long list of stigmas that must be reported. They range from violent deaths to suicides to sex crimes to drug activity -- specifically drug manufacturing at the location, since the chemicals used could seep into the walls or foundation.

In California, for example, a seller is bound to answer the buyer's question about any deaths that occurred in the home. Illinois statutes state that since ghosts would not have an effect on the "physical condition" of the home, they do not need to be disclosed. In New Jersey, on the other hand, real estate agents and sellers are specifically required to disclose "psychological impairments" inherent in a property -- and, yes, that includes the fact that it purports to be haunted. The same holds in Hawaii, where the culture of spirituality and respect for the land requires full paranormal disclosure.

In the last Gallup poll that asked the question, "Do you believe that houses can be haunted?" 37 percent of Americans said yes. Thirty-two percent agreed that spirits of dead people can come back in certain places and situations. So take heart -- if you tell a potential buyer your place comes with unexplainable cold spots, creaky nighttime sounds and floating apparitions, you might not shock them at all. Some buyers are actively looking for just such properties.

Back in the day, the magician The Amazing Kreskin was interested in buying the Ackley house. But then a team of paranormal investigators reported that the ghosts inside the old Victorian told them it wasn't much fun haunting the house without Helen Ackley in it. Someone else bought it -- fully aware of its controversial history -- and there have been no more public reports of hauntings ever since.

An Intriguing Plan to Create Urban Peace

May 10, 2014

Ten minutes on the phone with David Lockett and you realize this is a man of high integrity, compassion and vision. After a lengthy conversation with him, I came away believing that if there was ever a man we should follow in the fight against crime, it is David Lockett.

Lockett's business background is in the trucking industry. He also developed and has run a program for nearly 20 years that embraces society's toughest hardcore juvenile criminals and gives them the tools to turn their lives around. It's called the PACT LifePlan Coaching Program, and its guiding principle is the idea that if we help young people avoid a lifetime of crime, everybody wins. Spend a little time giving a kid some skills and a plan for his or her future and the country gets a law-abiding, contributing taxpayer in return. In the long run, it's a lot cheaper than paying for their trip (or trips) through the U.S. justice system.

Youth courts in and around Lockett's native Toronto, Canada, are so impressed by his track record with these kids they automatically funnel the toughest cases his way, sentencing young offenders to a term in this very unique program.

As the PACT staff explains, their approach isn't therapy or counseling; it is coaching kids on how to live a meaningful life. There are specially targeted programs for both young males, the category so often at the center of street crime, and for young women, who are so susceptible to early pregnancy.

For the dedicated PACT coaches it can be a constant, almost 24/7 job to keep track of their wards -- meetings, classes, outside projects with the kids, late-night phone calls and teary heart-to-heart discussions. The children come from abusive homes or live in foster care situations. Many have been in gangs, have mental health or substance abuse problems. During the year-and-a half long process, PACT coaches act like the dutiful parents these children never had.

The metaphor, Lockett told me, is simple: "Imagine a kid that's fallen into a deep pit. Many would rush in to pull up the kid. At our program, the coach comes to the edge of the pit and asks, 'Are you ready to figure out where your life should go? What are your goals? How do you plan to achieve them?'" And once the PACT coach gets satisfactory answers, Lockett says, "They go to Home Depot for lumber, nails and a hammer, and toss them down to the kid so they can build a ladder out."

For those who think the problem of youth crime is too widespread to tackle with a simple program, Lockett says he has proof that it really isn't. After much research and consultation with several police departments, the PACT program came to realize that a majority of crimes were being committed by a small group of troubled and forgotten teens.

Locket told me: "One youth court officer told me there were 60 kids in his area who were the worst. Those 60 kids committed 1,000 crimes." Those underage lawbreakers became PACT's target group. "It dawned on me," Lockett said, in the passionate tone he uses, "to break the cycle ... just help those 60 kids and your crime rate goes down!"

Now for the best part: Guess how much the PACT program's intensive, one-on-one mentoring costs Canadian taxpayers? Nothing, thanks to Lockett's creative and dogged approach to getting the community involved.

"From the beginning we decided we would not take government money because it just came with so much B.S. attached," Lockett said. "It just wasn't worth it. So I went and gave speeches to 30 Rotary clubs."

That is where PACT got its seed money back in 1995. And so it remains today. A combination of donations from service clubs, local businesses and corporations pays for everything. Right now there are 42 youngsters in the program, and the annual operating budget is about $300,000. That's less than the justice system spends on one teenage repeat offender. So far, 10,000 teens have graduated from the PACT program. The success rate of all those who enter is near 70 percent.

Lockett, who calls himself a "social entrepreneur," uses tried-and-true business practices to keep his program running in very creative ways. First and foremost, PACT is careful with its money as the staff goes about giving kids hope and teaching them skills that will take them into the future -- cooking, gardening, film production and light construction. One Lockett brainchild is a program that teaches kids patching, painting and how to place drywall, all with donated materials from local businesses. PACT then bids -- underbids, actually -- on local jobs and wins most of them. The money the team earns goes to pay some of the life coaches, salaries of up to $10 an hour for the most experienced teens, and the rest is distributed to the other kids as bonuses.

"Businesses are successful because they make plans, come up with a list of best practices ... and they thrive," Lockett said. "But we don't do that with social problems ... why not?"

Good question. Why don't we come up with concrete plans to creatively break the cycle of poverty and tackle the root issues that lure kids into crime, such as feelings of alienation and hopelessness, poor education, drug abuse, gangs and teen pregnancy?

Lockett's ultimate mission sounds lofty. He wants to "bring about urban peace" and convince communities and businesses that giving to his program is not a donation but an investment. As you might suspect, Lockett has his own wish list for the future.

"I want to build a social franchise and teach others how to create urban peace in the world," he told me. "Think about it. Our model really funds itself, it can be used anywhere and it works."

Any of you out there want to help create urban peace where you live? David Lockett will be glad to tell you how.

Paternity Fraud Hurts a Wide Circle

Aug. 29, 2015

Countless children go through life not knowing the true identity of their fathers. Shame on their mothers. And shame on the U.S. court system that, more often than you realize, forces child support on men with no DNA connection.

These false establishments of paternity, as they are called, happen in courts across the country. Our broken family court system is intent on getting someone -- anyone -- on record as being responsible for the child, so the state won't be.

The result is circles of victimized people. First, the children, who are denied the truth about who their biological father is, as well their heritage, extended family and inheritance rights. Then there is the innocent man and his family. They are robbed of hard-earned cash and emotional well-being. Living with an unfair court order, one that demands compliance for as long as 18 years, takes a terrible toll.

Here are some examples of how this could happen.

Sara has just given birth. Her husband, Andrew, who's on leave from the military and staying at home, is at the hospital with his wife and ecstatic about becoming a father and starting his own family. A hospital staffer presents Andrew with a paternity acknowledgement form, and he signs it without a second thought. Two years later, after a raging argument, Sara reveals the child is not his. She won't identify the biological father, and even after Andrew's DNA test proves he is not related, he is told that the time limit to challenge paternity has passed and he is legally bound to pay support until the child is 18.

Teenager Anita gives birth without the help of the father, and when she applies for state aid to help with her expenses, she is told that she must give the father's name and his last known address. Anita, scared and broke, puts down the name of a long-ago boyfriend and a phony address. When he doesn't show up in court -- because how could he? He was never notified -- an automatic default judgment is entered, and he is on the hook for 18 years of child support.

Jose faced a similar situation, except he was served with court papers. He shows up to court to explain that he hasn't seen his former lover for two years. His offer to take a DNA test is ignored, and without the money to hire a lawyer, the process rolls over him. He, too, is ordered to pay years of support for a child that isn't his.

Hospitals take such great care to connect newborns to their mothers by giving them matching identity bracelets and providing 24/7 security protection for the nurseries. But what do family courts do to ensure a defenseless child is connected to the proper father? Next to nothing. They take the mother's word on paternity, case closed.

Dianna Thompson is president of a nonprofit group called Women Against Paternity Fraud. The group wants there to be a federal law declaring that no paternity finding is final until a DNA test proves the identity of a biological father. The group also wants consideration given to any other women involved in these almost unbelievable scenarios, such as grandmothers, sisters, aunts, girlfriends and wives of falsely accused men.

Thompson wrote to tell me that this is more than just a problem for duped dads. She called it "a national epidemic" and recounted the personal stories of some of her supporters. One woman didn't discover her dad wasn't related to her until she was 50 years old and attending his funeral. Another woman found her biological father's family later in life and learned there was a history of breast cancer. Had she known, she might have avoided the trauma of her own breast cancer.

Then, there is the 13-year odyssey of WAPF's co-founder, Alicia Thompson. While waiting for her divorce to go through, Thompson began a relationship with another man. Months later, she became pregnant, and DNA proved the boyfriend was the father. No matter. The court cited the ancient common law of "presumption of paternity" and declared the soon-to-be ex-husband responsible for supporting the child. Thompson refused to let that stand and agreed to let her husband relinquish his parental rights. Her child was left fatherless in the eyes of the law -- no medical insurance, no Social Security benefits, no child support from her unsupportive biological father. Thompson continues to fight this injustice.

There is a lot in this world that isn't fair. This is one thing we have the power to change. Why don't we?

Elder Guardianships: A Shameful 'Racket'

Jan. 20, 2016

Betty Winstanley is a well-spoken, elegant and wealthy 94-year-old widow. And as she told me from her room at a south central Pennsylvania retirement facility, "I feel like I am in prison. My life is a living hell."

Welcome to America's twisted world of court-appointed guardianships for the elderly.

Quick backstory: Betty and her husband, Robert, were married for 72 years. They had three children, Richard, David and Betsy. For nearly seven years, the couple occupied a "lovely" apartment at the retirement home.

In early 2014, Betty, who uses a rolling walker to get around, said she felt faint. Seeing no staff nearby she lowered herself to the ground. "They said I fell," she told me. "But that is a bad, bad word around here. Once you fall they decide you aren't capable of taking care of yourself anymore." Betty was sent to the medical section of the compound for rehabilitation after a small fracture was found.

Robert, a doctor of ophthalmology with a keen interest in aerospace medicine, took ill shortly after and was also transferred to the medical unit. Betty stayed with him but longed to return to her apartment.

"They wouldn't let me," Betty said. Labeled as a resident who could no longer live independently, Betty was transferred to a smaller room where nurses could keep better track of her. Sadly, on June 16, 2014, Robert died of heart failure.

Soon after, Betty had to appear in court because a family member claimed she needed a guardian to make decisions for her. At this crucial initial hearing, Betty was without her hearing aids because the home collected them "for cleaning" and had not returned them. Still deep in grief, Betty was unable to understand the proceeding and her court-appointed lawyer never told her that she had the right to speak before the judge made a decision.

On July 17, 2014, a Pennsylvania common pleas judge heard testimony from one doctor and one nurse from the facility and ruled that Betty was "a totally incapacitated person." This, despite the fact that two independent neuropsychologists who tested Betty declared she was of sound mind. Depressed? Understandably, yes. Affected by dementia or Alzheimer's disease? No.

Those conclusions didn't seem to matter. Betty was appointed a guardian -- two, in fact -- and immediately felt cut off from the rest of the world. Her family visits were curbed, her checkbook was taken and she was restricted from leaving the facility campus. Her guardian did not even let her leave the campus at Christmas.

"They make me feel like a piece of protoplasm on a deserted island," Betty told me. "I just want to move to an assisted living home in Annapolis, Maryland, so I can be near David and Betsy. I have no family around here except Richard, who rarely comes to visit."

Interestingly, Betty is not allowed to pay for her own lawyer from her $1.9 million estate funds. Her son David, a flight attendant, told the court he has spent his life's savings trying to help his mother escape the grasp of a legal system that is supposed to help the elderly.

Groups fighting to change contested guardianship laws call the system a "nationwide racket," wherein an all-powerful judge appoints a guardian who, in turn, can hire a local attorney, any number of merchants and service people and, as in Betty's case, the elder has no idea how their money is being spent. Betty only knows that her monthly apartment cost was about $3,300 and now she's charged $8,500 for her smaller, skilled-nursing-care room.

In the words of Dr. Sam Sugar, an advocate for elders in Florida, "The mantra of the guardianship system is litigate, medicate and take the estate."

I've read hundreds of pages of court transcripts and documents about Betty's case, and while there is much more to her story -- including brothers who no longer speak and the prolonged focus in court on son David, who reportedly upset Betty in the past by yelling in frustration -- there is really only one important takeaway. Betty wants to leave the place where her husband died and live closer to her family in Maryland. The reason she can't move? Pennsylvania won't let her go, despite a state law that says a guardian must take into account what the ward wants. Betty's limbo has dragged on for 18 months.

"I get the impression they just plan to wait her out until she dies," Betty's attorney, Candace Beckett, told me. "I've watched my client decline during this prolonged fight. ... She is like a flower who's dying on the vine." There is an appeal pending but that will take months to be heard.

This is what happens in America when the kids can't -- or won't -- agree on what's best for Mom. Shameful, on many levels.

The Nationwide Problem of Court-Sponsored Elder Abuse

Feb. 6, 2016

I wrote about the plight of 94-year-old Betty Winstanley, who resides at a retirement home in Pennsylvania. She doesn't want to live there anymore. Now that her husband of 72 years is gone, she longs to move to a care home closer to her two children in Maryland. But the state of Pennsylvania won't let her leave.

To the state, Betty is case number 1201, just another old person the court has declared "totally incapacitated." Once someone is labeled as such, they're given a court-appointed guardian who literally takes over their life. The guardian decides all the ward's finances, who can visit and for how long, if and when they can leave the home -- everything.

This is widow Winstanley's lot in life now. Yet when you talk to Betty, she is still charming, articulate and highly intelligent, simply looking for a less lonely life during her last years.

I had no idea about the enormity of the nation's problems with elder guardianship, or how many individuals and organizations are fighting to change the now-bastardized set of laws that can turn an elder's life into a nightmare.

The aging baby-boom generation has probably already experienced this problem with their own parents. Be careful -- you could be the next one to get caught up in this awful system.

Reader Marcia Southwick wrote to tell me about Boomers Against Elder Abuse, a New Mexico organization fighting against abusive court-ordered guardianships.

"There is plenty of it going on in New Mexico but records are sealed here, and families gag ordered and made to sign no-sue agreements once the guardianship/conservatorship is over," she wrote. The group's Facebook page lists nearly 350 elder guardianship horror stories from just about every state.

From Austin, Texas, Kelley Smoot Garrett also wrote about New Mexico's system and the arrogance displayed by the court. "In New Mexico's Second Judicial District Court," she said, "The judges ... ALWAYS favor their court appointees and never listen to the families or the elderly because they are too busy allowing the 'incapacitated' person's property to be sold off -- frequently without the appropriate court order in place -- for pennies on the dollar."

There is no way for me to confirm judicial misconduct in sealed cases, but the sheer volume of complaints is staggering. They highlight citizens' attitudes about the legal system taking laws designed to help the elderly and twisting them to ensure continued employment for judges, lawyers, court-appointed guardians, social workers and those who own or staff elder care homes. And it is conveniently paid for out of the elders' estates.

"My mother has been shanghaied into a nursing home, drugged, assets disbursed," a woman named Frania wrote from Baltimore, Maryland. "The guardian of (her) property is like God. And the judge is cocky, completely confident, arrogant ... does exactly what she wants knowing nothing will happen to her."

It doesn't matter if the elderly person has a will or living trust -- it can be automatically overridden by the state. Once someone approaches the court for assistance with an elderly person -- say, a warring sibling or nosy neighbor -- they are in the clutches of this dysfunctional system.

Andy Skupaka wrote to say that he has experienced this: "For-profit guardian/conservatorship is now a big business with massive power. The elderly are being denied their civil rights and due process," he said.

"Their estates and legacies are being looted. ... Family members are slandered, libeled, vilified and driven into bankruptcy while trying to save their loved ones from this exploitation."

Some report they were tricked by unscrupulous lawyers. Darryl Steiner, a decorated and now-retired U.S. Army major wrote from Clearwater, Florida. He said that he went to his lawyer for financial advice and suddenly found himself in a plenary guardianship; now he has no control over his money for his son's education. "I do have a good monthly retirement income that disappears as soon as it comes in," he said. "I am desperately seeking help."

Several groups nationwide are working to change this awful system -- among them the National Association to Stop Guardian Abuse and the Catherine Falk Organization. Catherine, daughter of actor Peter Falk of the "Columbo" TV show, was denied visitation by her stepmother during her father's last days. Now, her group lobbies to pass a bill to remove the barriers of family participation while still providing ample protection for those in true need. Falk says that lawmakers in nearly two-dozen states have responded positively to changing the status quo.

Change couldn't come fast enough for Betty Winstanley. Since July 2014, she has had to live where her husband died, without the family she so desperately craves. Her estate was worth $1.9 million before her guardianship began in July 2014. I wonder what it's down to now.

~~~

CHAPTER 10
When the Justice System Fails -- The Human Toll

"Our criminal justice system is fallible. We know it, even though we don't like to admit it. It is fallible despite the best efforts of most within it to do justice." ~ **Eliot Spitzer, former governor of New York**

It's often said that the United States has the finest justice system in the world, but that doesn't mean it is perfect. Wrongful convictions, overly authoritarian or biased law enforcement, overburdened courts and misguided or uncaring judges are just some of the inherent problems with our system. It is as fallible as the human beings that populate it.

Unfairness -- or even the specter of unfairness -- erodes the public's faith in the justice system, and I feel it's my duty to report on those cases, as well as those that right the wrongs done to innocent human beings.

To wit: the Mississippi sisters who spent nearly two decades in prison because a white sheriff had a beef with their daddy. Frantic parents who could possibly get vital information on the whereabouts of their missing children if only the IRS would cooperate. And the countless Americans who are getting divorced turn to the courts for help only to face a horrifically dysfunctional family court system that promises to bankrupt them.

Again, no justice system is perfect. But ours could be a lot better and much more responsive to the citizens it was established to serve.

An Anniversary of Murder

March 5, 2008

I have a friend named Danielle Parker -- Dani for short. She is celebrating an anniversary. March 6 marks the 15th anniversary of her mother's murder. To this day, the case remains unsolved.

Fifty-one-year-old Gail Parker, a vivacious, altruistic, well-dressed resident of Tucson, Arizona, stopped by a Circle K Store on Saturday March 6, 1993. A surveillance camera caught her quick transaction, and maybe even a glimpse of the killer. But because the crime happened on a weekend, no one thought to preserve the tape.

Parker's body was found later that night in a stretch of desert -- her head bashed in, her pocketbook and jewelry gone. Her husband, Barry Parker, happened to be watching the news, waiting for his wife to come home, when he heard the chillingly familiar description of a Jane Doe's clothing. In a state of shock, he called police.

On that night so many years ago, Dani and her father's lives changed forever. So did the life of Gail Parker's elderly mother, who began a sad decline of Percocet overuse to try to dull the agony. Her emotional distress drove her to attempt suicide on more than one occasion. She died in 2005, never knowing who took her daughter from this Earth.

Parker's murder left a hole in the heart of the family, a hole that cannot begin to heal until the person responsible for creating it is found, put on trial and found guilty of the crime.

First denied of their loved one, the Parker family has also endured the denial of seeing justice done.

I've studied a lot of statistics about murder in America. None are so sad as those of unsolved cases. Of course, the numbers vary from week to week, month to month, as more cases hit the books and more are solved. But consider the latest government statistics: As of 2004, there were 16,137 reported murders in the United States. And 37.4 percent of these cases were unsolved, meaning more than 6,000 people got away with murder.

Now, think of the survivors of homicide, like my friend and her family. Grief expert Lu Redmond estimates there are seven to 10 close relatives for each victim. It's a horrific domino effect that leaves thousands of wounded people to grieve and mourn for the rest of their lives.

It all seems so simple when we watch TV shows like "Cold Case" and "Without a Trace." Crimes seem to get tied up in a nice little bow by the end of the program. That is not reality.

Over the last 15 years, Dani Parker has gone through life's normal ups and downs: She suffered a painful neck injury that nearly left her paralyzed, and she got married to a wonderful man named Michael. These are events in life for which you need your mother, but that was impossible for her. Her father couldn't bear to stay in Tucson without his beloved wife of 27 years, so he moved east to be closer to Dani, his only child. Today, his life revolves around simply getting through the day. Over the years, Dani has tried to introduce her father to other women. But he says that Gail was the love of his life, and he'd rather be alone with his memories.

As for Dani, I marvel at what she has achieved in life and wonder what more she could have accomplished if she hadn't had to operate with part of her heart and soul ripped away. Always successful in the public relations area, she opened her own PR business recently in the ubercompetitive New York. She's already building an impressive clientele.

But she wrote to me recently, saying: "Every day is a struggle for me ... to get up in the morning, to work, to put a smile on my face when all I feel like doing is crying. To the outside world, I seem like a person who has it together, but I am a complete mess inside."

You would never know to look at Dani, and I'm torn up inside knowing how tough every day must be for her. Now, multiply her life-numbing pain by the thousands, and you'll understand the amount of pain felt by other homicide survivors out there.

If lawmakers are struggling for grounds to fund victims' assistance programs or cold case teams, the reason is staring them in the face.

Free At Last -- The Scott Sisters' New Life

Jan. 8, 2011

Over the years, there have been torrents of tears, rejected legal appeals and heartfelt rallies, and now, after nearly 17 long years, there is finally clemency for Gladys and Jamie Scott. It's a case that has had injustice written all over it from the get-go.

The Scott sisters' 1994 conviction came on a crime they insist they played no part in -- an armed robbery in which no one was hurt and about $11 were stolen. Testimony at trial was completely contradictory, and in later years witnesses admitted they'd committed perjury.

On Friday Jan. 7, 2011, Gladys and Jamie jubilantly left the Central Mississippi Correctional Facility, yelling, "We're free!" and "God bless y'all!" They plan to move immediately to Pensacola, Florida, to start new lives.

At the core of the African-American sisters' bad luck was a simmering feud between their father and a local white sheriff. Instead of taking it out on Dad, it was the daughters who bore the iron fist of Mississippi justice.

The young men who wielded the rifle that December day finally admitted they had been threatened by authorities to sign statements implicating the sisters and testify against them. The men were each sentenced to eight years in prison and got out after serving just three. Yet the sisters, who had no prior criminal record and had young children waiting for them at home, were inexplicably slapped with life terms -- two for each sister. Even if they had been active participants in the crime, there was never a justification for that unequal punishment.

The sisters have endured in prison, taking various self-help classes and praying for a miracle. Thirty-eight-year-old Jaime suffers from life-threatening illnesses, including diabetes and kidney failure. She's been receiving costly dialysis three times a week, and without a transplant she may not survive much longer. The prison never bothered to place her on a transplant list, apparently figuring she would spend the rest of her life there. Gladys had offered to donate a kidney to her sister, but again, the prison never took any action to see if they were a match.

Yet, according to a legal assistant who met with the sisters just this week: "They've never been negative. I'm not sure how religious they are, but they always say they've been praying for this day to come."

Since they were housed in separate wings of the prison, the sisters were not able to share the joy of the monumental news that came last week: Mississippi Gov. Haley Barbour was vacating their sentences! Thirty-six-year-old Gladys revealed she only learned about her release when she happened to be watching a TV newscast.

She said at a post-release news conference: "I just started screaming and hollering. I'm still screaming and hollering."

In the governor's proclamation, he muddied the waters by writing, "Gladys Scott's release is conditioned on her donating one of her kidneys to her sister." But Chokwe Lumumba, the Scotts' champion and pro bono attorney, told me this is not a strings-attached release.

"The governor's office says (none of) this will affect Gladys' release," he told me. If she's not a match, she still gets out. And no, she doesn't have to donate an organ to anyone else. And besides, there are laws against giving something of value in exchange for a human organ.

When they were imprisoned, Jaime left three children behind. Gladys left one, and she was pregnant at the time of her conviction. Their mother, Evelyn Rasco, raised all five of her grandchildren while continuing to fight for her daughters' freedom from her home in Florida. That's where the sisters are now headed, to be reunited with their children. They will remain on probation for the rest of their lives.

They have catching up to do. There's a whole new technological world they have no experience with. They've never owned a cellphone or a computer. And they don't know how the family will pay for Jamie's life-sustaining dialysis or the transplant she must have to survive.

Believe me when I say an entire book could be written about the travesty that was the trial for these sisters. I've read the transcripts. And even now, at the end of their long ordeal, there is a distinct ugliness in the way Gov. Barbour dismissively referred to the Scotts in his announcement. He made no mention of the injustice of their sentences, no concern expressed for Jamie's perilous medical condition. Barbour simply wrote, "Their incarceration is no longer necessary for public safety or rehabilitation, and Jamie Scott's medical condition creates a substantial cost to the state of Mississippi."

Something tells me the state of Mississippi isn't done paying the cost of what has been done to the Scott sisters. I predict a major wrongful prosecution lawsuit in the future and a top actress -- maybe the socially aware Halle Berry -- starring in a compelling feature film about this travesty. Now, that would be justice.

How to Find a Missing Child -- Start at the IRS

April 16, 2011

Hardly a week passes without hearing something about missing children in this country. Some are believed stolen for sexual purposes, some are found murdered, and thousands of others are kidnapped by one of their own parents.

Today, let's focus on parental abductors.

For the parent left behind after a former spouse has kidnapped their child, there is the agony of not knowing when -- or if -- they will ever see their baby again. Even the tiniest clue as to their son's or daughter's whereabouts is vitally important if there is ever to be a reunion.

To those heartsick parents, I say: The IRS may very well know where your missing child is, but the agency won't tell you.

Believe it or not, there are some parental abductors who file tax returns and blatantly claim their kidnapped child as a dependent! Some of them apparently need the refund money, while others don't want to attract attention for failure to pay. When they file their return, they list their employer and their home address, along with the child's name and Social Security number.

All are major pieces of information the abandoned parent would love to know. But the IRS cloaks itself in Watergate-era privacy laws, shrugs its bureaucratic shoulders and says it just can't help the grieving parent locate the missing child.

I might be risking a tax audit here, but can't the IRS do better than that?

Apparently not. As it stands now, privacy laws prohibit the IRS from revealing any tax return information unless the parental abduction case is being investigated by federal agents. The reality is that these cases are most often investigated by local or state law enforcement. And on the rare occasion when the FBI does get involved in a parental kidnapping case, federal judges almost never grant requests for IRS information. Child advocacy groups say it's because judges most often believe this type of case more properly belongs in a state's family court, not a federal one.

What a bunch of Catch-22 type logic! It seems the bureaucrats are more worried about the privacy of a kidnapper avoiding a fugitive warrant than the well-being of a child torn away from everything that is familiar and who is being forced to live life on the run.

How many of these children are out there? Well, precise numbers are hard to come by. The Justice Department's latest figures show there are about 200,000 parental abductions reported every year.

However, a vast majority of them are cleared quickly, as they often stem from a non-custodial parent failing to return with the child in a timely fashion. The DOJ reports that every year there are some 12,000 cases that last longer than six months. These are considered actual parental kidnappings.

This problem has been going on for years. Yet no one can say for sure how many of those 12,000 children might be located by tracking their Social Security number or the tax return of their kidnapping parent. We get a hint, though, from an experiment conducted by the Treasury Department back in 2007. Researchers gathered up the Social Security numbers of 1,700 missing kids and the suspect parents. It was discovered that more than a third of those numbers had been used in tax returns filed after the kidnapping took place.

One woman I read about recently learned her son was alive only after she listed him on her tax return and the IRS reported back that she couldn't claim him because someone else already had. Mother and son were finally brought back together (no thanks to the IRS) when he was 15 years old. They had been separated five long years.

When you do the math and realize how many children could be reunited with their court-ordered primary caregiver, it's plain to see that the IRS guidelines must be reviewed. I would think the agency would want to be out front calling for changes in the laws that force it to keep this vital information covered up.

Some courageous lawmaker in Washington needs to grab hold of this issue and craft legislation that allows the IRS to lift its ironclad curtain of secrecy when court orders are being ignored and the safety of a child is at stake. I'm certain that custodial parents would be fine with the IRS handing over confidential information about their child's whereabouts -- not to them, but to a family court judge. That judge could then be directed to issue an instruction to law enforcement to work with counterparts in other jurisdictions to retrieve the child and take the kidnapper into custody. While we're at it, specific new penalties should be adopted for those parents who abduct their children.

Cindy Rudometkin of the Polly Klass Foundation was recently quoted saying she believes there are hundreds of cases that could be resolved if only the IRS would give up what it knows. "And even if it helped solve (just) one case," she said, "imagine if that child returned home was yours."

Annie McCann Is Dead

April 14, 2012

How did 16-year-old honor student Annie McCann die? Her parents have been agonizing over that heart-wrenching question for too long. Definitive answers have been few, but these determined parents refuse to give up asking.

On Oct. 31, 2008, Annie left a note in her bedroom that mentioned suicide, but she had also added the hope-filled line: "But I realized I can start over, instead. ... If you really love me, you'll let me go." Then, she inexplicably ran away, taking $1,000 in cash, jewelry and the family Volvo. It was a shock to Dan and Mary Jane McCann, whose daughter was a devout Catholic and a quiet and studious girl, a child who had never given them any trouble.

Two excruciating days later, the McCanns got a phone call informing them Annie's body had been found at a housing project in Baltimore, Maryland, about 70 miles from their home. They were dumbfounded.

The Maryland medical examiner ultimately declared Annie's death was due to lidocaine poisoning and concluded she had ingested the bottle of Bactine she carried to treat her newly pierced ears. The company that makes Bactine, along with a well-known medical examiner, Dr. Michael Baden, would both later declare that drinking one bottle would never be fatal.

After reviewing the autopsy and other reports, prominent psychiatrist Dr. Keith Ablow concluded, "It strains the imagination ... to believe that a person intent on dying would choose this obscure and extremely uncertain method of attempting to take her life."

While the official cause of Annie's death is still listed as "undetermined," Baltimore Police Department spokesman Anthony Guglielmi told me this week that "Police believe it was a suicide." Translated: While the case is listed as "pending," it might as well be closed.

The McCanns hired a private detective to figure out how Annie, who always had a lousy sense of direction and hadn't been driving that long, got all the way to Baltimore. P.I. Jimmy Kontsis followed the lead of a fingerprint found on the window of the McCann's' recovered car. That led to a group of local teens who admitted one of their group, a kid named D.J., had stolen the McCanns' car. But each of them insisted Annie was already dead in the back seat, so they tossed her body and took a joyride. Police said they could find no evidence to charge them in Annie's death, and auto-theft charges were never pursued, either.

Noting that Annie's autopsy remarked on "fresh injuries to her face and head," Baden suggested Annie might have died from homicidal suffocation.

Was she victimized for the $1,000 she took with her? Police made note of Annie's clean white socks but could never find her shoes. Might they have been left at the same place she ingested the lidocaine?

"That's the mystery," Kontsis told me. "Even the police were like, lidocaine? They didn't get it, either." Drug addicts have been known to try to smoke lidocaine, but Annie never experimented with drugs. Classmates called her sheltered and naive.

Kontsis canvassed people at spots where Annie had been -- her church, a Virginia Costco, even a pastry shop in the Little Italy section of Baltimore. He discovered a consistent description of an older, apparently homeless Hispanic woman seen speaking with Annie at all three locations. A sketch of the mystery woman (who claimed to be from Honduras and was seeking immigration information) brought in no helpful information.

And then, last November, the teenager known as D.J. -- whose real name is Darnell Kinlaw -- was arrested in Baltimore for murdering a woman and stealing her car. It was revealed that Kinlaw's extensive police record lists eight charges of auto theft. Annie's parents figured it was the perfect time to get more information from Kinlaw about the day their daughter died.

The McCanns travelled to meet Baltimore police, and while they were treated politely, they feel they have been lied to and ignored. Police say they are sympathetic but maintain they've already conducted a thorough investigation.

Look, maybe Annie McCann did manage to get a stash of lidocaine and poison herself. But that seems unlikely, and after researching this case and counting up the loose ends -- the odd trip to Baltimore, the missing money, the mystery woman and Kinlaw's past -- I can't help but feel that in the absence of concrete evidence, Annie's half-used Bactine bottle gave police a convenient reason for her death. It was easier to declare it a suicide and move on. Left in the wake of that decision are Dan and Mary Jane McCann, who cannot find peace. They still wonder why they never got Annie's clothes back and why no one will tell them whether she had been raped the day she died.

The sad fact is there are countless families mourning the loss of their murdered children every day in America. They are black, Hispanic, Asian and white. But their tears are all the same color.

In the end, it really isn't race or ethnic background that matters when a child is murdered. It is the fact that families often feel that no one cares enough to find the truth, that there will be no justice, that hurts so much.

Maybe our overburdened, understaffed police departments can find some way to work on making families feel more included in the heartbreaking process of homicide investigation.

The Buying and Selling of Babies

June 15, 2013

It is not some science fiction movie plot. It is real. Human beings are being manufactured and sold right here in America.

Even more shocking is the fact that decades after the first commercial U.S. sperm bank was opened (1971), after the world's first test tube baby was born (1978) and after the first U.S. court case regarding surrogacy played out (1986), this country still has no uniform law regulating how surrogate babies are created in a lab and brought into the world.

Let's be clear at the outset. No one wants to deny a childless couple the right to have, raise and love a child. I cannot imagine the pain an infertile couple feels longing to have a family. But at this late stage in the commercial surrogacy game, there ought to be an agreed-upon set of rules, regulations and laws on how it works and what should be done when things don't go as planned. There are lots of cases on record of surrogacy arrangements that have gone terribly wrong.

In 1986, I was assigned to cover a New Jersey custody case that resulted in America's first court ruling on the validity of surrogacy. The so-called "Baby M" case was fascinating! A married mother of two named Mary Beth Whitehead answered a newspaper ad and agreed to be the surrogate mother for two New Jersey doctors,

William Stern, a biochemist, and Elizabeth Stern, a pediatrician. Elizabeth suffered from multiple sclerosis and worried about the health effects of pregnancy.

Whitehead signed a contract and agreed to have the Sterns' baby for $10,000. A doctor inseminated Whitehead's egg with William's sperm, and she became what is now called a "traditional surrogate," one who has a biological connection to the baby. After the birth, Whitehead could not bear to give up the child, who the Sterns named Melissa, and she and her family fled to Florida. Police found them and returned the baby to the Sterns. The stage was set for the precedent-setting court case.

During the trial, Whitehead was vilified. Mental health experts labeled her as suffering from "narcissistic personality disorder" and called her stability into question. Her attorney referred to her as an "exploited" woman. Ultimately, a superior court judge ruled the surrogate contract was valid and that in "the best interests of the child" the baby should live with the Sterns. Whitehead was stripped of her parental rights and shut out of her daughter's life.

To underscore the legal vacuum surrounding surrogacy at the time, just 10 months later the New Jersey Supreme Court ruled that contracts to buy and sell babies went "against public policy" and should not be allowed.

Whitehead's parental rights were re-established, and she won visitation rights to the little girl nicknamed Sassy.

This legal limbo continues to exist today nationwide and at a time when the surrogacy market is "exploding," according to a report from the Council of Responsible Genetics. Many states have no surrogacy laws on the books. Some appear to permit such arrangements. New Mexico, New Jersey, Oregon, Virginia and Washington, for example, allow uncompensated surrogacy. But many other states hold that any contract for a baby born for money is simply unenforceable. Florida, Nevada, New Hampshire, Tennessee and Texas are the most surrogate-friendly states -- as long as the buyers are a married couple.

To add to the confusion, surrogacy is no longer just about a willing woman being inseminated with the sperm of a known potential father. Advances in science have opened up all sorts of possible combinations -- and potential for trouble.

Surrogates today can be the traditional kind, like Whitehead, or a "gestational surrogate mother," who agrees to carry the fertilized egg and sperm of two other people. She acts only as the host womb and has no genetic relation to the baby. You might think that this type of surrogate could cause no trouble after the birth.

Well, consider the case known by the initials: A.G.R. v. D.R.H & S.H. Again, it played out in New Jersey. And it came to court 20 years after the Baby M case. Two men, a legally married gay couple, decided to start a family. Lab technicians created an embryo for them using sperm from one husband and an anonymous donor ovum. The embryo was then implanted in the sister of the other husband. Are you following this? In 2006, the sister gave birth to twin girls and turned them over to the couple as stipulated in their surrogate contract.

A year later the sister was in court fighting for her parental rights, even though she had no biological connection to the babies. Having no law to guide them, the New Jersey courts again disagreed with each other. At first, the sister was recognized as the girls' legal mother. The trio continued fighting over the twins until December 2011, when a superior court decision awarded full custody to the husband who had donated the sperm.

Thank goodness the anonymous egg donor never came forward to claim custody! You see how convoluted things can become when we mess with Mother Nature?

It is far past time for states to pass laws that create a clear-cut, irrevocable path for participants in surrogate arrangements to follow. Failure to do that is an open invitation to more and very painful legal battles. It can also create lifelong scars for the child everyone professes to love.

Our Family Court Fiasco

Aug. 17, 2013

We in America like to say that what happens behind closed doors is nobody else's business. But what if what happens between consenting adults results in the rest of us having to pay out billions of dollars when things go wrong?

It is happening year after year. Taxpayers are footing the bill for countless ugly divorces, separations and couples who have babies out of wedlock. Experts who keep track of this call it "family fragmentation" and estimate that we, collectively, pay more than $112 billion annually in an oftentimes vain effort to fix the problems of troubled couples.

The Institute for American Values, a conservative group with a mission to "study and strengthen civil society," added up the public's cost of supporting divorcing and unmarried households. Using figures from 2008, they looked at the justice system's cost of dissolving a typical marriage, the average amount of a custodial parent's reliance on government programs like food stamps, Medicaid, Head Start, housing assistance and cash payments. Over the course of the previous decade, the institute concluded that taxpayers shelled out more than $1 trillion.

It found the biggest annual bite was the $19.3 billion that went to operate our justice system. What is happening in family court to rack up this kind of a bill? Well, first understand that since the mid-'70s about half of all marriages fail. At any given moment, there are millions of Americans in the court system fighting their partner for divorce, custody or a change in a previous order.

Family courts are overwhelmed. Judges often have no particular expertise in dealing with domestic issues and often let the warring factions repeatedly go at each other in court. Hearings are held months apart, and many judges hope the frustrated couple ultimately gets together long enough to reach their own settlement. In the meantime, the clock and the meter keep ticking. Often, the only winners are the lawyers who can rack up enormous fees.

Various states have appointed task forces to look at ways to streamline the process, but still words like "national crisis" and "flawed and frustrating" are used to describe family court's enormous backlog.

California's Elkins Task Force studied the problem for two years and in April 2010 announced 117 recommendations to streamline court inefficiencies. What's changed since then? Not much for the women and men who seek judicial help.

Adam Bram of Los Angeles says his contentious divorce case is typical. After living together as a couple for just 11 months, his wife filed for divorce in March 2010. Now, more than three-and-a-half years later, their case is still stuck in court.

A proposed settlement blew up last December, and Bram has not been able to see his almost 4-year-old daughter since then.

From the outset, the wife claimed that Adam was a drug addict who could not be trusted alone with their child. Adam, who had gone through a stint in rehab back in 2004, was eager to prove his wife wrong. For more than two years, he submitted to court-ordered random drug tests, which found nothing in his system but doctor-prescribed drugs for his prolonged back pain, muscle tension and his attention deficit disorder.

Superior Court Judge Mark Juhas, who happened to have served on the Elkins Task Force, never ordered Sarah to return any of the $200,000 she admitted taking from Adam. By the spring of 2011, court documents show, the money was gone. She was not punished for defying the court's order not to spend the money.

Juhas never declared that Adam was indeed fit to parent the child alone even after he passed drug tests and agreed to go to co-parenting classes, and a psychiatric evaluator concluded that he did not need to have his visitations monitored. (Repeated calls to the wife's divorce lawyer were not returned.)

Adam, who happens to be an entertainment lawyer, could not grasp the willy-nilly way family court worked. He admits he became frustrated with the indecisiveness of the system. He likely made the judge unhappy and worked against his own best interests when he filed motion after motion. Nonetheless, Bram paid the $4,400 monthly bill for a monitor just so he could see his daughter. Finally, he could no longer afford to pay for the monitor, the drug testing, the co-parenting classes and his legal bills.

"We were in court longer than the marriage was," said Adam's lawyer C. Brian Martin. "And it all comes down to the huge backlog of cases that goes on. The judge gives you 20 minutes today, and then the next hearing is 45 or 60 days away." Martin, a family court veteran of 30 years, says that the system is so broken he can't even suggest fixes or foresee a change.

In the meantime, we taxpayers continue to pay for this albatross of a system.

As for Bram? The couple is now officially divorced, but the court still has Adam's claim for joint custody on the calendar. "My next hearing is now set for October," Bram told me with a choke in his voice. "Which means I'm going to miss my daughter's fourth birthday."

"Lawyers often have no concept of the psychological effect of all this on the children," attorney Martin added. "And judges often don't care."

And that comes back to why we should all care about why the family court system is failing in America: the children. Warring adults and their lawyers scream louder and longer than the countless kids who need to be nurtured by both parents. Whatever happened to deciding things in the best interest of the child?

Divorce: American Style

Sept. 7, 2013

Are you or someone you know contemplating a divorce? Are there plans to hire a lawyer and take the matter to court? At the risk of raising the ire of matrimonial lawyers, I say, you might want to rethink that idea.

I've written in this space about alternative ideas to divorce court, the less painful process called "collaborative law," where specially trained lawyers act as mediators, not adversaries. More recently, I wrote about how the family court system is overwhelmed with divorce and custody cases. Some divorces take years to wind their way through the courts. In the meantime, the warring factions continue to funnel money to their divorce lawyers -- lots of money -- that would likely be put to better use establishing a new household or college funds for the children.

I have been with the same man for three decades, happily married for more than 20 years, but since I began researching the family court crisis, I've been unable to stop thinking about the state of marriage today. The cold hard statistics reveal shocking facts: Fifty percent of all marriages in the U.S. end in divorce. There is a divorce every 13 seconds. Apply a little math, and the staggering totals add up to 6,646 divorces each day, 46,523 divorces per week.

If the outcome is only 50-50, at best, why do people keep taking the plunge? And more importantly, when faced with the realization that the partnership is doomed, why do we fight so bitterly for the spoils -- the house, the car, bank accounts and, of course, custody of the kids. What makes us turn so ugly?

It's not the job of the court system to try to figure out the human dynamics behind a divorce. So for answers, I turned to those who study the human condition.

"The attitude toward marriage and its longevity has changed," clinical psychologist and author Dr. Patricia Farrell told me, as she described why marriage is no longer a sacred institution. "Divorce is now a right that comes with marriage. Why else would people have pre-nups? There is flexibility in marriage now that didn't exist before."

In what other part of your life would you throw absolute caution to the wind knowing there's a 50-50 chance of failure? Yet millions of us marry every year. Why?

Dr. Patricia Saunders, Ph.D., a psychologist trained in psychotherapy, explained it by saying that humans are hard-wired to need an intimate relationship. "It's the 'attachment' hormone that we've all got vis-a-vis evolutionary biology," she explained. "Primitive parts of the brain release it, and our higher brain centers don't have much control over it." The end effect, says Saunders, is that it's really easy for us to "miss red flags or rationalize them" when looking at our partner's foibles.

In other words, love is blind.

OK, I get that. But once the glow of contentment is gone and spouses have morphed into someone we can't stand to be in the same room with, why don't we take the easy and logical way out? Fill out some forms, split the material goods and go on their separate ways. Why do we so often see the prolonged animosity depicted so well in the film "War of the Roses"?

Dr. Robi Ludwig, a nationally known psychotherapist, told me that in many divorces all ability to calmly communicate and compromise goes out the window. At that point "They're probably lucky they're not killing each other," she said. So, these couples often turn to matrimonial lawyers to advocate for them in court.

"A partner may like the idea of a pitbull lawyer successfully fighting their battles for them; even if it costs them a fortune," Ludwig said. "Our more primal emotions are to win and to survive. Fighting helps us to feel -- on a primal level -- that we are right, we can win, and then, ultimately, we will survive."

Farrell, also a best-selling author, whose latest book is "Fired Up: A Shrink's Musings," blames lawyers for escalating tension and perpetuating the idea that you will suffer financially if you go the do-it-yourself-divorce route. "Couples are easily convinced in their emotional state that they need this service and that each of them needs a lawyer (now there's two fees) in order for each of them to have their interests protected. It's lawyer PR all the way," Farrell said. Saunders agreed: "The saddest part is that the kids are the ones who suffer from the chaos, anger and vengefulness. They can't understand why Mom and Dad are acting like different people and often wonder if that level of negative emotion will be turned on them."

According to Forbes in 2006, matrimonial law work is a $28 billion-a-year industry.

I will concede that in the case of a stay-at-home parent who is up against a wealthy and vengeful partner it is a good idea to have a legal advocate on board. But I'm not referring to a high-powered or celebrity-type divorce where millions are at stake. I'm talking about average Joe and Jane, who will spend about $15,000 (lawyer's fees, court costs, filing fees and refinancing) to undo their union, according to the latest statistics. The more simple mediation route will still cost several thousand dollars.

In these strained economic times, isn't it smarter to keep all that money in the family, even if it is a disintegrating family?

Doesn't someone out there have a better, easier idea for couples that no longer want to be married? Send me your ideas. If they seem plausible, I'll share them in a future column.

Paternity Fraud Begs the Question: Who's Your Daddy?

Feb. 23, 2015

There is a lot of unfairness in the world. The American justice system stands ready to counter that, right? Not so fast.

When it comes to men and allegations of paternity, women have a decidedly upper hand. Whatever the woman claims in court most often becomes fact. And once a court has ruled on paternity and established child support, it can be next to impossible to change, even if a DNA test excludes the man from any possibility of parenthood.

Across the country, men of all ages, colors and social statuses have been ordered by family courts to pay child support for children that aren't theirs.

In one infamous case in New Mexico, a man shelled out years of support for a daughter who never actually existed. His deceitful ex-wife simply told the court there was such a child, and no proof was ever requested.

Some victims of paternity fraud find out the truth while they are still married. In Michigan, Murray Davis discovered that two of his three children were actually fathered by his best friend. But by that time the kids were nearly teenagers, and it was well past the legal deadline for Davis to contest paternity in that state.

Carnell Smith, of Atlanta, Georgia, discovered that the daughter he'd been raising with his girlfriend wasn't his. But the courts didn't want to hear it. Smith was stuck. Like Davis, this falsely identified "father" began to lobby for changes in his state's law.

Smith started a group called U.S. Citizens Against Paternity Fraud and got Georgia to join Ohio as the only two states that allow an unlimited time for a man to challenge paternity as long as the child-support case is open.

Many states require a man to file a challenge before the child's third birthday. The federal law gives a man just 60 days.

"That's pretzel logic, isn't it?" Smith asked me. "Don't tell a man the truth and then penalize him for not correcting the record fast enough. Some men don't realize what's happened," Smith said, "until they are under water with child support payments and then have no money to pay an attorney to fight for them."

Also working against the wronged man is the Bradley Amendment, a federal law that prohibits state judges from retroactively modifying child support orders.

None of it sounds fair, does it? But it happens all the time. Judicial reasoning ranges from "It's in the best interest of the child" to "He didn't challenge the paternity claim immediately."

Carnell Alexander of Detroit has been under a court-ordered cloud for nearly 30 years.

In 1987, his ex-girlfriend applied for welfare to support her new baby. She put Alexander's name down as the father even though he wasn't. A process server swore he served Alexander with papers demanding that he appear in court, so when he didn't show up he was declared a "deadbeat dad."

The truth is, Alexander was never notified. He was in prison at the time on an unrelated charge stemming from a youthful crime. He didn't find out about his problem until a traffic stop in 1991.

The mother in question now admits, "Everything is my fault." She told a Detroit TV station: "He shouldn't have to pay it at all. I want everything to go away for him so he can get on with his life."

Despite the mother's lies to the state, despite a definitive DNA test excluding Alexander as the father, he still owes $30,000 in support for, as he puts it, "A child that I did not father ... that I was not involved in raising." He adds, "It is not fair."

There's that phrase again: It is not fair.

Murray Davis, who established the National Family Justice Association after his painful experience, says that Alexander "is only one among tens of thousands in this state and possibly hundreds of thousands or millions around the nation who are victims of this abhorrent crime of paternity fraud."

Fair seems rare in these cases, but a creative-thinking judge in Virginia found a way around that pesky Bradley Amendment. He ruled that a defrauded man who still legally owed $23,000 in back child support could pay it off at a rate of one dollar a year for 1, 917 years! You gotta love that.

This kind of fraud happens to young men going off to college, soldiers going overseas, men of all ages and occupations. And it ruins lives. The biological children, new wives, grandparents and others related to the falsely identified are all profoundly affected by paternity fraud.

Having the best interest of a child in mind is knowing the child's lineage and medical history. The best interest of society is to have a respected family court that is fair to all.

DNA tests cost about $30 these days. It's time for automatic court-ordered DNA testing in all child-support cases.

The True Hollywood Horror Story

Sept. 12, 2015

This is not your typical Hollywood film. It's the movie Hollywood doesn't want you to see. It's a documentary called "An

Open Secret," and it pulls the ugly scab off Hollywood to reveal what has happened to some vulnerable young boys who have tried to break in to the entertainment industry.

I got a special screening, and I hope throngs of people go to see it. The secret referenced in the title is how so many of these youngsters have so easily fallen prey to pedophile agents, acting coaches, photographers and public relations people.

These "entertainment professionals" haunt Hollywood and stalk unsuspecting children, grooming them into thinking their way is normal, just the way business is done. In the process, of course, parents are also manipulated into thinking everything is fine.

You'll recognize some of the former child actors featured in this riveting and raw documentary, who publicly say they were sexually abused.

Todd Bridges, from the 1970s-80s sitcom "Diff'rent Strokes," is shown discussing a previous two-part special the writers had produced to highlight the problem of pedophilia.

With a pained expression, Bridges says: "I didn't want to be around it. I ask them, 'Don't write me into this ... write me out of most of this." When Bridges' wish was not granted, he was heartsick.

He said, "I, myself, had gone through that, and watching it happen on the show -- it was like ... reliving the whole thing all over again." Bridges was molested by his public-relations agent.

Child star Corey Feldman, whose hit movies include "Gremlins," "Stand by Me" and "The Goonies," also appears to say that Hollywood predators ruined his life, propelling him into addiction and failed marriages.

"I can tell you that the number one problem in Hollywood was and is and always will be pedophilia," Feldman says. "I was surrounded by them. They were everywhere. Like vultures." Feldman's frequent co-star, the late Corey Haim, was also a sexual abuse victim. The pair openly discussed it on their A&E reality show, "The Two Coreys."

Anne Henry, who works with a group called Biz Parentz and is the mother of child actors, reveals how she came to realize that some of Hollywood's top professionals were selling the headshots of young actors on the internet.

Non-sexual PR photos of young girls, but mostly boys, inexplicably sold for more than $800 each. Tracking down the photographers led to an ugly circle of Hollywood insiders, some of whom have now been convicted on charges of child pornography, committing lewd acts and other sexual crimes.

In one case, a man convicted of sexually abusing a Nickelodeon child actor is now out of prison and back working in the entertainment industry. His jobs include a Disney show and a horror movie set in a high school.

Besides the celebrity stories, the sad tales of several less recognizable Hollywood hopefuls are told. One always looked much younger than his years; another was an opera lover cast in several movies; and another was a young man named Evan who displayed amazing singing talent. Each adult man explains how as children they found themselves surrounded by the industry's sexual predators. Evan signed with an agent at age 11, and the sexual seduction soon followed. Years later, Evan bravely tape-recorded his abuser discussing their sex acts, and the man was convicted.

I've expressed hope that throngs go to see this documentary but, not surprisingly, the producers have had a difficult time getting movie theaters to agree to show it. Are movie-house operators afraid of offending Hollywood executives?

The union representing actors, SAG-AFTRA, has threatened to sue Amy Berg, the director of the film, since its former Young Performers Committee chairperson is featured in an unflattering and even pedophiliac light. And now, because the director has refused to help promote the film (maybe for fear of Hollywood retribution), the producers have taken her to arbitration.

All of this, of course, dilutes the core message of "An Open Secret," and that is a shame. Child sexual abuse can happen anywhere, anytime.

Note that you haven't heard a peep from studio executives, big talent agencies or entertainment unions about steps they've taken to protect young actors against sexual predators. Yet in the words of victim Corey Feldman, "There are people who did this to me ... who are still out there, still working and they are some of the richest, most powerful people in this business."

Remember that next time you watch a movie featuring children. I know I'll never look at those films the same way again.

~~~

CHAPTER 11
Challenges for Cops

"Let me be clear -- no one is above the law. Not a politician, not a priest, not a criminal, not a police officer. We are all accountable for our actions." ~ **Antonio Villaraigosa, former mayor of Los Angeles**

Police officers are not perfect. Just like all other human beings, they succumb to weakness, anger and fear. I try hard to write about both sides of law enforcement -- the positive and the negative.

Consider that there are more than 900,000 sworn law enforcement officers now serving in the United States, according to the National Law Enforcement Officers Memorial Fund. And NLEOMF reports that "On average, one law enforcement officer is killed in the line of duty somewhere in the United States every 60 hours."

Can anyone quote me a statistic regarding any other line of duty where one employee dies every day and a half? I doubt it. Those who wear a badge leave home every day knowing they may never return. Their families live with that feeling of pending doom, too. And this all in the name of keeping the rest of us safe.

But an officers' sacrifice does not mean they get a pass on bad or criminal behavior. Just because they encounter unique challenges and stressors on the job, they don't get to engage in violent responses to situations without consequences. Officers who engage in domestic abuse at home or overly aggressive actions in the field should not be excused. Trigger-happy cops who shoot unarmed suspects should not escape punishment. And officers who cause the death of a prisoner should face the full force of the law.

That said, we should all realize that the instances of completely unwarranted police aggression are miniscule compared to the number of officers on the street.

Could police academies teach better, more up-to-date training techniques? You bet. Do some officers need an intensive course in interpersonal communications? Without a doubt. On the other hand, citizens must be less combative, too. Running away from police will only bring more trouble and disobeying a lawful command is never the answer.

The Big Blue Secret

May 16, 2009

She dug her heels into the carpet and put all her weight into trying to hold the door shut. Blood trickled down her face, her hands shaking uncontrollably. As she fumbled to engage the lock she heard him on the other side of the door, cursing, promising to kill her this time. Despite the terror, she never thought to call police for help. Her husband still wore his patrol uniform, his service revolver at his hip. One move toward the phone to call his office and it would be bullets coming through the door.

Domestic violence happens everywhere. In poor, middle-class and wealthy households, terrible secrets are being held. Overwhelmed by the pressures of life, some people snap and lash out at the person they are supposed to love the most.

This column is about a specific type of domestic violence: the type perpetrated by police officers once they go home. It's the "Big Blue Secret," violence made extra horrifying because the person meting it out is supposed to help keep the peace, not disrupt it. Fellow cops know or suspect but they stay silent.

Studies show police households are up to 4 times more likely to erupt in domestic violence. A full 40 percent of them report they've experienced violence from their armed family member.

More disturbing, the studies report, is the resolution of complaints lodged by police family members. "Exceedingly light discipline" is reported in domestic abuse cases from California to New York. Many of those officers charged often get a slap on the wrist. Others go on to be promoted to higher ranks within a short period of time. This, of course, gives them even more power over their cowering families.

It's understood that few underlings will step forward to go against a ranking officer.

The recent (and some would say long overdue) arrest of ex-cop Drew Peterson underscores this national problem. The Bolingbrook, Illinois, police department sergeant, Peterson had four unhappy wives. His last two complained to confidants that he was controlling and violent and had convinced them his police colleagues would never help them.

Peterson is now charged with the 2004 murder of wife No. 3, Kathleen, who was found badly beaten in a dry bathtub. Her death was ruled an accidental drowning. A new autopsy prompted the murder charges. His fourth wife, 23-year-old Stacy, disappeared in October 2007 and is widely presumed to be dead.

The Peterson case is just today's most visible police-involved domestic abuse story. There are reams more. And while it is uncomfortable for law enforcement agencies to admit it, in almost every case there were warning signs.

In 2003, the chief of police in Tacoma, Washington, shot his wife and killed himself as their now-orphaned children watched in horror from a nearby car.

Crystal Brame said that her husband David had long been violently cruel. In her divorce papers, she alleged several harrowing encounters, including times when the chief would point his service revolver at her and menacingly say, "Accidents happen." The implication was clear. He could kill her and get away with it.

In February 2008, Canton, Ohio, police officer Bobby Cutts was found guilty of killing his pregnant girlfriend and their nearly full-term baby. Another girlfriend of Cutts, mother to another of his children, said that the officer was always very violent and that "he feels that he can do certain things and get away with them."

In the late '80s, police family member/survivor Susan Murphy-Milano convinced her mother to move away and divorce her abusive father, a top detective with the Chicago violent crimes unit.

"My big mistake was not moving her far enough away," Susan says today. In January 1989, she found the bodies of both her parents -- a murder-suicide -- dead at her father's hand. She said: "He always said he was going to kill her. He finally did."

The men -- and yes, sometimes the women -- we train to police our nation are programmed to use force and even kill if need be. The problem comes, of course, when the synapses criss-cross and the officer's family takes the brunt of it.

And those terrorized by officers are faced with a triple threat. The aggressor has a gun, knows the location of local battered-women's shelters and knows how to manipulate the system to avoid penalty or to shift suspicion to the victim.

Murphy-Milano, an author and victim's advocate, trains women how to devise their own "exit plans" from police brutality. She suggests departments offer mandatory training for police spouses so they can learn how to diffuse threatening situations. And victims need to be assured that action and punishment will be pursued even if the accused wears a badge.

Their families deserve as much protection and respect as the rest of us, right?

Where Guns Go to Die

June 13, 2009

We want police to get dangerous guns off the street, right? Well, they are, and in record numbers. Now the problem is what to do with all those confiscated guns.

At a routine traffic stop, you see a rifle in plain sight in the back seat of a car driven by a convicted felon.

A domestic abuse call uncovers two unlicensed pistols inside a home where a woman has called 911 after being battered by her husband.

A takedown of a local drug deal nets police a cache of illegal weapons, from semi-automatic to half a dozen .357 Magnums.

What happens to all those weapons?

First, they're stored as evidence until disposition of each criminal case in question. Then, once they're no longer needed, it's up to each department to decide what to do with them.

You'd think that with all the white hot heat surrounding gun control in this country we'd have a uniform policy on this. We don't. The FBI referred me to the Bureau of Alcohol, Tobacco and Firearms, where I got nowhere. The National Association of Chiefs of Police had no answer either. No guidance, no policy.

It used to be that police departments along America's coastline, from California to New York to Florida, would dump these guns into watery graves far out into the ocean, creating artificial reefs of rusting revolvers and rifles. Sometimes financially strapped departments kept the firearms for their SWAT team's use or traded them with neighboring law enforcement agencies. Other departments have been known to auction off confiscated guns or sell them to registered dealers for much-needed cash. That, of course, puts the guns back on the street again.

So, more and more these days, guns seized from those who aren't supposed to have them, or those weapons turned in during "No Questions Asked" neighborhood collection and buy-back drives, are being destroyed. They're literally shredded in huge metal-chomping machines called "alligators" that have 200 tons of cutting force. The weapons are pulverized into small pieces of scrap metal and sold for about 25 cents per pound.

There are other places these guns are sent to die. At foundries and smelters across America, armed police guards are arriving with tens of thousands of pounds of confiscated weapons, and they stand by to make sure they are completely destroyed.

The guns are subjected to temperatures of more than 3,000 degrees for as long as it takes to make them liquid again.

This death sentence for guns means life for more practical items. Some of the melted metal is used to make chain-link, pipes or manhole covers. In Southington, Connecticut, there is just such a sewer cover that declares, in raised metal, "Made from 172 pounds of your confiscated guns." Ironically, it's placed right outside JoJo's custom-made gun shop and about 15 miles from the main Colt Fire Arms Manufacturing Company in West Hartford. It's a constant reminder to gun owners to keep their weapons safe and to stay out of trouble.

In Rancho Cucamonga, California, the TAMCO Steel foundry has been melting down guns for years. They call the program "Project Isaiah," named for the biblical passage about beating swords into plowshares and spears into pruning hooks. One TAMCO official put the project goals into a modern version. He said, "We shall melt their guns into rebar and build a community for all to live in peace and harmony."

The rebar fashioned out of the 12,000 guns TAMCO melted into uselessness helped build, among other structures, the Staples Center and the New York, New York Casino in Las Vegas. They also used it to repair the Oakland Bay Bridge in San Francisco and various earthquake-damaged freeways.

A great swap, right? Lethal guns in exchange for products that produce jobs and safe places for citizens. But not everyone is happy with the gun-destruction programs.

Gun enthusiasts complain police don't really try to find the true owners of stolen guns before they condemn a weapon to the smelter.

Others mourn the deliberate destruction of weapons that qualify as historically valuable antiques. Then there are the pragmatic who point to the latest FBI stats and grimly remind us that no matter how many guns are destroyed in this fashion, the American people buy an estimated 5 million new guns every year.

The destruction programs are a literal drop in the smelter bucket. Me? I acknowledge the U.S. Constitution gives citizens -- law-abiding citizens -- the right to bear arms, and that's fine. But these are guns taken from outlaws. And outlaws use guns to commit nearly 70 percent of all the murders in this country. I've got no problem drowning, grinding or melting them into oblivion.

Stopping Domestic Abusers Can Start at Home

March 26, 2011

Oh, boy, am I ever going to take heat for this. But it must be said. There are some women caught up in the awful throes of domestic abuse who are to blame. Domestic abuse occurs because they allow it.

The women of whom I speak stay when they should leave. They repeatedly call police to come to their rescue after their partner's anger erupts. Then, they repeatedly refuse to press charges. These abused and humiliated women forget the panic they felt at the moment they scrambled to the phone and dialed 911 for help. They imagine they can't possibly make it in life without their abusive mate. They're caught in a terrible cycle of co-dependent violence.

The harsh reality is that when one of these women fails to follow through by pressing charges, she may be sealing a death warrant for others who will cross paths with the lout later.

Case in point: Jeffrey Maxwell of Corsicana, Texas. In 1987, he was arrested for slitting his wife's throat. He never went to trial because Martha Martinez Maxwell returned home and declined to cooperate with prosecutors. Five years later, Maxwell mysteriously disappeared.

Now, 24 years after the vicious attack on his wife, Jeffrey Maxwell is once again in trouble for assaulting a woman. Police traced his car to the home of a kidnapping victim. When they arrived at Maxwell's house to question him, officers found the missing woman, who had been shackled, sexually abused and badly beaten during her 13 days in captivity. Maxwell, known for his charity work and as an officer in his local Kiwanis Club, is now charged with kidnapping and rape.

If only Martha had pressed charges! Police now suspect she was murdered by Maxwell, and they're trying to prove that. They also believe he is to blame for the disappearance of a third woman, Amelia Smith, who went missing in 2000 and is also presumed dead.

Another example: George Villanueva is a career thug with 28 priors, including three open cases of battering his girlfriend, Kim Dykstra. Police in Brooklyn, New York, responded to at least a dozen of Kim's calls for help. Every time Villanueva was arrested and jailed for assaulting her Kim signed an affidavit saying she would not testify against him.

In mid-March, Kim called police a final time, saying George was threatening to kill her. When police moved in to arrest Villanueva, a violent scuffle on his stoop ended with veteran officer Alain Schaberger being shoved over a 9-foot-high railing.

He broke his neck and died a short time later. Villanueva is now charged with aggravated murder.

If only Kim had found the courage and self-esteem to press charges!

Every cop on the beat will tell you the most dangerous call they get involves domestic violence and the most heartbreaking DV calls are the ones that include children. Anger mixed with passion can be a deadly combination. In candid moments, officers might admit they'd like to ignore the 911 calls from women like Martha and Kim, those who routinely flake out when it comes time to testify.

Please, don't accuse me of being unsympathetic to victims. I am not. I've interacted with battered and terrified women as a reporter and in my personal life. I know their plight and the lack of services offered them when they finally decide to stand up for themselves and their children. I know the law often considers a spousal beating a minor infraction.

Manhattan District Attorney Cyrus Vance recently wrote: "With so many of these cases ... the abuser faces the same sentence on his hundredth misdemeanor conviction as he did on his first. A punch to the face month after month is (considered) the same level crime as not paying a subway fare."

That's got to change. We have to instill a system-wide attitude adjustment on how we handle habitual batterers. A three-strikes policy might be a fine solution. But the women at the center of this horrible cycle must also take personal responsibility.

Society cannot remove an adult woman from a perilous domestic situation. She must walk out on her own, resolved to find a better way of life. Can we do a better job of helping her find the courage to leave and a safe place to go? Yes. But more educational opportunities, job training and child care won't help until the woman helps herself.

After he was charged with murder, Villanueva told the New York Daily News he wasn't guilty of killing officer Schaberger. From behind bars at Rikers Island, he cockily said, "The only thing I'm guilty of is domestic abuse." As if beating a woman is really nothing much to worry about.

The most immediate way to stop serial abusers like Maxwell and Villanueva is for their punching bags to take a permanent walk away. The best long-term solution is for the women to cooperate with prosecutors and for judges to throw the book at the abusers.

That's really the best chance we have to stop the cycle of violence from being handed down to future generations.

Disabled Americans Deserve Full Protection Under Law

Aug. 31, 2013

Ethan Saylor wasn't like you and me. He was born 26 years ago with Down syndrome. He was a happy, loving, "goofy" brother to younger siblings Emma and Adam. His parents adored him. At one point, Ethan had moved out to live independently, but he had recently moved back to an apartment on his parent's property.

By now you've noticed I speak of Ethan in the past tense. Sadly, he died in a confrontation with law enforcement officers who apparently had little training in how to deal with people who suffer from disabilities that make them unable to comprehend, feel or react as the rest of us do.

The officers, members of the Frederick County, Maryland, sheriff's department, were moonlighting as security cops at a mall at the time of the fatal confrontation. They had no way of knowing that

Ethan was captivated by police, and that he loved the TV program "NCIS" and would sometimes call 911 just to ask questions. They also didn't know that Ethan, who was famous for his hugs, had an aversion to being touched by strangers.

On Jan. 12, 2013, Ethan went to the movies to see "Zero Dark Thirty." He enjoyed the film so much he wanted to see it again, and his 18-year-old aide could not convince him otherwise. In fact, she called home to Ethan's mother to tell her that he had become frustrated and upset at the prospect of having to leave.

In the interim, Ethan wandered back into the theater and settled in to see the movie again. He either didn't realize or didn't stop to think that he needed to buy another $12 ticket and, in any case, he had no more money in his pocket. An assistant manager called in mall security to eject Ethan.

According to witnesses, when the first plain clothes officer told him he had to leave Ethan stubbornly replied, "I'm not leaving." (If they had only been wearing a uniform and a badge the young man who was so fascinated by police might have reacted differently.) The aide urgently told them Ethan required time to process the situation and begged for their patience. She warned them about his phobia of being touched and specifically said Ethan would "freak out" if they forced the situation. Her warnings went unheeded. As patrons began to fill the theater for the next showing, the officers may have felt pressure to quickly resolve the issue.

Now let's pause a moment here to describe the man officers were speaking to. Ethan was 5 foot 6 inches and weighed 294 pounds. One glance at the young man would immediately communicate that he was disabled. His chromosomal disorder had left Ethan with widely recognized Down syndrome characteristics: Eyes that slanted upward, small ears, a large forehead and a thick-tongued speech pattern.

Eyewitness statements say as the officers tried to pull Ethan out of his chair he both verbally and physically resisted. During the ensuing wrestling match, the officers struggled with three sets of handcuffs (made necessary due to Ethan's short arms and girth) and told him he was going to jail. One witness said Ethan was crying and calling out for his mom, clearly unable to process what was happening. As the scrum scuffled toward the exit, they fell in a heap with Ethan at the bottom - face down.

Ethan's sister Emma would write about the incident online. "Ethan died from a crushed larynx. He stopped breathing and went into cardiac arrest. In just a few moments he was dead." She then asks and answers her own question. "His crime? Not buying a $12 movie ticket."

The official autopsy report ruled the cause of death was, "Asphyxia ... complicated by Down Syndrome, obesity, atherosclerotic disease and some cardiac abnormalities."

I forgot to mention that having heart problems is another characteristic plaguing those with Down syndrome. The medical examiner's office determined the manner of death was homicide.

Homicide - so you'd think charges would be filed, right? No. The sheriff's office conducted an internal investigation and found its deputies - including a sergeant and a lieutenant - had done nothing wrong. Prosecutors took the case to a grand jury, which heard from 17 witnesses. No indictment was issued.

Emma, who happens to work for the National Down Syndrome Society, started an online petition at Change.org calling for Maryland's governor and attorney general to reopen her brother's case. The petition asks that the deputy's behavior be re-examined by outside investigators because as Emma bluntly observed, "They investigated and cleared themselves of any wrongdoing."

Emma's employer asked the Justice Department to investigate whether Ethan's rights were violated under the Americans With Disabilities Act. According to ABC News, a Department of Justice official confirms they are "reviewing" the case.

The most important point for other families with specially challenged children? The Saylor petition also calls for more training so deputies understand that a person such as Ethan isn't capable of responding automatically and should not be treated like a usual suspect. At last check, more than 300,000 people had signed that petition. It's a testament to how many families struggle with physically and emotionally disabled loved ones.

Look, no one thinks the officers deliberately set out to do harm to Ethan that day. But the fact remains he died because of their actions. Ethan had the bad luck to be born with an extra chromosome, but that doesn't mean he forfeited his rights as an American to respectful due process.

The justice system already gives special treatment to those who are targeted by hate crimes or those with alternative lifestyles. Now it's time to give disabled Americans a break, too.

After Deadly Disputes, Policing Can Never Be the Same

Dec. 15, 2014

Note to Sheriffs and Police Chiefs: If you aren't actively seeking ideas to foster better relations between your community and your officers, you probably should resign.

If you are still operating under the illusion that social unrest could never come to your town, you better think again.

If you don't realize that a new day has dawned in law enforcement - a day where a growing number of citizens automatically mistrust cops - you might want to get back out on the street and walk a beat for a day or two.

There is now a nationwide, colorblind call demanding a change in the way law enforcement interacts with the people they have sworn to protect.

There is no turning back now. The bad apples in the policing barrel have spoiled it for the rest of you.

Most recently, a cop in Cleveland gave a 12-year-old black child - who was unfortunately playing with a realistic-looking toy gun - just a few seconds to live before pulling his gun and shooting him dead. Other officers reportedly then restrained his mother, telling her to "calm down," and then tackled, handcuffed and tossed his 14-year-old sister in the back of a squad car.

There was, of course, the headline grabbing Ferguson, Missouri, shooting of unarmed black teenager, Michael Brown, in August. Before that, in July, the much-publicized death of an unarmed black man named Eric Garner who was selling single cigarettes on a street corner in Staten Island, New York. In March, Albuquerque police shot and killed a homeless white man following a more than four-hour standoff over his illegal camping.

Each of these cases has a backstory, of course, but the cold, hard fact is that there have been too many recent cases involving the use of questionable deadly force by police. Their seemingly callous actions after the fact only add to the growing anti-law enforcement feeling.

Across the country, people of all colors are asking, "Isn't there a more humane way for peace officers to respond to tense situations? Can't police be trained to defuse disputes in a way that does not include fatal gunfire? Why are so many unarmed citizens losing their lives?"

I'm wondering if it really is all about race, or might it have something to do with the poverty and sense of hopelessness that traps so many minority Americans in gang-infested neighborhoods? Have those consumed with surviving the desperation simply forgotten to teach their children to respect law enforcement, to acquiesce when an officer tells you to stop an illegal action?

Why did young Brown decide to confront Ferguson Officer Darren Wilson in the street that day? Why hadn't Garner stopped illegally selling cigarettes after police had repeatedly warned him not to? This isn't blaming the victim; it's trying to understand motivations.

Anyone who reads this column regularly knows I am a friend to law enforcement officers and completely understand their daily challenges. To those who wear a badge, I say you've got another challenge on your plate now. A good chunk of the population has come to see your profession as one to automatically fear and mistrust. It is way more than just a public relations problem, and multiple steps are required to fix things.

Police academies have to adopt better ways of weeding out psychologically unsuitable cadets. Instructors need to include more non-confrontational training and stress the art of street-level problem solving.

Police unions need to stop automatically going before cameras to defend questionable shoots and do more to pressure departments into providing state-of-the-art training and crime-fighting tools such as Tasers and body cameras. Demand qualified dispatchers who know the full facts of a situation to convey them to officers in the field.

The cop on the beat who displays the uber-macho, bad-guy attitude when dealing with the public needs a slap upside the head and a reminder that the arbitrary enforcement of the law is the mark of tyranny. Citizens will always fight against it.

And, finally, back to the sheriffs and chiefs of police. Learn a lesson from what's occurred recently - from the tiny 'burb of Ferguson to the inner city of Staten Island. You set the tone for your department. Even if you don't think adjustments are necessary, take another look. Citizens of all colors are demanding change.

The 911 System Needs Help

Feb. 14, 2015

Each day across this country, lives are saved because a dedicated 911 operator dispatched emergency personnel to help a panicked person. Every year there are some 240 million urgent calls made to this "one nation, one number" system. The value of the 911 organization is beyond question.

But how many times have you heard a recording of a 911 call in which the operator seems bored, uninterested or downright rude?

The latest incident occurred when a 14-year-old called from the back seat of a car to report her father and his fiance had been struck by a hit-and-run driver while changing a tire. Sitting alone on the Baltimore-Washington Beltway, she and her little brother were scared to death.

"They just laying here. Nothing. They are just laying here," she sobbed.

"OK, let's stop whining. Let's stop whining. It's hard to understand you," the uncompassionate-sounding operator told her. And then when she continued to beg for help to come he scolded her in a dismissive tone.

"Let's stop worrying about 'hurry up and get there' ... we're already on our way." The young girl's father and his fiance died at the scene.

There has got to be a better, more compassionate way to handle calls from people who are experiencing the worst moments of their life. Something more than an operator's condescending and repetitive admonition to, "Calm down, calm down ... " as heard on so many of these 9-11 tapes.

Dr. Brian Russell, a psychologist who has worked with law enforcement, believes operators need to learn to think like the victim they're talking to. The rote message to "calm down," is the wrong one.

"There's a reasonable chance that you're going to hear that as me (the operator) minimizing what you're experiencing," Russell said during a conversation from his Kansas headquarters. "And if so, there's a reasonable chance that you're going to become even more emotional in your desperation to get me to understand how bad the situation is."

There are countless examples of callers becoming more and more agitated as the 911 operator dispassionately asks questions. Many times the operator doesn't bother to tell the caller that help is already on the way, leaving them ever more frantic and believing the seriousness of the situation is not being understood.

Time is the enemy in all these situations, so getting a proper location of the emergency -- be it a crime-in-progress, a fire or the need for medical rescue - should be paramount.

Yet one widely referenced dispatcher-training manual suggests this order of questioning:

--What happened?

--Weapons?

--When did it occur?

--Where did it happen?

--Suspect description?

There is no national protocol on how to question a caller, but departments using this training method (offered in 2013 by the National Emergency Number Association) may be wasting valuable time by not asking for an address until question No. 4.

Dr. Russell thinks one of the first things an operator should say - in a composed and empathetic sounding way - is a question like, "Let's figure out where you are so I can send you help." He stresses that callers might very well be in shock and may have to be asked several times before it "registers" with them.

I'd like to see operators who get exasperated with sobbing, cursing or rambling callers re-trained, suspended or even fired if they do it repeatedly. I'd like to see better personality screening at the point of hire. Paying operators more might attract more suitable applicants.

None of this is to say there aren't wonderful 911 operators out there. I've listened to countless recordings of heroic conversations. An operator in Iowa helped a woman trapped in a runaway SUV travelling at speeds of up to 119 miles an hour successfully disable the vehicle and walk away. An operator in Kentucky helped a frantic mother save her 17-month-old baby whose eyes had rolled back in her head. And there are too many instances to mention where a 911 operator successfully handled a call from a child reporting an incapacitated parent.

But it's those cringe-worthy calls like the "stop whining" one we remember. They embarrass their departments and, worse yet, expose cities to multi-million-dollar lawsuits. Many filed by members of minority communities. The very group, according to Dr. Russell, that law enforcement cannot afford to offend.

We all pay for the sins of the 9-11 operator who responds poorly. We should all demand they do better.

More Female Police Officers, Please

March 30, 2015

When you were growing up and there was a dispute between siblings, who stepped in to bring about a peaceful solution? Probably Mom, right?

And when mediation was necessary to decide the evening's curfew, your punishment if you ignored it or when you were mature enough for driving lessons, I'm guessing it was Mom who was front and center.

Soothing raw nerves, introducing diplomatic distractions and solutions and hugging away bruised feelings are all female specialties. It's just human nature.

So at a time when conflict resolution is so obviously needed on the mean streets of America, why don't we have more female cops?

After all the violent and deadly events we've heard about recently -- from Missouri and Ohio to Wisconsin and Georgia -- where young men lost their lives during encounters with male police officers, you'd think police departments would be recruiting as many candidates skilled in de-escalating situations as they possibly could.

They have not.

Estimates on the number of female officers in the U.S. vary. John Wills, a former Chicago cop and FBI agent wrote the book, "Women Warriors: Stories from the Thin Blue Line." He reports that in 1970, only 2 percent of all law enforcement officers were women. In 1991, that number rose to 9 percent. Using the latest Bureau of Justice statistics, Wills writes the latest figures indicate, "The number of women involved in policing is almost 100,000, or just over 15 percent."

Although officer recruitment is no longer focused solely on military bases and other male-dominated venues, and recruitment billboards routinely feature female patrol officers, departments don't seem to be actively seeking out female nurses, social workers, mediators or psychologists with skills that could reduce instances of excessive or deadly force. Wonder why that is?

Penny Harrington, the first woman to head a major police force in the U.S. (Portland, Oregon) puts the need for female officers succinctly. "Women tend to talk, to reason, to try to deescalate violence," she told Ms. Magazine. By contrast, Harrington said, "Men have been taught - through sports, through the military - that you use physical force to get situations under control. Those are two hugely different approaches."

I'm thinking that state-sanctioned brawn isn't cutting it anymore. Communities across the nation are marching in the streets protesting what they see as overt aggression and ingrained hostility from their police force. Instead of bold brawn, we now need brains and conflict resolution tactics to be introduced to defuse the oozing hostility - from both officers and suspects - seen on today's streets.

Recent cases make my point. In Chamblee, Georgia, Anthony Hill was spotted naked and wandering erratically around his neighborhood one afternoon. When he approached (or ran toward) the responding police officer - obviously unarmed - he was shot dead. That, even though the officer carried a Taser gun and could have subdued Hill.

It's the overkill -- absolutely no pun intended -- that galls most clear-thinking people.

It was the third police shooting of an unarmed -- or apparently unarmed -- black man within a week. The other killings occurred in Aurora, Colorado and Madison, Wisconsin. All the cases involved male police officers. Besides possible machismo and racism, it feels like there's an element of institutionalized law enforcement arrogance at work here, too. Which exists, of course, because it is allowed to exist.

Look, the threat against police officers who patrol our neighborhoods is clear. And there will surely be more justified police shootings. But it's equally clear that something has to change if we ever expect police/community relations to improve. These days more and more citizens say they are afraid to call police for help, and no one wins in that culture of distrust.

Will having more strong women wearing badges -- talking reconciliation instead of flexing muscle -- be the kick in the culture police departments need? I say yes. Law enforcement administrators with vision need to start looking for them. Like, yesterday.

~~~

CHAPTER 12
Special Victims

"Stand up for the underdog, the 'loser.' Sometimes having the strength to show loving support for unacknowledged others turns the tides of our own lives." ~ **Alexandra Katehakis, Author**

There are all sorts of victims in this world, and sometimes one must look below the surface to realize that.

The murdered are certainly victims, but so are their survivors. Family members of mass murderers or serial killers have also been victimized, living the rest of their days with the shameful acts their loved ones perpetrated. The children of criminals become victims of a stunted childhood. Those citizens who, through no fault of their own, live in dangerous, gang-infested neighborhoods are victimized every day as they fearfully traverse their way to and from home, school and work. Those who join cults frequently find that, in the end, they were duped, robbed and left directionless.

I write about all types of victims to open minds and enlighten readers about the real-life, far-reaching ramifications of crime.

We hear a lot about victims on our favorite prime-time television dramas - especially stories of women in peril - but the real life criminals often look nothing like the TV version.

I strive to put a face on victims for a very simple reason. There but for the grace of God go each of us.

Let's Talk About Prostitution

May 25, 2008

Following every prostitution roundup, I can tell you with certainty that at least some of the women involved become despondent about the course their lives have taken. They may even be on the verge of suicide.

National figures bear me out. In an article by Dr. Melissa Farley called "Prostitution: Fact Sheet on Human Rights Violations," it's reported that 75 percent of women engaged in escort prostitution have tried to kill themselves.

Dr. Farley follows up with a lot of other numbers regarding a lot of other dreadful categories. The bottom line is, the majority of prostitutes report they were victims of incest or childhood sex abuse, have been violently raped on the job and physically assaulted with weapons, and have struggled with hunger, homelessness, drug and alcohol abuse, and diseases, such as HIV. Most meet the criteria for post-traumatic stress disorder. The average age of entry for a prostitute is 14- to 16 years old, and most spend more than a decade selling their bodies.

In other words, these women don't go into this line of work because they think it will be a good, long-term career move. They go into it because they know no other way to survive. I don't imagine there was ever a well-adjusted little girl who declared, "I want to grow up to be a call girl!"

Most chilling is the murder rate among prostitutes. According to a Johns Hopkins study, the workplace homicide rate for a woman who sells sex is about 7 times higher than that of a person in other high-risk occupations.

It doesn't sound to me as though prostitutes can be considered happy-go-lucky "ladies of the evening." It seems clear they have been and continue to be victimized on several fronts, often by their own bad judgment.

I can understand why police arrest the women. They're breaking the law. But aren't the male customers breaking the law, too? Why are the clients so rarely charged?

Case in point: Deborah Jeane Palfrey, the madame of a high-priced service in Washington, D.C., catered to the powerful, including Republican Sen. David Vitter of Louisiana. Once he was exposed as being a Palfrey client, the senator publicly apologized to his wife and constituents and promptly went back to work making the laws of the land.

Palfrey, on the other hand, was convicted, and was about to be sentenced to several years in prison when she was found dead, hanging in a shed on her mother's property. Two suicide notes were found.

In January 2007, one of Palfrey's "girls," a former college professor named Brandy Britton, hanged herself on the eve of trial. It was learned that the single mother of two had been facing foreclosure on her home and had lived through a history of domestic abuse. She had lost her teaching job at the University of Maryland-

Baltimore after filing a sex discrimination suit against the school, and had turned to selling sex to pay the bills.

They say that if you bite off the head of a snake, it dies. But where exactly is the head of the prostitution problem? Is it the women who sell themselves? The pimps who arrange the liaisons? Or the men who buy the services?

We arrest people who buy and sell illegal drugs. We convict people who buy and sell child pornography. So why don't we go after men who buy sex? Why is there a different standard when it comes to prostitution? If laws are being broken, aren't the women and the men equally guilty?

Convicted Sex Offenders -- The Other View

Aug. 1, 2008

David is a convicted child molester, a registered sex offender, who has served his time and currently lives in Albuquerque, New Mexico.

So what should society do with him now that he's out? Watch him like a hawk? Well, that's already being done via the registry through which he must regularly report his every lifestyle move -- where he lives, where he works, what car he drives, where he spends his time.

For many of us the quick answer would be, "Lock him up, and throw away the key!" And until I met David, I would have joined in that chorus. Once a sex offender, always a sex offender: That had been my mantra.

To make a very long story short, David's estranged wife accused him of sexually touching their 5-year-old daughter during visitation. Their 7-year-old son allegedly saw it happen during nap time, when all three of them had laid down to take a quick snooze.

At trial, stories changed, and physical examinations proved no wrongdoing. But David was sentenced to six years in prison. He says that everything you've heard about life for a convicted child molester in prison is true. It is the hardest time you can do.
David says that he never ever would have done what he was charged with.

Now that he's free, he is not in communication with his children, who live with his mother-in-law. His wife died of a methadone overdose while he was serving time.

David is getting on with his life. For the last two years, he's been diligently working a job where they don't mind his past; going to church; showing up for his court-mandated checks like clockwork; and spending time with Alice.

Alice is how I came to know David. She is a remarkable 79-year-old woman who gently tells me that I've had it all wrong about convicted molesters.

The media, Alice politely scolded me, never talks about the convicted innocent or the released offenders who truly want opportunities to live a better life -- a job, a place to live, a break from society -- none of which come easy to them.

"It doesn't matter to me what they did," Alice said, while stressing the faith that she and her late husband, Pastor Don, shared. "My mission is to make sure they don't re-offend."

"We have redefined the word rape in this country," she told me as she detailed what she'd learned in recent classes about the eight levels of sex offenses we punish. Many include the kind of behavior that teenagers often engage in: removal of an item of clothing, skin-on-skin contact, nonpenetrating acts.

Alice and I discussed the case of 17-year-old honor student Genarlow Wilson of Georgia, who got 10 years for engaging in an oral act with a willing 15-year-old girl at a New Year's Eve party. His life was ruined.

In her quiet, dignified way, Alice says that the media fans the flames of ignorance. Reporters stress only the most extreme accounts of perverts who kidnap and kill children. They don't adequately explain flimsy trial evidence or today's rampant zeal to convict at just a hint of inappropriate behavior.

Alice followed in Pastor Don's footsteps, visiting the convicted in prison. Her grown children think she's "losing her marbles," as she meets and becomes involved with more of these convicts, determined to help them when they get out.

"I believe God can change anyone's life," she explained.

Take cross-country truck driver Robert, for example. Alice says that he had sex with a mature-looking 16-year-old waitress. He gets out next year after serving 10 years. While in prison, he has been attacked several times and now must walk with a cane.

Jose served 10 years for something he did with a minor when he was 16. When he was released, he wanted to go live with his dad, but the courts said no, since Dad had a 30-year-old felony on his record. Nothing comes easy for convicts.

Back to David. When he recently showed up for his regular 90-day check-in, he was suddenly handcuffed and told there were two warrants for his arrest. Never mind that the spelling of the last name, the date of birth and the Social Security number that the state had didn't match David's. He was taken into custody, and it was Alice who was there to pick him up when the snafu was finally figured out.

"Alice gives me the benefit of the doubt," David says. "That holds me up to a higher standard and makes me want to life a better life."

Maybe we could all learn a lesson from Alice. She and David gave me a reason to rethink my mantra.

Locking Away Evil -- Finally

Nov. 28, 2009

On this Thanksgiving weekend, I want to tell you about a group of young people who are giving thanks for the first time in their lives. This year, they are extremely thankful that their tormentor, the self-proclaimed preacher Tony Alamo, has finally been brought to justice.

In U.S. district court in Texarkana, Ark., the 75-year-old Alamo was recently sentenced to 175 years in prison on charges of engaging in sex with minor members of his so-called "church." One of the five brides identified was just 8 years old. My sources, escapees of the church, tell me there were many more Alamo brides.

Alamo's real name is Bernie LaZar Hoffman. He was a phony from the get-go. Back in the early '70s, he and his wife Susan dreamed up the "Alamo Christian Ministries" to rescue drugged-out homeless people from the streets of Hollywood. They gave the unfortunates a cot to sleep on, food to eat, a rousing sermon and an odd job or two to perform as payback. City fathers donated money to show appreciation for the more tourist-friendly streets.

Those first Alamo followers settled in, coupled up and gave birth to a second generation. The poor kids never had a chance.

The Alamos had up to three dozen moneymaking enterprises -- from restaurants to hog farms -- and their loyal disciples were their workforce. Instead of a salary, the workers got meager living arrangements, irregular meals (many consisted of whatever food had been donated to the ministry) and all the preachin' about Jesus the Alamos could muster.

The Alamos got rich. When Susan began to suffer from cancer, they moved their headquarters to a hilltop near tiny Fouke, Ark. -- far away from the prying eyes of outsiders.

A big source of income was the uber-expensive, handmade rhinestone- and sequined-studded denim jackets the disciples churned out. In the day, it seemed all of Hollywood was wearing one! Dolly Parton, Brooke Shields, Mr. T, among others, wore the flashy fashion statements, and sales skyrocketed.

In 1994, Alamo went to prison for failure to pay taxes on the jacket earnings. At the time of the trial, there was evidence that children at the compound were being brutally beaten, held aloft by four burly church men while Alamo beat them bloody, "baseball style," with a wooden paddle. That testimony was never allowed at the tax trial, however.

Once in prison Alamo still ruled his flock with an iron fist.

In a series of exclusive interviews with those born into the Alamo cult, I've heard unforgettable horror stories.

The children were schooled but now realize, as adults, that on orders from Alamo their education was sorely lacking. If they asked an inappropriate question about the day's lesson, they were beaten. If they were tardy, laughed too loud or wore the wrong clothing, they were beaten. After classes, they were ordered into hours of mandatory prayer. One young man named Jared remembers after Susan died of cancer in 1982 all followers were ordered by "Papa Tony" to keep up a round-the-clock kneeling prayer circle for her "certain resurrection." Alamo kept Susan's corpse for 16 years, until a court finally ordered him to return it to her family.

These Alamo captives now reveal it was they -- the exhausted, terrorized children of the group -- who often worked until midnight laboriously turning out those denim jackets. A young mother named Becca tells me that growing up in the ministry brought no joy -- ever.

She worked in the communal kitchen cutting away the rotten parts of donated food. She fantasized about Papa Tony's promise to get her a "jar of pickles for my birthday." There was no real medical care, not even for one poor epileptic child. Jared remembers watching the girl beaten every time she had a seizure.

Several other former Alamo Ministry children who wish to remain anonymous told me how underage girls were routinely married off to much older male church members. After Alamo got out of prison in 1998, they say, Papa Tony chose multiple underage brides for himself. Finally, in September 2008, at a roadside stop in Arizona, Alamo was arrested with six girls in his vehicle and charged with transporting them across state lines for sexual purposes.

I tell you this story because society needs to learn from it. Our justice system took way too long to stop this monster, knowing since the early '90s that children were suffering at his hand. The doctrine of separation of church and state caused authorities to shy away.

We need to do better. While the second Alamo generation is now thankful he's locked away, authorities admit there are other religious-based predators out there. No one wants to curtail freedom of religious practice, but allowing charlatans to victimize the innocent and enslave people isn't acceptable, either.

Some Sex Crimes Get a Pass -- Why?

April 17, 2010

Sometimes the simplest-sounding questions spark the most profound discussion.

What's our purpose on earth?

Why is the sky blue?

Why do we have a statute of limitations on sex crimes?

I mean, really, why give the criminal any break at all? By placing a limit on how far back the prosecutor can go to punish a sex predator, aren't we telling countless victims that the justice system doesn't apply to them?

Experts in the medical and law-enforcement fields will tell you the career sex offender has probably committed dozens of attacks over a long period of time before they're ever caught. An FBI profiler once told me the bureau stopped a serial molester who was in his 90s. Imagine how many victims he'd left in his wake.

Let's say a career sex offender - maybe a priest, a teacher or a family member - routinely molests children and tricks them into staying silent for 10 years. (Statutes of limitations vary from state to state.) When the offender is finally brought to trial, the prosecution is often not allowed to tell the jury about their past pattern of bad behavior - not even if a dozen other people come forward to claim the defendant did the same thing to them. Too bad, the law says, it doesn't matter anymore.

That's a horrible thing to tell victims, that what happened to them doesn't matter, that no justice can be had by them.

I know a lot of people who work in the justice system, so I called them to pose the question, "Why is there a statute of limitations on sex crimes?"

Mickey Sherman is a noted Connecticut-based defense lawyer. "The system is designed to protect a defendant's rights. Every person has a right to be notified in a timely manner as to potential criminal charges against them," he told me. It's just not fair for someone to be able to say, 'Hey, 26 years ago last Tuesday this man raped me!'"

When I contacted Boston attorney Wendy Murphy, known nationally as an adamant victim's advocate, she offered a much more sinister assessment of the status quo.

"The way these silly rules work should make any decent person cringe because limitation periods mean a perp who raped 25 children can, as soon as the clock runs out, walk into the middle of main street and brag about his crimes -- and there's nothing anyone can do about it."

Many others I contacted didn't want their names used.

Most seemed puzzled when I asked if we could simply do away with the statute of limitations for sex crimes.

A federal prosecutor in New Mexico told me: "That's what the state legislature wants. ... (They) determine what S.O.L. will apply to every crime."

A retired district attorney from California said, "It doesn't have to be that way. ... A state legislature could pass a law and change it. Maybe it is time to change some laws."

I also asked a sex-crimes prosecutor who answered in an exasperated tone of voice: "Why is there a statute of limit on anything! I guess so the cases don't linger forever ..." And he admitted how tough it is to prove a crime happened years earlier. Details get fuzzy, witnesses move away, evidence can get lost, and defendants have the "right to a speedy trial."

I came away thinking the real answer as to why we allow this is because that's the way it has always been done ...

That's not to say that some adjustments haven't occurred. Some states now give childhood victims 30 years to come forward, and some wave the time limitation and start the clock anew if psychiatric treatment has helped a victim recover their memory of abuse or if DNA evidence from a current attack matches the DNA from a dormant case.

Long ago, law enforcement started collecting DNA samples from rape victims, and now forensic matches in current cases are helping past victims find resolution. Finally, they are able to come face-to-face with the shadowy criminal who stole their dignity.

I like Wendy Murphy's suggestion. "Someone," she told me, "needs to confront the head of the judiciary committee in (every) state legislature where the time limits are short and ask only one question: "Why do you want a child rapist to EVER stop looking over his shoulder, wondering if the cops have finally caught up with him?"

The truth: There is no constitutional right to have the clock stop running on a crime. The lawmakers in your state have simply failed to act.

There is no statute of limitations for murder or treason, and I would submit sexual assault is just as life-damaging and heinous a crime. Let's demand we abolish this foolish statute.

Life After a Tabloid Scandal

Dec. 7, 2013

I went to a wedding this past weekend, and while you may not immediately recognize the name of the groom, I'll bet you know of him.

Despite a lifetime of obstacles, Gavin Arvizo -- once at the center of a sensational child sex abuse scandal -- has worked his way through to a triumphant life. At 13, Gavin accused Michael Jackson of molesting him, and the superstar was arrested.

It seemed life was stacked against this kid from the very beginning.

As a youngster he lived in a one-room apartment in East Los Angeles with two siblings and his parents. Poverty and domestic abuse was a way of life.

At the age of 8 this young Hispanic boy and his little brother were instructed by their father to walk out of a J.C. Penney store with clothing that wasn't paid for. Out in the parking lot the boys watched in horror as their father was surrounded by security guards and wrestled to the pavement. His mother, emerging from another store, soon joined in the melee, and both parents were handcuffed and taken to the police station.

At just 10 years old, Gavin was diagnosed with a rare and deadly cancer. As he laid helpless in an L.A. hospital bed feigning sleep, he heard his parents being advised to plan his funeral. Following months of grueling treatments, this plucky kid pulled through.

While in the hospital, the boy's plight came to the attention of the King of Pop. Jackson sent a basket full of toys and good wishes. When he was well enough to travel, the boy and his family were invited to visit the singer's Neverland Ranch. Knowing of their poverty, Jackson even sent a limousine to drive them. What a wonderful respite for a recuperating cancer patient and his exhausted parents!

But once back home, things got worse. Violence. Restraining orders. Divorce. Yet the limousines kept arriving, and the sleepovers in Michael Jackson's master bedroom at Neverland continued.

The rest is history. Authorities in Santa Barbara, California charged Jackson with child sexual abuse, giving intoxicating substances to a minor to facilitate child sexual abuse, conspiracy to cover up the crimes and more.

During the trial Gavin, then 15, was vilified as an accomplished liar. Jackson's lawyer, Tom Mesereau, called him and his family "grifters" and "thieves," and he repeatedly warned the jury that the Arvizos were only "in it for the money."

The jury also heard about two other boys who said they, too, had been molested by Jackson. One was a maid's son, the other the son of an L.A. dentist. Both boys received generous payouts from Jackson in return for keeping quiet. The dentist's family got nearly $20 million.

The defense called a group of young men to the witness stand, leading off with dancer/choreographer Wade Robson. Each testified they had often slept in Jackson's bed when they were youngsters and nothing sexual had ever happened.

ackson was acquitted of all charges in June 2005.

In a stunning turnaround, Robson recently admitted he perjured himself at trial. He is attempting to file suit against the Jackson estate, claiming he suffered two nervous breakdowns because of the sexual abuse secret he harbored for so long. During a "Today" show interview, Robson said of Michael Jackson, "He sexually abused me from 7 years old until 14. He performed sexual acts on me and forced me to perform sexual acts on him." Robson bluntly added, "Jackson was an amazing talent, but he was a pedophile."

To this day attorney Mesereau continues to vilify Gavin as a dishonest character. Nine years later he still ridicules the only youngster with enough courage to have actually gone to court against an international superstar. Mesereau continues to claim Arvizo's allegations were money-driven.

The fact is the defense lawyers and their teams are the only ones who made money from the Jackson criminal case.

Gavin, now 24, has also endured years of being hounded by paparazzi and tormented by a worldwide legion of die-hard Jackson fanatics who have vowed to kill him, maim him and stalk him for the rest of his life for saying their idol molested him.

One of the more vicious fans recently discovered Gavin was about to wed a preacher's daughter and urged others to inundate the church with menacing phone calls about Gavin's integrity.

Gavin steadfastly refuses to speak up for himself, believing a man's actions speak for themselves. So let me tell you a little bit about him.

Gavin worked two and three jobs at a time (in restaurants and landscaping) to put himself through community college. Through sheer perseverance he won partial scholarships to attend prestigious Emory University. He double-majored in history and philosophy, made the honor roll, was president of the student union and he still found time to volunteer frequently at his church.

Gavin doesn't drink, use tobacco, drugs or foul language. He is currently working as a paralegal in a law firm, preparing to take the LSAT and is applying to more than a dozen law schools. His dream is to go to Harvard.

Most telling about the character of Gavin Arvizo? He has never accepted any of the outstanding six-figure offers to sell his story. Newspapers and television shows continually dangle tempting deals, but Gavin is adamant that the passage of time will best tell his story.

He says he knows the truth and believes it will be revealed to the doubters of the world when the time is right.

As I sat in church and watched this resilient young man joyfully take a wife, I thought back to all his trials and tribulations. Poverty, violence, near-fatal cancer, his punishing and unsatisfying ride through the justice system. Amazing.

At the reception, the unknowing DJ played "The Way You Make Me Feel" by Michael Jackson. I caught Gavin's eye as he sat on the dais with bride, Shelby. He just smiled, grandly shrugged his shoulders and went back to living his life as anonymously as possible.

Homegrown PTSD -- America's Dangerous Neighborhoods

Feb. 22, 2014

Think about the least desirable neighborhoods around you. You know the places I'm talking about - the areas you think twice about going to in the daytime and deliberately avoid at night. Those zones where police officers are most often called to respond to reports of shootings, stabbings and murders.

Now, think about the people who live in those crime-infested neighborhoods. Think of the young people who grow up watching the violence all around them and fearing it will come for them.

A recent article by journalists at ProPublica.org quoted a growing list of studies that have compared what happens to people who live in dangerous neighborhoods here at home with what happens to soldiers serving in war zones. The unanimous conclusion is that residents of violent neighborhoods can suffer from Post-Traumatic Stress Disorder just as so many of our soldiers do. Just like veterans, civilians can experience flashbacks, nightmares, paranoia and social withdrawal.

While the military has established protocols for diagnosing PTSD in soldiers, there are barely any programs in place to help civilians. You can count on one hand the number of hospital emergency rooms that bother to question victims of community violence, those who come in seeking treatment for a severe beating, a stabbing or gunshot wound.

We know from research on military personnel that PTSD is a very real, very terrifying syndrome in which the sufferer has a sudden and distorted sense of being in imminent and extreme danger. They become horrified, hyper-aggressive and violent in response. They gather weapons to help them fight off their perceived threats.

If these recent studies about the growing number of civilian PTSD cases are on target - (one from Drexel University, for example, found homegrown PTSD victims are more likely to carry a weapon in order to "restore feelings of safety") - doesn't it behoove us to pay closer attention to neighborhoods that could be producing human ticking time bombs?

It doesn't take a risk assessment expert to peg this problem as a solid public safety issue.

After a catastrophic event such as the 9/11 attacks, the Oklahoma City bombing or a devastating hurricane, mental health experts flood in to offer counseling and follow-up treatment. Currently, however, only one U.S. hospital performs routine PTSD screening.

ProPublica contacted top trauma centers in the 21 U.S. cities with the highest murder rates. Only the Spirit of Charity Hospital in New Orleans has their emergency room doctors routinely monitor for PTSD and offer treatment options to the incoming wounded.

At Cook County Hospital in Chicago's inner city, a pilot program began in 2011 to identify PTSD symptoms in pediatric patients. Now, social workers report 42 percent of all patients examined for gunshots, stabbings and other violent injuries had signs of PTSD symptoms. Most of them were male but, when questioned, women and whole families reported "significant levels of PTSD."

Researchers in Atlanta questioned 8,000 inner-city dwellers and learned that two-thirds had been violently attacked, about half of them knew someone who had been murdered and 1 person out of every 3 interviewed reported having had PTSD symptoms sometime in his or her life.

"The rates of PTSD we see are as high or higher than Iraq, Afghanistan or Vietnam veterans," Project leader Dr. Kerry Ressler said. "We have a whole population who is traumatized."

ProPublica reports that at Detroit's Receiving Hospital, psychologists talk with susceptible patients about PTSD, but there's no real program in place. Staffs at hospital trauma units in Birmingham, Alabama, and St. Louis, Missouri, say they hope to begin routine PTSD screening by the end of the year. And, doctors in Baltimore, Newark, Memphis and Jackson, Mississippi, all said they would like to have such a program, but their hospitals simply don't have the money.

The bills of low-income patients are most often paid by Medicaid, which doesn't cover PTSD screenings. Maybe the program should reconsider, as a bit of public money spent now could save a lot more in the future.

Regular readers of this column know the rate of crime has been going down, nationally, but still there are pockets in America where rates of violent crime continue to escalate.

There are whole neighborhoods in the United States that are so dangerous that they are creating a clinically definable group of people who could violently lash out at any given moment. Think of the damage done in terms of getting an education, family relationships, parenting skills and, in many cases, the frequent inability of adult PTSD victims to hold down a job. You know who pays for their unemployment benefits? We all do. We also pay for food stamps, child welfare, housing allowances, the cost of family and juvenile court and incarceration costs.

There are so many politicians who, during election cycles, wax eloquently about working for the well-being of all citizens, doing what's best for the economy and society at large. Funny, I don't hear many speak about crime, justice or concrete ideas to make us safer where we live.

I guess it comes down to this: Do we want to offer better policing, meaningful counseling and maybe even a relocation stipend to those who have endured violent acts in their own communities - or do we want to wait until something awful happens and pay the increased freight on the back end?

There's no getting around it. Researchers have been studying this problem since the late 90s and all have come to the same conclusion. There are parts of America that are as damaging to human beings as the worst foreign war zones.

Cyber Stalking Just Got Harder

June 8, 2015

What if you got a message on your Facebook account from someone you knew was angry with you that read, "There's one way to love ya, but a thousand ways to kill ya." You might be a bit worried, right?

What if that person continued to write things like, "I'm not going to rest until your body is a mess, soaked in blood and dying from all the little cuts." And they followed up with musings about putting your "head on a stick" and making a name for themselves with "the most heinous school shooting ever imagined."

Would the phrase "Hell hath no fury like a crazy man in a kindergarten class" prompt you to pick up the phone and alert the police? I sure hope so.

Well, thanks to a new ruling from the U.S. Supreme Court, there may be no grounds to arrest someone who writes such terrifying threats.

What has happened to our common sense?

The case stems from actions by Anthony Elonis of Bucks County, Pennsylvania, after his estranged wife got a restraining order to keep him away from her and their two children. Elonis was ordered not to post threatening messages about his wife, but he ignored the order.

About a week later he wrote on Facebook, "Fold up your protective order and put (it) in your pocket. Is it thick enough to stop a bullet?"

He also wrote about slitting the throat of the female FBI agent who came to investigate his threat against school children.

Elonis, then 29, would tell a judge he didn't mean to frighten anyone. He insisted his words weren't true threats but therapeutic rap lyrics he composed during a rough period of his life.

A jury ultimately convicted him under a federal law that makes it a crime to communicate any threat to injure another person. Elonis was sentenced to nearly four years. He appealed, and his case advanced to the U.S. Supreme Court.

In handing down their ruling, the high court vacated Elonis' conviction. The Justice's majority opinion declared that the point of siding with the defendant had nothing to do with his claim of freedom of speech but, rather, the prosecutor's failure to prove the defendant's intent at the time he wrote those brutally violent taunts.

Really? The justice system is supposed to prove what was on the mind of someone -- their intent -- when they wrote terroristic messages?

As an investigative reporter for many years, I've been on the receiving end of some of the most hateful online messages you can imagine.

Those that question my motives or impugn my honesty roll off my back. But some contain violently sexual threats, brutal ways to kill or maim me, including this most memorable one as I covered a controversial criminal trial: "My friend and I will push you down outside the court. While she scrubs your face with steel wool I will scoop out your eyes with a spoon."

The L.A. Cyber Crimes Unit got involved once, the FBI on another occasion. Both ultimately told me there was nothing they could do to make the intimidating writers stop.

For me, it comes with the professional territory, but not so for the countless victims of domestic abuse and other crimes who are virtually paralyzed by these terrifying threats. That the nation's highest court now dismisses their abject fear by ignoring the long standing "reasonable person standard" -- the idea that any reasonable person would find such words threatening -- in favor of "proof of intent" sends a shiver down my spine.

Anti-stalking statutes nationwide rely on the reasonable person standard. Now that guideline is in doubt, and it is a sure bet that prosecutors will be more reluctant to bring charges against these cyber terrorists.

It is way past time for Congress and/or state legislatures to pass meaningful cyber-threat laws. Vulnerable citizens should not have to live in fear. We condemn threatening hate speech on the street. Why not on the Internet?

If cyber bullies realize there is jail time attached to their hate-filled actions, they may think twice before hitting the "send" button. These ubiquitous messages of hate are not only clear-cut verbal assaults but they can be early warning signs from disturbed criminals-in-waiting.

Must we wait until they explode in actual physical violence before the system allows them to be punished? Not fair.

Deny, Deny Until They Die: Agent Orange and the Government Response

June 27, 2015

So, the U.S. government has finally decided to help some 2,000 Air Force personnel exposed to Agent Orange residue left over in airplanes used during the Vietnam War. They are now eligible for disability, medical and survivor benefits.

"Opening up eligibility for this deserving group of Air Force veterans and reservists is the right thing to do," Veterans Affairs Secretary Bob McDonald announced.

Really? Then why didn't the VA take this step long ago? These new recipients flew in Fairchild C-123 aircraft from 1969 to 1986. That's between 46 and 29 years ago!

And if it's the "right thing to do" for those folks then what about the countless other Vietnam-era military personnel whose cries for help have been ignored even though they suffer from some or many of the 14 diseases needed to claim Agent Orange benefits?

The longstanding rule says if a veteran had boots on-the-ground in Vietnam they are automatically accepted for special benefits. All others making Agent Orange disability claims have to prove they handled the toxic chemical or worked near it.

Over the decades I have spoken to dozens of vets who suffer from an "approved" disease. Among them: Hodgkin's, Parkinson's, prostate or respiratory cancers, soft tissue sarcoma, diabetes mellitus (Type 2), chronic B-cell leukemia, ischemic heart disease and debilitating chloracne. Many fear they have passed their ill health on to their children and grandchildren.

These veterans are ignored, according to the few lawyers willing to challenge the VA on their behalf, because the Defense Department claims they can find no records proving they were in proximity to Agent Orange. Records were poorly kept, lost and, in at least one case, destroyed by fire.

If ever there was a deserving group of citizens with a reason to sue for redress, this is it. But, oh yeah, the U.S. government is conveniently immune from lawsuits.

These men and women who loyally served their country are convinced that the government's strategy has been to "deny, deny, until they die," since Agent Orange benefits already account for one out of six disability checks issued by the VA.

Take the case of Air Force Master Sergeant LeRoy Foster who spent 10 years (from 1968 to 1978) assigned to the 43rd Supply Squadron at Anderson Air Force Base in Guam. His duties included spraying herbicides around the base to get rid of weeds. In sworn testimony to the U.S. Congress, and in several affidavits to the VA, Foster swore that Agent Orange -- which contains deadly TCDD dioxin -- was among the defoliants he regularly loaded into his 750-gallon, trailer-mounted sprayer and dispersed base-wide. Other military personnel on Guam at the time -- such as Sgt. Ralph Stanton -- confirm the account and reported they were "routinely soaked" by Foster's spray.

They gave me personal photographs from their days at Anderson AFB showing stacks of chemical barrels they swore carried the telltale Agent Orange markings. Other photos showed G.I.'s cooking on barbecue grills fashioned out of the empty drums.

A U.S. government analysis of the island's soil confirmed the presence of Agent Orange toxins. Guam currently has an extraordinarily high cancer rate. Yet, to this day the DOD maintains it has no records proving the military ever transported Agent Orange to that strategically important Vietnam-era island.

The Pentagon also denies Agent Orange was ever present on Okinawa, another location U.S. vets maintain was an AO hot spot where they first began to experience major health issues.

Checking in this week with Foster and Stanton I discovered both men were still alive but deathly ill. Foster is battling devastating rectal cancer.

"I am down to 150 (pounds) now," Foster wrote. "The weight is falling off of me. I believe there is no reversing it."

Stanton wrote of his health, "It's kind of like a juggling act because of the number of things wrong with me."

Hundreds of Guam- and Okinawa-based veterans have filed VA claims citing exposure to Agent Orange as the cause of their health problems, but the vast majority were rejected. And none of the 200,000 so-called "Blue Water" vets who say they were exposed to Agent Orange while serving aboard deep-water naval vessels stationed off Vietnam's coast has been awarded special benefits.

Who can't be happy for the 2,000 Air Force vets who were recently added to the Agent Orange rolls? But excuse me if I don't applaud the VA's massively delinquent action.

Our government did a terrible thing when it continued to spray millions of gallons of deadly Agent Orange long after it was clear it caused devastating health problems. But what's worse is its obstinate refusal over the years to take full responsibility for all sick and dying veterans.

Deny, deny until they die. Shameful.

~~~

CHAPTER 13
Consequences of Our Actions

"The sower may mistake and sow his peas crookedly; the peas make no mistake, but come up and show his line." ~ **Ralph Waldo Emerson**

Remember when your parents warned you that the decisions you made in life would come with consequences? The truth is that, oftentimes, the actions of others can also come with consequences for all of us.

Misbehavior by drug addicts certainly affects us, as we taxpayers foot the bill for their arrest, prosecution, incarceration and maybe even their period of rehabilitation. Bad conduct by politicians and idolized professional athletes goes a long way to degrade our faith. Criminal behavior by parents directly impact the children they leave behind when they go to prison. Gun violence causes our citizenry to become divided in the red-hot issue of gun control.

It is important to highlight these issues because as independent Americans like to think we are, the reality is we are all in this together. What one does can affect many.

Too Many Lawsuits and It Costs You!

June 2, 2008

Have you heard about the crazy lawsuit filed in Washington, D.C., last year by former Judge Roy Pearson? He demanded $54 million from a dry cleaners because the Korean couple that owns it allegedly misplaced a pair of his trousers.

The hardworking Jin and Soo Chung nearly had their American dream stolen. Donations from outraged citizens helped fight the injustice and showed the Chungs that America really is the land of opportunity.

At trial, the judge, Judith Bartnoff, allowed Pearson's past behavior of "creating unnecessary litigation" (during his 2005 divorce proceedings) to be presented. Ultimately, she ruled in favor of the Chungs and awarded them court costs. Later, Pearson's contract as an administrative law judge was not renewed. His reaction? You guessed it: Mr. Fancy Pants is now suing to get his job back!

This kind of frivolous misuse of the legal system is not as rare as you might think. Our court systems are tied up in knots by ditzy attempts to make money or punish people for a perceived act of disrespect. Something's got to change.

The mere possibility of a lawsuit forces businesses and public institutions to pay for all sorts of safeguards. And naturally, that cost gets passed on to us.

According to the Institute for Legal Reform, the average American family shells out an extra $3,500 annually for everyday goods and services. I don't know about you, but I'd rather keep my $3,500.

Your kids' after-school activities cost more because their club has to carry extra accident insurance. So does your supermarket, home improvement store and pharmacy. Perhaps one of the businesses you deal with has already been hit with a lawsuit and is paying off a settlement. You may be shouldering the burden, whether you realize it or not.

The ILR, working as an affiliate of the U.S. Chamber of Commerce, has studied the legal fairness of each state and ranked them in terms of how often a state allows the average American's dream to be turned into a nightmare.

You can find the entire 50-state list on the ILR website and learn about several small-business people whose livelihoods have been impacted or completely destroyed because some numbskull complainant with a willing attorney decided to try to get a payoff to go away.

Can anyone say, "tort reform"?

Now, hold on. If you are a member of the Bar Association and you're getting set to fire off a missive lambasting me, I concede that there are countless lawsuits of merit filed every year by deserving plaintiffs and earnest lawyers. That's not what's being discussed here. This is a discussion about bringing some common sense back into our judicial system.

A man who uses a table saw incorrectly and injures himself shouldn't automatically get a million bucks from the store that sold it to him, as compensation for his stupidity. An inmate shouldn't automatically get to sue because he doesn't like the prison food. A suspect who forces cops on a high-speed chase shouldn't be compensated for injuries sustained in the inevitable car accident. A burglar who sues a homeowner because he was hurt during the break-in should go to prison, not to the bank with a settlement check in hand.

And think about this: If you live in a state with a lousy litigation atmosphere, how many new businesses do you think will move in and offer new jobs to you and your neighbors? Ummm. I'm thinking none will find your state attractive enough to invest in.

We like to blame people for our troubles. But who is really to blame for the litigation mess in which we find ourselves? Is it the complainant? The lawyer who thinks more about the 33 1/3 percent he might rake in and less about the actual merits of the case? Maybe it's the insurance company that routinely goes for out-of-court settlements rather than fighting the good fight in court. Perhaps it's the judges, who should take a cue from the jurist in the Mr. Fancy Pants case and toss out more lawsuits that don't pass the common-sense smell test.

It's a combination of all of the above, of course. I vote for a system in which these type cases to have to pass a merit panel of former judges before actually getting anywhere near a courtroom.
Oh. And in the meantime, I want my $3,500 back.

When Parents Go to Prison, Children Are Punished

July 19, 2008

When I was a rookie TV reporter covering crime I got the chance to go on an early-morning drug raid with the Newark Police Department in New Jersey.

We met at a station house in downtown Newark at 3 a.m. -- sleepy-eyed, coffee in hand, but ready for the pre-raid briefing. Naturally, I had brought along a camera crew.

We filmed the squad room briefing, the crew filmed me being outfitted in a bulletproof vest (the crew got vests, too), and then we captured the scene as we set off in a slow, quiet convoy of police cars toward the intended target's home.

The residents in the neighborhood were mostly lower-middle class and minorities. Think Archie Bunker's house in "The Jeffersons."

There were no sirens or flashing lights that pre-dawn morning, and everyone spoke in whispers -- if they spoke at all. Every step of the operation was carefully planned, including the fact (that was initially unknown to me) that a social worker was coming along.

Once we were out of the cars and at the foot of the front stoop, we were instructed, via hand signals, to get behind the first few officers -- those directly behind the officers with the battering ram.

Then, WHAM! In an instant, we were inside the house, and police were shouting instructions to those about to be arrested. A man and woman lying on a mattress on the dining room floor were rousted from sleep. A stash of drugs and at least one weapon were located not far from where they slept. He was being handcuffed; she was shouting. Then, as the seriousness of the situation sunk in, her cries turned into rattling shrieks.

My attention was suddenly jerked away by the sound of a sobbing child. As my eyes adjusted to the dim light, I saw there were two children. The girl, who was dressed in a sweet little nightgown, appeared to be about 7 years old and was crying, with her shaking arms outstretched toward her mother. The toddler boy in diapers was oddly quiet but alert.

That's when I noticed the social worker steering them away and out the front door.

As a mother, I've never forgotten that scene. It still brings a lump to my throat.

And since that day, I've wondered: What about the children of those who are taken away to prison?

Here are today's startling facts: At least 2 million children in this country have a parent behind bars. Some experts in the field believe 10 million children currently have or have recently had a parent in some sort of detention facility. Numbers are hard to come by because adults often won't admit they have children and the children often don't come forward out of shame.

Many children who are old enough to understand the situation become angry and ashamed and suffer feelings of isolation and depression. They do poorly in school, especially if they're separated from their parents for a long time. They endure financial and psychological hardships. None of it is their fault, of course. But they often feel as though it is. They worry about the safety of their absent parents.

As the parent is punished, so is the child.

No one argues that people shouldn't be incarcerated for the sake of their children. But there are many who argue that we should be doing more for these kids. Some studies conclude that if we fail to help them maintain their equilibrium, many will be condemned to follow in their parents' footsteps. Other studies are cited indicating that children of offenders are 5 to 10 times more likely than their peers to end up in prison.

Failing to help now could mean that a terrible cycle will continue and our prisons will remain full in the future. In other words, pay now for some programs, or pay much more later for lengthy incarcerations.

I can't tell you how many times over the years I've thought about those young kids I saw in Newark during what had to have been the scariest moment of their lives. I tried to follow up on their story, but juvenile privacy laws prevented that. The public would never know.
Did they go into foster care or to live with relatives ? Did they get to visit their parents? Did they get a good education? What was society obligated to do for them, after their parents took such a wrong turn in life?

Next week, I will discuss prison-based programs for these kinds of kids, and why putting children and parents together helps them both.

Kids of Criminals -- Part 2

July 25, 2008

Warden Ralph Logan, a man the inmates used to call Idi Amin for his stern attitude, had an epiphany one day while entering the Eastern Correctional Institution in Westover, Maryland.

He saw a little 5- or 6-year-old girl wearing a beautiful Sunday-best pink dress, who was obviously there to visit her incarcerated father. As she stepped up to go through the metal detector, Logan watched as she automatically reached up to take off the religious medals hanging around her neck.

Logan said: "I thought to myself, this little thing knows how to clear a metal detector! What are we doing when our babies know this -- and do it without even being prompted!?" Right then and there, he told himself things had to change to make real rehabilitation work.

In prisons across the country, as many as 75 percent of the inmates are parents. Some won't admit it. Men fear their failure to have paid child support will add time to their sentences. Women fear the welfare system will take away their kids forever. So estimates of how many kids they left behind vary tremendously -- from 2 million to 10 million American children.

Imagine millions of kids growing up with the stigma of a criminal parent. Study after study reports these kids are often profoundly affected. They suffer from combinations of shame, anxiety, fear, sadness, low self-esteem or aggressive behavior. Their grades often suffer, they can become antisocial, join gangs and many turn to drugs or alcohol. The number is in dispute, but various reports conclude these children are 7 to 10 times more likely than other kids to enter the criminal justice system themselves.

A weekend for most youngsters means sports or cheerleading practice or going to the movies. But for these kids it all too often means getting on a bus or cramming into a car along with others to visit a parent in prison. The worst part is, they think it's normal.

Back before the events of Sept. 11, 2001, rocked our nation, Warden Logan teamed up with the Urban Family Institute to adopt a program called Salisbury's Promise. Logan and UFI founder Kent Amos believed in the program so deeply they cobbled together government and corporate funding to make it a reality.

The college-designed curriculum was intended to nurture the kids, to give them quality study and face time with their incarcerated parent. The program kit provided age-appropriate interaction cards to guide both parent and child in reading, studying and social skills -- a different take-away card for every day so the lessons continued in between the one-on-one visits.

Logan says that the misbehavior rate among participating inmates "went down to almost nothing," because they didn't want to be frozen out of this precious time with their children. And the prison itself was made more hospitable to visiting children and their mothers. Kids left with smiles on their faces instead of tears.

It was a program that truly made a difference and was practiced in at least 24 facilities nationwide. But funding dried up after 9/11.

The good news is that today programs like this are cropping up at prisons all over America, helping both the criminal and the child see that the future is worth planning for.

The Justice Department and the Girl Scouts of America initiated a mother-daughter visitation program called Beyond Bars that now operates in 37 prisons, servicing hundreds of young girls and their mothers. One chapter in Ohio takes girls to visit their incarcerated fathers, too.

The Boy Scouts of America aren't so active, but there's a troop in Gig Harbor, Washington, that takes boys to visit their moms at the women's prison there. Daughters also get visitation during what are, in effect, troop meetings behind bars.

The Peanut Butter and Jelly program in Albuquerque, New Mexico, not only delivers children to see their incarcerated parents but also offers the kids therapeutic counseling before and after the visit.

In New York, the Osborn Association gets private donations to put kids and parents together even if it means flying children to far-flung state prisons. Lutheran services in Pennsylvania set up video visitations so children can see their parents while talking to them on the phone.

These programs don't cost much money; many services are donated. It's all about thinking outside the box. They are win-win ideas. The child gets real-life lessons in right and wrong while keeping the parental bond. The inmate learns discipline and the pleasure of accountability and parenting skills. Sometimes there are disappointments but these pairs often form a new union and goals for the future.

It's all about helping people step up to the plate and be responsible for their actions. Maybe once they learn to do that the generational revolving door at our prisons will slow down.

Halloween Harassment Campaigns Must End

Oct. 20, 2012

Here we go again. Law enforcement officers nationwide are about to stage their annual pre-Halloween effort to make sure everyone listed on the local Sex Offenders Registry knows (imagine this being said in a spooky, Vincent Price-like voice with a scary laugh at the end) THEY ARE BEING WATCHED!

This annual charade is also supposed to help the community feel safer. I'm here to tell you it is nonsense.

The intimidation campaign is a silly diversion of manpower and a waste of your tax dollars. Police and the politicians who are in search of tough-on-crime votes will tell you otherwise, but don't believe the myth that Halloween is the night child sexual predators wait all year for. The facts tell a different story.

Those on the registry -- convicts who have done their time and are trying hard to blend back into the population -- will likely get a personal visit from officers. Depending on the state in which they live, they may be told that they must stay home Halloween night, that they must keep their lights off and not answer the door. Many will be required to display a sign that reads something like "No Candy at This Residence."

There could be other restrictions, too: no holiday decorations outside the home; no dressing up in costume; no attending holiday parties, haunted houses, hay rides or any other Halloween activity where children gather.

Now, let's look at the facts. Over the last several decades, there has not been one reported instance I can find of a convicted sex offender molesting a child on Halloween night. Shall I repeat that? Despite all the hysteria, I couldn't find evidence of even one case. Furthermore, a huge majority of these convicts never reoffend. The only Halloween tragedy my research turned up was back in 1973 in Milwaukee, Wisconsin, where a little 9-year-old girl who was trick-or-treating by herself went to the home of a stranger named Gerald Turner. Turner, a man with no criminal record, raped and killed the child. Using today's guidelines, Turner wouldn't even warrant a visit, since he was not a known molester.

Fact: Our sex registry system is foolish. It lumps in everyone who ever mooned or streaked or urinated in public with hardcore career pedophiles. A registrant may have been a teenager caught with a girlfriend in the back seat, the victim of a vindictive ex-wife who made abuse allegations or a man who legitimately believed his partner was over 18.

Whether they are a public urinator or Jerry Sandusky, they all occupy the same space on our misguided registry. And in four states -- California, Alabama, South Carolina and Florida -- once placed on the list, the offender is there for the rest of their lives.

Anyone with half a brain knows it is the dedicated pedophile -- that person who will always choose a child for sex over an adult partner -- whom we should spend our time watching. So why aren't we?

Fact: No matter what you've heard, sex offenders rarely repeat their crimes. Studies by Dr. Jill Levenson (funded by the U.S. Department of Justice) have concluded the recidivism rate for sex-related convicts is about 5 to 5.3 percent. That is a whole lot lower than the recidivism rate for burglars, robbers, murderers and those who commit assault or drive drunk. Yet none of them are restricted in how they can live their lives after the justice system is done with them.

In my opinion, every time an officer hassles a registrant around Halloween, they are violating that person's civil rights. These people are already severely restricted on where they can live, work, worship and seek entertainment. Their home address and past crimes are listed on the internet for all to see. What will the pols and the police think up next? How about curbing their movements around July 4 or Christmastime?

California attorney Janice Bellucci has just filed suit to stop Simi Valley, California, from enforcing its new ordinance mandating Halloween harassment. The suit claims the law "suppresses and unduly chills protected speech and expression."

Bellucci, the wife of a minister, became interested in the issue after her longtime plumber wrote a book, "We're All in This Together" by Frank Lindsay, about his experience as a sex registry lifer.

"When I read it, I was shocked," Bellucci told me on the phone. "So shocked that any group in our society would be treated that way."

Bellucci worked with rape victims for years, so she sees both sides of the problem. But she filed suit on behalf of 10 registrants and their family members because "people naturally like to commit mischief on Halloween," she said. "I fear someone could see that sign outside their front door and set the (registrant's) house on fire ... or shoot a gun into the home."

She's hoping the California court will act in time to strike down the law before the end of October. The fact is, worried parents and police should be watching everyone on Halloween, not just one segment of the population that statistically is so unlikely to commit a crime. To do otherwise puts our children in danger. How about diverting manpower to check for drug dealers or drunk drivers careening through darkened neighborhoods full of costumed kids?

Think about this. These Halloween laws are really no different than isolating segments of the population and branding them with a scarlet "A" as an adulterer or with a Star of David as a Jew. Shame on us. It is time to declare these Halloween laws for what they are: unconstitutional.

Grant Edward Snowden Amnesty Now

Dec. 21, 2013

As any member of organized crime will tell you, it is best to "Keep your enemies close to you." Why no one in the Obama administration has latched on to that concept while contemplating the Edward Snowden National Security Agency scandal is beyond me.

Snowden is, of course, the former NSA computer analyst who fled the country with about 1.7 million classified documents proving that America has been involved in a massive telephone and Internet surveillance campaign.

Snowden has released some 200,000 documents so far, and the world has learned that the U.S. routinely scoops up the phone data and Internet traffic of millions of Americans who are not suspected of any crime. There are separate U.S. spying programs abroad with such tremendous reach that they have even targeted the personal cellphones and emails of heads of state. Two of the victims, Brazilian President Dilma Rousseff and German Chancellor Angela Merkel have asked the United Nations Human Rights Counsel to investigate America's actions.

After the initial document dump, Snowden has been cooling his heels in Russia. It's ironic, I think, that the man who declared America's surveillance programs violated human rights would land in a country with a far-worse record on the issue. The Russians took him in for a year only after he promised to temporarily stop releasing any more classified information.

After six months living in what is surely a 24/7 surveillance atmosphere, Snowden is indicating he's thinking about moving on. At least 20 countries have denied his asylum request, but he recently penned an open letter to the country of Brazil, perhaps hoping that their offended president might change her mind and approve his sanctuary request.

"American Senators tell us that Brazil should not worry, because this is not 'surveillance,' it's 'data collection,'" Snowden wrote. "They say it is done to keep you safe. They're wrong. These programs were never about terrorism: They're about economic spying, social control and diplomatic manipulation. They're about power."

And Snowden made clear his determined mindset: "I will not be the one to ignore criminality for the sake of political comfort. I would rather be without a state than without a voice."

This makes Snowden a formidable foe. He doesn't care about his own fate. He is an ideologue whose only goal is to continue to reveal the contents of the remaining 1.5 million classified documents he took with him.

It's time to staunch the damaging flow of secret information. During this temporary hiatus in Snowden's revelations, it is time for the brain trust in Washington, D.C., to come up with an amnesty package for Snowden and get him back on American soil.

Even the chief of the NSA's investigation into the scandal seems to agree. Richard Ledgett told "60 Minutes" he is extremely worried about highly classified documents not yet made public and that amnesty for Snowden, "is worth having a discussion about."
Naturally, there would have to be strict conditions such as securing the remainder of the secret documents and positively confirming there were no copies made.

This will be difficult because federal prosecutors have charged Snowden with several felony counts, including some under the Espionage Act.

Any defense lawyer worth his or her salt would insist the charges be reduced or dropped before Snowden would consider returning. They may demand a presidential pardon or other far-reaching immunity. Maybe the feds could offer a protective custody deal where Snowden remains under guard for a pre-determined period of time while details of the document recovery are worked through.

Another problem? Snowden surely won't want to keep silent. He craves a public discussion about what he sees as the illegal actions of U.S. intelligence agents. And if the feds are smart, they will want to question him about how he achieved the theft of all those classified files. How about granting Snowden closed-door conversations with select members of Congress? Lawmakers who have felt lied to by NSA officials would jump at the chance to question the man.

Yes, Snowden would ultimately be allowed to walk free. But isn't that the price we should pay for recovery of America's most top-secret information?

There have been terrible miscalculations made about Snowden. He has proven he is smarter and craftier than our entire intelligence community. He quietly conceived and then carried out his plan; he deftly escaped the reach of American law enforcement and expertly began to reveal what he had learned through pre-selected media. Snowden has engineered a protective sphere around himself designed to help him release more of the incriminating information he took with him. It is safe to assume he has deposited computer drives containing the documents somewhere accessible to friendly reporters.

Some view Snowden as the ultimate traitor, someone never to be negotiated with. Others see him as a selfless patriot who was compelled by his conscience to reveal the unconstitutional actions of his government. Indeed, a federal judge recently ruled that the NSA's daily habit of collecting virtually every American's phone records is likely unconstitutional. In 2010, another federal judge ruled the NSA's warrantless wiretaps were illegal.

I say it's time to do something other than wait for Snowden to come in out of the cold.

America is strong enough to withstand past bad deeds. We have re-examined sanctioned actions, such as slavery and World War II Japanese internment camps, and we've come out stronger on the other side of the discussions.

If Washington played it right, granting Snowden amnesty and engaging in an open dialogue about what has occurred could be used as an incredibly poignant mea culpa to the rest of the world.

There are only two alternatives here: Allow Snowden to remain at large, free to release more of America's secrets, or grant him amnesty.

I vote for the "Keep your enemies close to you" solution.

Why The Erosion of Public Trust?

Jan. 11, 2014

If you robbed a bank and got caught, you would go to jail. If you waited in the getaway car while your cohort robbed the bank, you would go to jail as an accomplice, right? Of course you would. That's what the law mandates.

So how come after a bank stands mute as customers are robbed it gets "deferred prosecution?"

I ask these questions after this week's decision by the feds to merely fine JPMorgan Chase for failing to report their very real suspicions about mega-fraudster Bernard Madoff. No criminal charges, no one is held responsible and faces jail time -- just $2.5 billion in fines and penalties for an organization that experts say will likely make as much as $23 billion in profit this year.

Under the settlement agreement, announced by the U.S. Attorney in Manhattan, New York, any criminal charges were deferred for two years -- and maybe forever, if the bank keeps its nose clean. All JPMorgan had to do was admit it's bad conduct, pay the fine and agree to strengthen its anti-money laundering policies.

JPMorgan immediately issued a statement saying, "We recognize we could have done a better job pulling together various pieces of information and concerns about Madoff from different parts of the bank." Really?

Pulitzer Prize-winning business reporter Michael Hiltzik, writing in the Los Angeles Times, declared that the JPMorgan admission "resembles hay after it's been passed through the digestive system of a horse." Hiltzik also believes JPMorgan has rewritten the history of what it knew about Madoff's criminal practices -- and when it knew it.

"JPMorgan, where Madoff kept his major bank accounts and which profited handsomely off its relationship in numerous ways, knew Madoff was crooked. Bank executives had him figured out ... early," Hiltzik wrote.

Look, I don't know much about high finance. But let's review some facts about what JPMorgan did -- and didn't do -- after it had reason to believe Madoff was a conman of mammoth proportions.

Keep in mind the Bank Secrecy Act of 1970 requires banks to file what's called "suspicious activity reports" with federal regulators if they think a customer is dealing in ill-gotten gains. JPMorgan consistently stayed mum about its Madoff concerns, and under the law that is a felony.

In Oct. 2008, the bank's branch in London apparently saw great financial doom looming and finally registered their concerns about Madoff with British regulators. While required to file the same report in the U.S., JPMorgan did not. Over the next few weeks, the bank quietly withdrew some $300 million of its own money invested in various Madoff funds. By December, Madoff was in handcuffs, paraded as a master Ponzi perp before his horrified investors -- and the world.

In other words, JP Morgan never lifted a finger to help protect clients, but when it came to protecting itself against risk, bank executives made sure they were ahead of the curve.

JPMorgan executives likely consider the just-imposed $2.5 billion fine as simply the cost of doing business.

Over the last year the organization has agreed to pay out a collective $20 billion for various serious banking violations.

Imagine if you robbed a bank of, say, $1 million, and prosecutors agreed to let you pay $1,000 to make the criminal charges go away. Being able to pay away your crimes would never happen with an individual, but when it comes to financial institutions, the legal playing field is suddenly different. Why is that?

Because our Department of Justice says that's OK.

Remember the days when prosecutors actually came to the aid of cheated investors to punish those responsible? The days when charlatan convicts actually went to prison and names like Mike Milken, Ivan Boesky, Jeffery Skilling and Charles Keating made the news?

Today, swindlers like former Countrywide Financial Services CEO Angelo Mozilo -- a man widely considered to have been a kingpin of the sub-prime mortgage crisis -- can walk away from the financial messes they create by simply opening up their fattened wallets. Mozilo was four days away from the opening of his criminal fraud trial when the Security and Exchange Commission suddenly dropped the charges in exchange for his payment of a $67.5 million fine.

That's justice? Is it any wonder so many Americans have grown distrustful of both the federal government and big institutions? This is why so many citizens have come to believe that there are two justice systems in this country -- one for the average citizen and one for those with money and connections.

While watching the U.S. attorney's news conference announcing the latest settlement, I couldn't help but notice not one word was said regarding the federal government's failure to monitor Madoff's years-long misdeeds. Certainly the bank was wrong. But where had the SEC, the FBI and other government agencies been all those years that Madoff was scamming people? If someone as blatant as Madoff slipped through the cracks, how many other financial fraudsters are operating unnoticed today?

There seems to be no end to the number of fingers of blame that can rightfully be pointed. Yet, hardly anyone has been held personally responsible for the myriad of financial crimes we've seen over the last few years.

U.S. District Court judge Jed Rakoff recently wrote a brave essay about Wall Street's watchdogs. Rakoff, who has an expertise in securities law, wrote that exacting fines and promises to do better from institutions is "little more than window dressing," and he lambasts the shift in DOJ policy toward negotiating with companies.

"Companies do not commit crimes," the judge wrote. "Only their agents do ... So why not prosecute the agent who actually committed the crime?"

Is anyone at the Justice Department listening?

When Do We Listen to the Experts on Drugs?

Sept. 22, 2014

Here's a riddle: How many knowledgeable people does it take to suggest a policy change before society adopts their sage advice?

Buried in all the recent news about ISIS, horrific weather lashing the United States, the violence of NFL players and the like came a hardly noticed news item about the idea of legalizing drugs.

Now, stay with me on this. It's important.

The Global Commission on Drug Policy, an illustrious panel including former U.N. Secretary Gen. Kofi Annan, former U.S. Secretary of State George Shultz, former chairman of the U.S. Federal Reserve Paul Volcker, former presidents and prime ministers of nearly a dozen countries and others issued a detailed study about why it's smart -- for reasons both humanitarian and financial -- to legalize marijuana and other drugs.

Yes, all drugs.

Maybe it's time to consider their suggestion.

After all, our decades-long war on drugs has been a miserable failure. Actions to curb drug production and violence in other countries and along our border have obviously not worked. Over the last 40 years, countless billions of dollars have been spent trying to corral the scourge, and the result is more drug addicts than ever before. Our prisons are overflowing with dealers and addicts. Yet the supply and demand keeps flowing and growing.

So how long do we keep doing what obviously doesn't work?

The Commission's study has several main recommendations and one guiding goal: The "health and welfare of mankind," including widespread access to essential medicines and pain control. The idea being, I surmise, that patients in pain often graduate to the ranks of full-fledged addicts. Help them early and they don't graduate.

The Commission calls for an end to the criminalization and incarceration of low-level users, instead diverting the money we spend on court costs and prisons to treatment strategies. And to undermine the massive profits of organized crime the panel recommends, law enforcement specifically target top-level criminals and the most violent organizations. In other words, cut off the head of the snake instead of worrying about its tail, as we so often do today.

Governments are called upon to totally rethink their drug problem and not be afraid of new ideas.

Gee, it sounds so simple.

This isn't the first distinguished bunch of thinkers to put forward these suggestions.

In 2002, an influential group of American law enforcement professionals, including police chiefs, high court judges and lawyers, got together to formulate better ways to handle the drug plague in America.

They formed Law Enforcement Against Prohibition, which has already advocated many of the Commission's ideas, and believes prohibition of drugs is at the center of the problem. Remove the ban, LEAP's leaders say, and you remove both the colossal profit motive and the violence inflicted upon those who get in the way of the cartels. In the process, you've eased the burden on police departments, overcrowded prisons and families whose breadwinners are behind bars.

"We believe that by placing drug abuse in the hands of medical professionals instead of the criminal justice system, we will reduce rates of addiction and overdose deaths," says LEAP's mission statement. "We believe that in a regulated and controlled environment, drugs will be safer for adult use and less accessible to our children."

Can all these people who have stared the drug problem in the face and now advocate decriminalization be wrong? They have lived, breathed and been part of the system that was designed to find solutions. How can we ignore their learned advice?

Oh, there are plenty of outstanding questions about these revolutionary suggestions. If drugs are legalized, regulated and taxed by governments, won't there still be a black market for those who don't want to be tracked by Uncle Sam? Isn't there the risk of creating another bloated government entity? Would hardcore drugs like heroin and meth be available, or would substitutes be offered? How can we know if more money, time and expertise will really be dedicated to treating addicts?

I don't know the answer to all these questions, but several states have already taken the step of legalizing marijuana, and the gates of hell have not opened. Locking up millions of addicts with the hope that the suppliers will dry up hasn't worked. So, how long do we keep hitting our heads against the wall with zero positive results?

Doing the same thing over and over is, to me, the definition of stupidity.

I say it's way past time to seriously consider alternatives.

What Glorifying Football Says About Us

Oct. 27, 2014

This question is going to sound like blasphemy to some, but here goes: Why do we glorify the game of football and its players the way we do?

I'm not really an NFL fan, but I occasionally watch games with my husband. I can take it or leave it, but I know there are millions of others who live breathe and eat the game. But why?

In the aftermath of yet another round of NFL scandals, I've been thinking about what the game of football and the fallout from its disgraces really says about us. I wonder what football's influence has done to generations of America's boys.

Kids as young as six suit up for Pee Wee league games and are taught that winning equals aggression and is rewarded with cheers and praise. Older boys who play football are the idolized the "big men on campus," their heads often filled with dreams of playing for the pros. If their parents and coaches fail to instill real life lessons of good character along with the rules and strategies of the game, all the kid may come away with is the idea that violence is acceptable and steroids may be just the thing to help them achieve their dream.

Take the group of high school players in Sayreville, New Jersey, who became so pumped up on their own self-importance that they viciously set upon freshmen in their darkened locker room and then sexually attacked them. The boys called it hazing. The cops called it felony assault.

Criminal complaints against college football players happen nationwide. They range from public drunkenness to discharge of a firearm and sexual assault. There has been a scandal brewing at Florida State University where players have been accused of domestic violence, auto theft and rape among other charges. According to The New York Times, "Investigations have stalled, and players have escaped serious consequences."

Coaches, police and judges frequently look the other way as player transgressions pile up. If and when punishment is meted out it often seems far more lenient than regular folks get.

These kids get the idea that just because they can play a ball game, they get to live life outside the law.

Indeed, the NFL players they watch on nationally televised games each week (now airing on Sunday, Monday and Thursdays) often seem to get away with thumbing their nose at the law.

Since 2000, dozens of NFL players have been arrested for drunk driving, and on at least three occasions people have died as a result.

Pro players have assaulted strangers, their lovers and even their children as seen in the recent case of Minnesota Vikings' Adrian Peterson, who bloodied his four-year-old with a wooden switch. Many fans seemed to buy the star running back's excuse that he had only disciplined the child the way he had been disciplined as a boy. As if that made it OK. Pending felony child abuse charges apparently weren't sobering enough for Peterson. He showed up for a court date and was forced to admit (right before a random drug test) that he had just smoked marijuana.

And everyone who follows the NFL knows that the Baltimore Ravens' Ray Rice dodged charges after he sucker-punched his fiance, knocking her like a noodle into an unconscious heap. Only after two damning videos surfaced and the public outcry became unbearable did the NFL Commissioner indefinitely suspended Rice from the game.

More recently, Joseph Randle of the Dallas Cowboys -- a dude who earns $495,000 a year -- was arrested for inexplicably shoplifting cologne and a package of underwear. The upshot? After quickly posting a small bond, his spin team cooked up a PR stunt with MeUndies, an underwear company that announced a deal in which the admitted thief would donate $15,000 worth of clothing to needy kids.

Are these players stupid, or do they simply believe there are no consequences?

The game of football can, of course, be a great tool to instill discipline and teamwork in young males. And the majority of NFL players are good and wholesome citizens. But what I worry about is that this billion-dollar-a-year industry has polluted our young males' idea of what it is to be a man. I worry about the culture of professional football and how it has infused so many of us with the ability to look the other way and shrug when crimes occur.

Like I said, this will be blasphemous to some, but I hope it spurs some deep thought about what the game of football has wrought.

An Open Letter to Camille Cosby

Jan. 5, 2015

I have finally had enough of the smarmy sexual revelations swirling around Bill Cosby.

It's more than the latest reports that Cosby's pitbull private detectives are digging up dirt on women who have accused him of sexual assault. It's what this whole sordid mess says about us: We, the fawning fans, who have ignored for years the growing number of females who claimed they were drugged and raped by the comedian.

It was easier to cling to the idea that Cosby was just like his charming Dr. Heathcliff Huxtable character than it was to accept that he might be a sexual predator.

I'm increasingly embarrassed for his wife, Camille, who recently issued a cringeworthy public statement professing her undying love and insinuating that Bill Cosby, who's 77, is the victim of a mysterious conspiracy involving the media and nearly 30 women who now claim they were sexually violated by her famous husband.

I feel compelled to write this open letter.

Dear Mrs. Cosby,

Let's look at reality, my dear. As you approach your 51st wedding anniversary, I suggest you drop the defend-at-all-costs attitude and count the ways your man has let you down.

The publically admitted extramarital activity, the admission that besides the five children he had with you he may very well have had a daughter with a mistress in the early 70s. Your husband sent weekly $750 checks to the woman for years. She now joins a chorus alleging the same modus operandi: After being invited by a celebrity to a private meeting, her drink was spiked, she passed out, and upon awakening realized she had been raped. Like the others, she didn't report it because she was convinced no one would ever believe her.

This husband of yours, I'm sad to say, has heaped shame on your doorstep.

Didn't you wonder when the first lawsuit was filed in 2005? It wasn't just one woman's allegations. Thirteen other women signed on to testify against your husband. Weren't you suspicious when the case was settled out of court? Did you ever wonder what those 13 other women might have said, under oath, from the witness box?

You married the "love of your life" in January 1964.

The earliest allegation goes back to 1967; a woman who says she was just 15 when Cosby grabbed her at a party and forcibly kissed her. He would have been 30 then and riding high after several top-selling comedy albums and starring in the acclaimed TV adventure series "I-Spy."

In 1971, an actress says your husband forced her to perform a sex act on him in a Tonight Show green room; a nurse says that in 1976 Cosby drugged and raped her. In the mid-80s, another woman claims that after having coffee with the man who would be dubbed "America's favorite Dad" she groggily awoke in a car, her bra undone, her blouse untucked, wondering what in the world had happened.

The list goes on and on with shockingly similar tales. The latest allegation stems from an alleged incident in 2008 -- two years after your husband reached that out-of-court settlement. Is everyone lying?

Do you see a pattern here, Mrs. Cosby? Or do you buy the idea espoused by your husband's legal team that it is all "utter nonsense" and a "media-driven feeding frenzy?" And what about the impression your husband left when he told Stacy Brown, an African-American reporter, "I only expect the Black media to uphold the standards of excellence in journalism ... go in with a neutral mind." Do you believe your husband's troubles are because of racist white journalists?

Please don't tell me, Mrs. Cosby, that you actually buy the idea that all these women are after your husband's money. Only a couple of them filed lawsuits since the one in 2005 was settled. One who said she was raped when she was 15 after your husband snuck her into the Playboy Mansion. Another accuser filed a defamation claim only after your husband's attack-dog attorney called her a liar. I'd call that a self-inflicted problem.

You may think this is all a big mistake that can be rectified by attacking the accusers, but cancellations of Cosby performances by networks, theatres, universities and withdrawn honors from the U.S. Navy tell another story. The word "rapist" scrawled across your husband's star on the Hollywood Walk of Fame gives you a stark glimpse at the public's opinion.

Mrs. Cosby, tell your husband to come clean with you. And call off the lawyers and detectives. Otherwise, you might find yourselves in a very public courtroom.

Office Surveillance: Are You a Target?

July 25, 2015

Is your boss spying on you? There's a good chance. These days, employers are monitoring their workers in all sorts of ways you might never have thought about.

Your employer can look back at anything you've done on your office computer -- check what websites were visited and what was written in interoffice emails, and even capture keystrokes to see what was typed on outside sites, such as your personal email, Facebook or Twitter. If they are the snoopy-snoop type, they're probably already watching your social media output anyway.

Management can also monitor the time spent on a desk phone and the numbers called. They can listen to worker's voicemails, even the deleted ones. And if you drive a company car or use a business cellphone, the boss can tell via built-in GPS systems where you are at any given time and how long you linger.

Supervisors may say the surveillance cameras in your workplace are watching for consumer theft, sabotage or vandalism. But they also capture employees' performance, conversations with customers and with each other. Grouse about the person in charge and run the risk that a supervisor is listening or may hear the conversation later on playback.

You may think, "Well, my boss would never do any of that." You sure about that?

The American Management Association conducts surveys about this kind of activity and reports that 66 percent of the small, medium and large companies responding admitted they monitor employee's Internet use. Forty-five percent log workers' keystrokes, and automation can recreate what was written. Forty-three percent track their staff's emails.

Undercover employer monitoring is widespread. It just makes good business sense if you stop and think about it -- for the company and for you.

Supermarket devices clock how fast cashiers scan groceries. So guess who gets the raise come evaluation time? The best performers, that's who.

Some hospitals require nurses to wear a special badge that registers how often they wash their hands. When the boss disciplines a lax hand washer, employees spread the word and the result is a healthier environment for patients.

A point-of-sale computer system at a restaurant can log more information than just a customer order or their credit card number. It can also keep track of how often a server steers a customer to the special of the day. Again, this is data that could be used to reward the most enthusiastic employees.

But you might wonder if all this surveillance is legal. Yes, it is. Privacy on the job is almost nonexistent, so keep that in mind. The only place recording devices are forbidden is in a locker room, restroom or in areas where union business is being discussed.

Only Delaware and Connecticut require employers to tell workers that they are subject to surveillance. But the aforementioned AMA survey discovered a majority of companies nationwide do inform their employees about their monitoring policies.

Myrna Arias, 36, of Bakersfield, California, was told when she took a sales executive job with the international wire-transfer service Intermex that her movements would be monitored. She was instructed to download an app on her company phone that kept track of her whereabouts. In a lawsuit she filed a few months ago, Arias claims she became uncomfortable with the 24/7 monitoring after her direct supervisor joked that he knew how fast she was driving on any given day. Arias claims she was not allowed to turn off her phone after hours, so she disabled the app and was fired. Now she wants $500,000 for invasion of privacy, wrongful termination and lost wages.

Ms. Arias' test case could change the employer-employee surveillance dynamic, but it seems unlikely she will change the status quo.

In the meantime, businesses determined to weed out slackers and get the most from their staff continue to explore their options. There's no dearth of think tanks and private firms studying what makes a single employee or group of employees more productive.

Sociometric Solutions of Boston is currently testing a new kind of employee ID badge at some 20 different companies. The badge helps gather data on how employees interact with each other. Among other things, they discovered that something as simple as a shared 15-minute coffee break not only fostered better staff interaction but also increased productivity and made employees 70 percent less likely to quit.

As creepy as the boss spying on you sounds, in the end, it is not against the law and it could make for a much more enjoyable place to work.

~~~

CHAPTER 14
Crime and Justice Warriors

"Nothing in this world can take the place of persistence. Talent will not; nothing is more common than unsuccessful people with talent. Genius will not; unrewarded genius is almost a proverb. Education will not; the world is full of educated derelicts. Persistence and determination alone are omnipotent." ~ **President Calvin Coolidge**

There is hardly anything that fascinates me more than a selfless person. They don't "do unto others" because it will gain them fame or fortune. They do it because, as one philanthropic woman energetically explained to me, "I have never had such a full heart. I have found my calling."

When one of these rare human beings comes in contact with the justice system they can, literally, save lives and solve crimes. A child kidnapped by a non-custodial parent is returned, human remains are positively identified, serial killers are unmasked and brought to justice and brave whistleblowers such as Michael Winston risk everything to expose massive white-collar crimes - in his case, at great personal expense.

I am compelled to write about these extraordinary people who work, fight and live to do what they know in their heart is the right thing. I write with great gratitude for all those who occupy this chapter.

The Patron Saint for Missing Kids

Aug. 30, 2008

When Sen. Barack Obama traveled to the Middle East not long ago, he had more than presidential politics on his mind. He was also on a secret mission to help an Illinois constituent get back her four kidnapped young daughters. Obama slipped a note to the Palestinian Prime Minister about Colleen Bargouthi, whose husband had refused to send their girls home after a visit to his family in Palestine. The prime minister said he'd look into it.

Sen. Obama should have turned to my pal, Bazzel Baz.

He's got an unusual name and an even more unusual vocation. He clandestinely rescues missing children that authorities can't find or have given up trying to reunite with their custodial parent.

Baz has long operated in the shadows, but now he's allowing me to publicly reveal his name and tell his story.

Baz is a former CIA agent who takes on the most impossible cases. And he doesn't charge the heartsick family of the missing a penny. With volunteer help from other retired intelligence officers, Baz travels all over the United States and the world, covertly getting in and out of countries some of us can't even pronounce.

His goal is to get children back to where they belong. So far, Baz and the boys have a 100 percent success rate. They've safely brought home 53 children.

Baz, an unmarried man who is a doting uncle to two nieces, founded the Association for the Recovery of Children. Unlike the National Center For Missing and Exploited Children, which recently got $40 million from Washington, D.C., Baz gets no government funds. He pays for his rescue missions out of his own pocket, using his savings or the money he earns from writing Hollywood screenplays.

You can't make up this stuff, folks. Somebody should make a movie about Baz.

Why does he do it? Because, he says, after what he saw happen to children during his days in Special Ops in places like Somalia, Afghanistan and Iran he understands he has unique talents that could make a difference. He knows how to get in and out of a place nearly undetected.

"I should have been dead three times over," he told me. "And now, I have this tradecraft I feel I have to do something meaningful with."

Baz and his operatives work with surgical skill. After carefully studying each case, they quietly move in on the target. They contact local law enforcement and tell them what they are up to. They never go in armed, they don't break any laws. And their average mission time is about 10 days. On average, mainstream law enforcement takes years -- not days -- to return a missing child. That's if they return the child at all.

"Amazing what you can do when you don't have to worry about all the red tape," he told me.

I wondered whether the terrified children ever resist rescue for being afraid of the strange men who've come to help them home. Baz says they're careful not to wear hoods or appear scary in any way.

"Diane, every single child -- when they see us -- they are ready to go," he said. "They just get it."

When Baz and his team went to Costa Rica to rescue 5 1/2-year-old Lily Snyder, whose father and half-brother had kidnapped her from Ketchum, Idaho, Baz's first words were comforting.

"Lily," whispered Baz, "Your mother sent us and she loves you very much." And a calm Lily whispered back, "I know. I've been waiting for you."

As for her father and half-brother? They are back in the States in prison.

75 percent of Baz's efforts are on behalf of mothers who've had their child torn away. Twenty-five percent are fathers who needed help, like the deployed soldier whose wife ran off with another man and took the kids with her. To Baz, every case is a noble cause.

I call him Baz the Magnificent, a sort of patron saint for impossible cases. Only after years of stealth operations has he come around to the notion that he could use some financial help. His Association for the Recovery of Children recently declared nonprofit status, meaning donations are not only welcome but desperately needed.

He said: "I'm looking at four boxes full of cases right now. I know ... 35 kids we could go rescue. We just don't have the money right now."

Does he ever consider charging the parents for his services, at least to cover costs?

"That doesn't sit right with me," he says. "If you take money from a grieving parent you're in it for the wrong reason."

Maybe the National Center for Missing and Exploited Children could send some of that 40 million bucks Bazzel Baz's way?

Blowback for a Whistleblower

Feb. 20, 2010

What would you do if your boss began to do questionable, maybe even criminal, things? Would your paycheck be at the top of your mind, or would you call authorities? What if you worked for a politician and you knew he or she was doing something wrong? Would you speak out?

Such was the dilemma for an impressionable young man named Andrew Young, who worked for former North Carolina Sen. John Edwards. While he believed passionately in his boss's political message, he allowed his loyalty to temporarily blind him. Young admits he did things for Edwards that he now regrets. Some of those things came to the attention of a federal grand jury investigating how Edwards spent campaign money, and Young was called to testify.

After dutifully serving the senator for more than a decade, Young has written a book that not only tears back the covers on a flagrantly unfaithful John Edwards, it also shines a white-hot light on the type of candidate often attracted to our nation's top offices: arrogant, devoid of character and supremely charming.

Young's book, "The Politician," reveals the ugly truth about how presidential politics works, especially how campaign fundraising -- both on and off the books -- drenches a candidate in so much money it's almost simple for them to spend it on things they shouldn't.

In Edwards' case, it appears he spent plenty on his mistress and their baby.

Young says he wrote the book to clear his reputation and make up for two years of unemployment. During that time, he says, John and Elizabeth Edwards sabotaged his job opportunities, and blamed him for their strained marriage and John's failed 2008 presidential bid.

The truth? John Edwards never had a chance in the race for the White House. He ran a deeply flawed and distracted campaign. As a wealthy man, he lacked credibility when he preached about "the two Americas," the poor vs. the rich. He was eliminated in the primaries.

Now we know what diverted the senator's attention. Young's book reveals a torrid affair Edwards was conducting with a staffer named Rielle Hunter. Young participated in keeping the steamy secret, hiding a pregnant Hunter from the media (and Elizabeth) by moving her to various clandestine locations. Remarkably, Young and his devoted wife, Cheri, even caved to the senator's request for Andrew to claim paternity of the baby.

Among the book's most fascinating claims is how the senator used government-paid aides to do so many personal tasks.

Washington, D.C., staffers were once used, Young writes, to load furniture and personal items into a truck he drove to North Carolina. Elizabeth often gave Young lengthy lists of chores, like helping to build and furnish the Edwards' new mansion, buying their children's Christmas presents or changing light bulbs in the Edwards' beach house. And Young was expected to make sure there was always chilled Chardonnay in the pick-up vehicle for the senator to sip.

As for funding "Operation Hide Hunter," Young's book details how massive amounts of cash, travel and housing from wealthy donors was used to keep Mistress Rielle in credit cards and luxury residences. Evidently, Edwards didn't pay a personal penny toward that. His cancer-stricken wife Elizabeth, reportedly, kept too close a watch on their personal accounts for that to happen.

There are many layers to this saga, including how Elizabeth bought the false story of Young being the baby's father and the savage campaign she waged against the Youngs. She left several chilling voicemails for Cheri. "This is not Andrew's first woman. ... We wash our hands of this filth."

Now that John has copped to paternity, Elizabeth has kicked him to the curb. She's not apologized to the Youngs.

And then there's the sex video Rielle made with the senator and carelessly left behind with Young and his family.

Backed by a team of high-priced lawyers, Rielle recently went to court to get Young to relinquish the video and other incriminating evidence she'd abandoned. He did so, but as I watched the proceedings it became clear Hunter's lawyers are out to destroy Andrew Young. They branded him a liar and demanded he be charged with perjury. The judge refused.

I'd like to know who is paying the unemployed Rielle Hunter's considerable lawyer fees. I suspect the money trail might lead to either John or Elizabeth Edwards. They may be angry at each other, but they are surely over-the-top furious with the embarrassing secrets spilled in "The Politician." The book spells the end to Edwards' political career.

As for whistleblower Andrew Young? This preacher's son may have come to the table of full disclosure late, but he's there, sitting tall, showing us how the game of national politics can become twisted and repulsive. We should pay attention to what this impressive man tells us.

I'm sure that federal grand jury did, and I can't wait to hear its verdict.

The Re-Composer of the Decomposed

Aug. 6, 2011

A man died recently that I want you to know about. He operated in the shadow of law enforcement, and you probably never heard his name. In his own very unique way, he developed an expertise that helped bring justice to those who would otherwise never get it.

His name was Frank Bender, and when he died recently, at the age of 70 at his home in Philadelphia, Pennsulvania, he was the best known of a rare breed of forensic sculptors.

Bender somehow knew how to take a fleshless mummified human skull and reconstruct its face into an eerily perfect facsimile. To compare a photo of the dead person with a finished, Bender's sculpture would take your breath away.

Bender started his career as a commercial photographer and had an innate curiosity about human anatomy. That lead the young Bender to visit the Philadelphia morgue, and he came away with a mysterious talent that would become sought after by law enforcement officials worldwide.

He reverently began each reconstruction by focusing on and minutely measuring certain points of the skull. Bender was then able to calculate how thick the tissue, muscles and skin would have been at any given point. Working with tissue-thin layers of clay, he painstakingly followed the unique bone structure of each skull and, as Bender once explained his process to a USA Today reporter, his fingers just "take over" and he "becomes" his subject.

His finished projects were stunning renditions of the forgotten dead seemingly brought back to life. Once released to the public, Bender's work brought in tips that helped identify dozens of discarded bodies that might have gone to unmarked graves had it not been for his efforts. Over the years, his work helped solve numerous murders and serial killings, and led to the arrest of high-profile fugitives.

Bender first reconstructed skulls for the Philadelphia Police Department, and when word of his success spread, he was called upon to help departments in other states. Then the FBI came calling, followed by Scotland Yard and the government of Egypt, and in Mexico his work identifying the remains of a string of murdered woman became the basis for a book called "The Girl With the Crooked Nose."

His most publicized reconstruction came in 1989 and originated not from a skull but an old photograph. Police in Westfield, New Jersey, had long been looking for a mild-mannered accountant named John List who was wanted for the 1971 murders of his wife, three children and mother.

The television program "America's Most Wanted" commissioned Bender to craft a sculpture of what List would look like 18 years after the crime. He created an age-progressed jowly bald headed bust, and because he thought an aging accountant might wear glasses, Bender plopped a pair of black horned-rimmed glasses on it. The glasses did the trick.

A woman in Virginia watching the program called the tip line to report her neighbor, an accountant named Robert Clark. A fingerprint check quickly revealed the man was really fugitive List. Sentenced to five life terms, List died in prison in 2008.

One of Bender's most notable reconstructions was on the skull of a young woman found near a stream in Boulder, Colorado, in 1954. Working with the Vidocq Society, a group of professional crime fighters who tackle cold cases (which he helped establish in 1990), Bender used his unexplainable sixth sense to reconstruct her face.

He also told investigators the victim had blonde hair and blue eyes. How could he possibly know that, they wondered? Fifty-five years after her remains were found, she was finally identified as 18-year-old Dorothy Gay Howard. A family portrait confirmed she was a stunning blonde with sky blue eyes.

Bender never made much money for his efforts. In the end, one of his meticulous creations brought in about $1,700. He worked as a fine artist and did various other odd jobs to help pay the bills.

Bender never discriminated over which skull to rebuild, but he had a passion to help solve crimes against children. Ted Botha, the author of the aforementioned book, was quoted in a New York Times obit saying the diminutive Bender was "a fighter for justice. He's almost like a little Captain America or something."

His last reconstruction, created while he was dying of mesothelioma, came on the skull of a young boy found discarded in high grass along a North Carolina roadway. The 10-year-old's skeleton was still wearing tube socks and brand new sneakers. In his pocket were neatly folded bills totalling $50.

The sculptor told a North Carolina newspaper why he had to make this his last work of art. "A child is so innocent," Bender explained. "They have a whole life ahead, and it's taken away. It all bothers me, but they bother me the most."

No, you probably never heard of Frank Bender before now, but as he playfully identified himself on the outgoing message of his home answering machine, he was indeed "a re-composer of the decomposed." A crimefighter par excellence.

Remembering Forgotten Vets

Sept. 28, 2012

For this Band of Brothers, the Vietnam War never ended. Forty years after the fighting stopped they continue their struggle to be recognized as part of the unenviable group poisoned by the deadly herbicide Agent Orange.

These men who dedicated years to the U.S. military were stationed at Andersen Air Force Base in Guam. In the mid-60s it was an important stopover on the way to war zones in Southeast Asia. B-52 bombing missions targeting the Viet Cong -- with names like Operation Arc Light and Operation Linebacker II -- were launched from Andersen. Two years after the conflict, the base became a way-stop for more than 100,000 Vietnamese refugees seeking a new life in America.

Andersen AFB was a well-oiled machine, thanks to the dedicated soldiers stationed there. Two of those men, Master Sergeant LeRoy Foster and Sargent Ralph Stanton, found each other late in life and began to compare their multitude of similar health problems.

MSgt Foster served at Andersen from 1968 to 1978 as a Fuels Specialists assigned to the 43rd Supply Squadron. Part of his duties, he told me, was to get rid of the vegetation and weeds on the base. Foster says Agent Orange, which contains deadly TCDD dioxin, was among the herbicides he regularly mixed and loaded into his 750-gallon, trailer-mounted sprayer. Back then no one knew how deadly it was.

Sgt Stanton worked at Andersen's fuels maintenance shop. He says he remembers the skinny little Foster always driving by, spraying herbicides that left him and his fellow soldiers with a stomachache or headache. Stanton also recalls using discarded 55-gallon Agent Orange barrels to burn off excess fuels. He showed me photographs of an old herbicide drum he had fashioned into a BBQ for cookouts.

Today, both these men, and approximately 270 others once based in Guam, have applied with the Veterans Administration for Agent Orange benefits. Many of their diseases are found on the VA's official list of 15 ailments recognized as being tied to Agent Orange exposure. Among them: Hodgkin's Disease, Parkinson's Disease, prostate or respiratory cancers, soft tissue sarcoma, diabetes mellitus (Type 2), chronic B-cell leukemia, ischemic heart disease and Chloracne, an oily, painful condition of cysts and pustules that erupt on cheeks, arms, chest and groin areas. Although the VA's rules say the benefit of the doubt should always go to the diagnosed veteran, fewer than a dozen Guam-based vets have been granted benefits. Why?

Here's the rub: The Defense Department has long maintained -- and told me again last week -- that there are no surviving records to prove that Agent Orange was ever sent to Guam. No proof, no benefits, except in the case of about nine claimants, including MSgt Foster.

He stands as a modern-day, human Catch-22. The DOD denies he could have been exposed to Agent Orange on Guam, yet the VA has awarded him disability payments specifically tied to the deadly herbicide's effects. Foster never set foot in Vietnam.

MSgt Foster told me he thinks his claim was approved because he's been so vocal. He has sent mountains of compelling research and sad testimonials to Congress. He has testified before House and Senate Veterans Affairs committees in 2010 and again in 2012. He has written directly to President Obama, asking that personnel stationed on Guam be given the automatic benefits awarded to soldiers who had boots on the ground in Vietnam, Laos and Cambodia. Foster told me he is motivated by the overwhelming guilt he feels for spraying the poison at Andersen for so many years.

As I researched this story I discovered that it is not just the veterans who believe Agent Orange was used on Guam. In 2008, the legislature of Guam passed a resolution asking the Congress to include the island on the list of those locations due benefits under the Agent Orange Equity Act saying, "The VA procedures have resulted in an unjustified withholding of benefits for military and civilian workers in staging areas for the Vietnam War such as Guam, through which military personnel, munitions, equipment and supplies -- including herbicides containing Agent Orange --- were shipped." The resolution has been ignored.

A Public Health Report issued by the Agency for Toxic Substances and Disease Registry in 2002 reported that water and dioxin soil contamination at Andersen AFB was an astronomical 19,000 parts per million. The EPA puts the safe level at below 1 part per billion. Even today, Andersen remains on the EPA's Superfund contamination list. Currently, there is a population of about 8,000 living at Andersen, with another 5,000 Marines set to be transferred in soon.

I found another compelling outside opinion in financial advisory reports for potential investors in Monsanto and Dow Chemical, two manufacturers of Agent Orange. The 2004 report stated, "Soldiers stationed on Guam who handled Agent Orange have become ill, and symptoms of TCCD (dioxin) poisoning are apparent in the general population of the island as well." Indeed, Guam does have a higher than normal cancer rate, especially rare leukemia-type cancers in children.

The saddest part of this story to me has to do with the birth defects reported in children born to these Andersen vets. Foster says his daughter was a victim, and her child, Foster's granddaughter, was born with 12 toes and fingers and is feared to be autistic. These birth defects mirror what has happened to generations of children born in Vietnam.

The latest Institute of Medicine report on Veterans and Agent Orange says more study is needed on the question of "paternally transmitted effects to offspring."

It has been 40 years, and these vets wonder how much longer it will it take. Many believe the VA is engaged in a program of, "Deny, deny until they die."

I find it hard to argue with that.

The Rise and Fall of a Patriot

Nov. 24, 2012

In 1970, a diminutive 18 year old from rural Cornwall-on-Hudson, New York, traveled 9 miles south from his parent's home and checked in at the front gate at what would be his new residence for the next four years. He had worked hard in high school to get the grades to qualify for this unique place, and in return he had pledged an additional five years of service to the organization.

The young man was David Petraeus, and by walking through the front gate at the U.S. Military Institute at West Point, he committed to spending the next nine years of his life connected to the U.S. Army. By the end of his military career, he had served 37 years and reached the rank of four-star general.

This country invested heavily in developing Petraeus into the successful and well-decorated military leader he became. We spent about a million dollars on his extensive education: West Point, Ranger School, the U.S. Army Command and General Staff College, and in the mid-'80s Princeton University, where he earned both a master's and his Ph.D. in international relations. And during that time, according to military and West Point sources, Petraeus would have been receiving take-home military pay of between $50,000 and $60,000 a year. Low-cost commissary goods and housing (or a housing allowance) was also part of the deal.

Multiply this government support over 37 years, and it is likely America has invested multiple millions of taxpayer dollars for the education, transportation and development of Petraeus.

To be sure, this country got a considerable return on its considerable investment. Among his long list of accomplishments, Petraeus commanded a division that helped liberate Iraq and steered the course for America's exit from the war in Afghanistan.

As we all know, last September Petraeus resigned from the military to become director of the CIA. And then he had a brief extramarital affair that forced him to resign as the nation's top spy.

The CIA director simply cannot compromise national security by allowing outsiders to get close to classified information, say, on his iPhone, laptop computer or briefcase. Even though Petraeus, now 60, was no longer operating under the military law that deems adultery a crime, he had to go. He fell back on the West Point Code of Honor, which states that no cadet will lie, cheat or steal or tolerate anyone who does. Petraeus resigned from the CIA, and it was the right thing to do.

Where I have a problem, however, is the pious and sometimes vicious condemnation of the man. Words like fraud, scum, hypocrite and even traitor have been used repeatedly to describe Petraeus.

Yes, he made a terrible mistake, but let's be honest. He succumbed to the most common and mundane of human weaknesses: a sexual affair with a 30-something woman.

When President Bill Clinton shamed the office by having sexual relations with a young woman not much older than his daughter and didn't have the decency to resign after being impeached for lying about it under oath, I was disgusted. Not so much with Petraeus.

A double standard? No, not really. There is no comparing a career politician to a career military patriot. Both pledged loyalty to America, of course, but in this equation only one has selflessly dedicated his whole life in service to the country.

Retired Major Mike Lyons told me that David and Holly Petraeus moved 22 times in 30 years to keep up with his burdensome reassignments. As a fellow West Point graduate, Lyons is friendly with many inside Petraeus' inner circle. He estimates that during the last six or seven years, Petraeus spent about five years deployed abroad. The entire Petraeus family, according to Lyons, has endured "tremendous instability" on behalf of the country.

Clinton, who deliberately never served a day in the military, seems to me to have been motivated more by his own personal goals and partisan politics. And unlike the head of the CIA, Clinton occupied the highest and most powerful position in the country -- and some would argue in the world.

So for those so quick to condemn a man like Petraeus, who briefly strayed outside his marriage, I have to ask: Shouldn't we consider his whole life? Petraeus' dedication to country for nearly four decades surely must count for something, right?

When I expressed this feeling to a pal of mine, a former U.S. Marine, he sent me an eye-opening email, saying: "Our warriors all understand they are held to a higher standard, and they accept that as a consequence of their service. We don't want people who compromise integrity or make excuses because we also have to rely on these extraordinary warriors to act with uncompromising valor on the battlefield."

He concluded by saying, "Only those who have served understand this, I guess."

Well, I have never served in the military, but several members of my family have. And I remember that awful time after Vietnam when America turned its back on brave warriors and called them names, too. Remember "baby-killers"?

If we respond to momentary lapses of judgment among our career military personnel with invectives like "psychotic" and "egomaniac" (as I heard Petraeus described recently), then where will we find the next generation of 18-year-olds knocking on West Point's front gate?

Let's stop kicking the dog while he's down, shall we?

Sex Trafficking Victim Fights for Justice

May 17, 2013

Danielle Douglas had a wonderful Mother's Day -- breakfast out, a trip to the zoo with her husband and two children, snuggly nap time and the gift of a colorful necklace and brooch.

This New Jersey woman looks like a modern-day young mother. She works at a pharmaceutical company, and in her spare time she experiments with fashion statements, such as different haircuts and hair color, and fanciful makeup to accentuate her beautiful hazel eyes.

But 30-year-old Danielle is far from typical. She is a survivor of human trafficking, victimized during her teen years by a vicious pimp who turned her out as a prostitute in the Boston, Massachusetts, area. Those violent years and how she survived is the subject of an upcoming documentary called "10,000 Men," to be released later this year.

Today, Danielle is a woman with a mission.

On the heels of news about the House of Horrors in Cleveland, where three young women were held as sex slaves, Danielle is pushing for heightened awareness about how pervasive human sex trafficking is, that it is nationwide. For Danielle, words matter.

"We have to start by changing the vocabulary that defines the crime," she told me. And for her, "It all begins with the pimp." For Danielle, that was the man who conned her, imprisoned her in a home with other women, brought in streams of strange men and allowed her only a few supervised phone calls home to her worried family. He lived off her labor.

Recently, Danielle turned to a dictionary to look up the word "pimp" and was floored at the milquetoast, turn-of-the-century definition she found in her Merriam-Webster: "A man who solicits clients for a prostitute."

"This is like a 1920s definition!" she said. "Anyone who works with the problem of human trafficking knows that isn't even close to what a pimp is! ... Nothing about the violence they perpetrate and what they actually do to people," she said with anger in her voice. "I decided, I've got to start a petition about this. ... We have to get real!"

Danielle's online petition calls for Merriam-Webster to understand that "pimps use fear, force and coercion to abduct human beings. They are usually violent and abusive, and can use various tactics to keep the human beings under their control." She asks the dictionary keepers, "How can we expect people to understand sex trafficking when the definition of one of the main aspects is incorrect?"

My repeated messages to Merriam-Webster in Springfield, Massachusetts, were ignored. But Danielle is a determined sort. She told me she finally got past the tape-recorded phone system and got a man in marketing on the phone. She calmly explained that she would like to discuss changing the definition of a word.

"He told me they only change definitions when they aren't current anymore. And 'We decide what needs changing.'" Danielle was told that the brainiacs at Merriam-Webster scour the Internet to study current word usage, and that is what determines whether changes are made.

Gee, a quick Google search, and I was able to find pages of information about physically violent and mentally abusive pimps identified in scholarly human trafficking studies. It took me no time to learn about the Trafficking Victims Protection Act of 2000, which equates pimps to slave owners. Let's not overlook the fact that many pimps sell defenseless children. On the Justice Department website, I found more than 115 recent entries by simply searching the words "Sex trafficking," "pimps" and "children."

The folks at Merriam-Webster may not know the term "pimp" means a lot more than just "a man who solicits clients for a prostitute," but we know. So let's take up the education campaign where the dictionary has faltered.

Armed with the knowledge of what a pimp really is -- a modern-day slave owner of women and children -- let's all do our part to make sure another Cleveland-like situation isn't happening right under our noses. Exact victim numbers are impossible to know, but a recent message from Congress estimates that "Every year as many as 17,500 people are trafficked into the U.S. from over 50 countries." That doesn't even count missing or exploited American citizens.

Obviously, the alleged Cleveland, Ohio, monster, Ariel Castro, 52, was not your run-of-the-mill pimp, but his brutality toward women had been well documented in a string of domestic violence complaints dating back to 1989.

In 2004, police went to his home after he was accused of mistreating a child on his school bus, but no one answered, and police never tried to speak to him at the house again. More recently, when neighbors say they called in a report of seeing a naked woman chained in his backyard, Castro should have already been on law enforcement's radar even though none of the numerous complaints against him ever wound up in court.

Things won't get better until we all get involved. Neighbors: Make it your business to know what's going on at that spooky house down the block. Call police with your suspicions because there is no telling what or who they might find behind those blacked-out windows. Call more than once if you have to.

To law enforcement, I say, please, give more awareness training, so officers don't just stop-and-knock but actually ask to come inside for a routine welfare check in all rooms of the house. And to politicians, I say, how about some tougher anti-pimp laws to ensure it isn't just the prostitute who gets arrested?

And while I've got your attention, why not sign Danielle's petition at www.change.org/petitions/? Words matter, and true definitions enlighten.

UPDATE: On May 23, 2013 Danielle Douglas became victorious! The Merriam-Webster Editorial Department wrote to Danielle and declared: "Thank you for your message regarding the definition of 'pimp.' We agree that the current definition is in need of updating and are researching the matter further. We expect the definition to be changed when the dictionary is next revised. Thank you again for helping to bring this matter to our attention."

Remembering the Dick Tracy of Wichita

Feb. 15, 2014

This is a story about a cop's cop, a hometown kid who devoted his life to keeping his community safe, a man who took on the duty no one should have to do: ministering to the murdered and help seek justice for their families.

This column is dedicated to the late Lt. Ken Landwehr, commander of the homicide unit of the Wichita Police Department, because he epitomizes the determination, integrity and ingenuity that all great detectives possess. His deeds will live on in the annals of America's crime and justice history.

Landwehr was the son of an aircraft worker and a homemaker. He was an Eagle Scout as a boy and devoured books about the investigations of the legendary Sherlock Holmes. He attended Bishop Carroll Catholic High School where he played tricks on the nuns and was no stranger to occasional bouts of brawling and drinking. At Wichita State University, he was, by his own admission, a mediocre student. He thought about joining the FBI but was unsure about his life's path until a fateful day in 1977 when he went to his job at a North Wichita clothing store.

Robbers burst in and hogtied Landwehr, the owner and several customers. As the young college student lay hogtied on the floor, he heard one of the robbers jack a bullet into the barrel of a handgun as he stood over him. Landwehr felt sure he was about to die. Everyone escaped unharmed that day, and that life-changing experience infused him with a deep empathy for victims and gave him a razor-sharp focus for his future.

Landwehr joined the Wichita P.D. the next year, and at the entrance interview, the rookie officer was asked how far he wanted to go in the department.

"I said, 'I want to command homicide,'" Lt. Landwehr told a television reporter years later. "Those victims cannot speak for themselves, so that's probably the only reason why I picked homicide."

His dream would come true, but not before he paid his dues by working in patrol, vice, narcotics, cold cases and finally, in 1987, he made detective in the homicide unit. There, he worked tirelessly, taking each murder case personally.

Over the years, Landwehr had a hand in working and mostly solving some 600 murder investigations. His wife, Cindy, says he felt deeply about each and every case.

His most famous case began in the mid-1980s when Wichita's police chief assigned the impressive young detective to a special task force called "Ghostbusters." The goal was to learn the identity of a serial killer who had murdered nine people and signed his taunting notes to local reporters with the moniker BTK (short for bind-torture-kill).

The investigation would span two decades until it finally went cold. There was one more BTK murder in Jan. 1991, but then the brutality stopped.

Many thought the killer must have died. Landwehr, who was promoted to Commander of Homicide in 1992, always kept his BTK files handy, firmly believing his department would ultimately solve the case.

He was right. Landwehr was at his wife's bedside in March 2004 as she was being prepped for gall bladder surgery when word came that BTK had suddenly resurfaced! After being dormant for all those years, a letter bearing the familiar BTK handwriting had been sent to the local newspaper. The author had included Polaroid photos of a BTK kill to prove his identity.

More communications followed, and Landwehr devised a strategy to play to the killer's ego to keep him engaged. The detective staged a number of news conferences about the investigation, knowing the attention would appeal to the killer's vanity. The pair began private communications via cryptic newspaper ads in a cat-and-mouse game in which Landwehr could feel the noose tightening. When BTK asked if he could be traced if he sent a floppy disc of information to Landwehr, the detective told him it was safe to send it.

It was not. Shortly after police got their hands on the disc, which was delivered to a local TV station, they discovered it had been created on a computer at the Christ Lutheran Church in Wichita by someone named Dennis. Dennis Rader was president of the church council.

When they first came face-to-face in an interrogation room, Rader reportedly confronted the commander about the trickery, asking, "How come you lied to me?"

Lt. Landwehr calmly replied, "Because I was trying to catch you."

Landwehr had been prescient enough to save a very small DNA sample recovered in 1974 from the first murder scene. That DNA was matched to Rader, who confessed to all 10 murders.

Landwehr was diagnosed with advanced kidney cancer just before his 2012 retirement. He died last month at age 59. I write about him because he was a bigger man than just the BTK case.

After his death, colleagues told touching stories of how the gruff and "sometimes blunt and cantankerous" raspy-voiced Landwehr responded to victims.

He once quietly took a victimized boy aside and described "the beauty of heaven" to the child to help soothe his trauma.

When speaking to families of murder victims, he always talked about when -- not if -- the killer would be caught.

In the emergency room bedside of a 5-year-old drowning victim, a detective was brought to tears when Lt. Landwehr suddenly appeared to lay a comforting hand on the child and whisper something in the little dead boy's ear. He then turned to the detective and said: "Touch him. You've got to touch him."

It was a lesson from a veteran homicide detective that a dead body deserves kindness, dignity and justice. It also signaled how much of himself Ken Landwehr gave to his job over the nearly 35 years he served. That compassion and doggedness-to-duty is why the mayor dubbed Landwehr "The Dick Tracy of Wichita."

We should all be so lucky to have such a dedicated detective on our local force. Maybe you do.

A Whistleblower's Worst Nightmare

March 22, 2014

Justice is supposed to be blind. But what happens when it turns out to be blind, deaf and dumb?

Sadly, there is not enough space here to tell you the entire seven-year saga of whistleblower Michael Winston, but the bottom line is this: He got royally screwed by the California judicial system.

Winston, 62, is a mild-mannered Ph.D. and a veteran leadership executive who has held top jobs at elite corporations such as McDonnell Douglas, Motorola and Merrill Lynch. After taking time off to nurse his ailing parents, Winston was recruited by Countrywide Financial to help polish their corporate image. He was quickly promoted -- twice -- and had a team of 200 employees.

It's almost unheard of for a top-tier executive turning whistleblower, but that's what Winston became after he noticed many of his staff were sickened by noxious air in their Simi Valley, California, office. When the company failed to fix the problem, Winston picked up the phone and called Cal-OSHA to investigate. Retaliation was immediate. Winston's budget was cut and most of his staff was reassigned.

Several months later, Winston says he refused Countrywide's request to travel to New York and basically lie to the credit ratings agency Moody's about corporate structure and practices. That was the death knell for Winston's stellar 30-year-long career.

When Countrywide was bought out by Bank of America in 2008 -- following Countrywide's widely reported lead role in the sub-prime mortgage fiasco that caused the collapse of the U.S. housing market -- Winston was out of a job.

In early 2011, after a month-long trial, a jury overwhelmingly found that Winston had been wrongfully terminated and awarded him nearly $4 million. Lawyers for Bank of America (which had assumed all Countrywide liabilities) immediately asked the judge to overturn the verdict. Judge Bert Gennon Jr. denied the request saying, "There was a great deal of evidence that was provided to the jury in making their decision, and they went about it very carefully." Winston and his lawyer maintain they won despite repeated and egregious perjury by the opposition.

Winston never saw a dime of his award, and nearly two years later, B of A appealed. In February 2013, the Court of Appeals issued a stunning reversal of the verdict. The court declared Winston had failed to make his case.

"This never happens ... this isn't legal," Cliff Palefsky, a top employment lawyer in San Francisco, California, told me during a phone conversation: "The appeals court is not supposed to go back and cherry-pick through the evidence the way this court did. And if there is any doubt about a case, they are legally bound to uphold the jury's verdict."

None of the legal eagles I spoke to could explain why the Court of Appeals would do such an apparently radical thing.

The Government Accountability Project, a whistleblower protection group in D.C., has been watching the Winston case closely.

Senior Counsel Richard Condit says that he believes the appeal judge wrongly "nullified" the jury's determination.

"This case is vitally important," Condit told me on the phone. "Seeing what happened to Winston, who will ever want to come forward and reveal what they know about corporate wrongdoings?" GAP and various legal academicians are trying to figure out a way to get Winston's case before the U.S. Supreme Court.

There have been whispers about the possible malpractice of Winston's trial lawyer failing to file crucial documents that might have satisfied the appeal court's questions. His appellate lawyer didn't even tell him when the appeals court was hearing the case and Winston was out of town. The LA district attorney and the Sheriff's Department refused to follow up on evidence that Countrywide witnesses, including founder Angelo Mozilo, had blatantly committed perjury on the stand. Some court watchers speak of the "unholy alliance" between big corporations and the justice system in California.

Winston, who says he spent $600,000 on legal fees, further depleted his savings by appealing to the California Supreme Court. That court refused to hear his case.

During one of our many hours-long phone conversations, Winston told me, "So, here I sit," the whistleblower. The good guy loses. And the bad guys, officials at the corporation that cheated and lied and nearly caused the collapse of the U.S. economy -- win."

There's a lot of talk out of Washington these days about "economic equality." But seven years have passed since the housing crisis, and the feds have not prosecuted one key executive from any of the financial giants that helped fuel the economic crash. Too big to fail. And too big to jail, I guess.

Bank of America has spent upward of $50 billion in legal fees, litigation costs and fines cleaning up the Countrywide mess. Their latest projections indicate they'll spend billions more before it's over.

To my mind, a stiff prison sentence for the top dogs who orchestrated the original mortgage schemes would go much further than agreeing that they pay hefty fines. That's no deterrent to others since they all have lots of money.

A recent email I got from Michael Winston, a proud man who has been unemployed for four years, said: "I have just received (a) court order mandating that I pay to Bank of America over $100,000.00 for their court costs. This will be in all ways -- financial, emotional, physical and spiritual -- painful."

If a top-tier executive can't prevail blowing the whistle on a corrupt company, if the feds fail to pursue prison terms and if a jury's verdict can be overturned without the opportunity to appeal, what kind of signal does that send to the dishonest?

You know the answer. We're telling them it is OK to put profit above everything else. We're telling them to continue their illegal behaviors because there will be no prison time for them. At worst, they may only have to part with a slice of their ill-gotten gains.

This is not the way the justice system is supposed to work.

The For-Hire Soldiers in the Fight for Justice

April 19, 2014

Time for a word about private investigators.

TV dramas of the past left the impression that the primary reason to hire a PI is to tail an unfaithful spouse. There was always the obligatory scene in which a semi-shady-looking private detective appeared with a stack of 8-by-10-inch photos as proof of infidelity and slithered away with a check from the not-so-shocked husband or wife.

Certainly, that is one of the services a PI can provide, but today licensed private detectives are much more valuable than just that.

These days, police departments are too busy, underfunded and undertrained to follow up on every complaint. Corporate espionage, computer hacking, identity theft and missing persons reports abound, and it is the ranks of private investigators that often come to the rescue.

Private detectives can also offer a valuable extra set of eyes when it comes to reviewing old police files and, specifically, working to help those who were wrongfully convicted.

Take the PI team of super-sleuths Bob Rahn and Kim Anklin of Management Resources Ltd. They are the unsung heroes in the recent case of exonerated prisoner Jonathan Fleming, who spent 25 years in prison for a murder he didn't commit.

In August 1989, a man named Darryl Rush was murdered outside a Brooklyn, New York, housing project. Fleming's car was seen speeding away from the scene, and an eyewitness said she saw Fleming. At trial, the jury heard evidence that Fleming was a thousand miles away -- in Orlando, Florida, with his family -- at the time of the murder. His attorney produced airplane tickets, video, photos and hotel and telephone receipts, and several members of the Fleming family testified that Jonathan was with them at Disney World when the murder took place.

But the prosecutor maintained that there were 53 different flights Fleming could have taken back to New York to commit the crime and that he then could have quickly returned to Florida. Despite the fact that no evidence was ever produced showing Fleming took any extra flights, he was convicted and sentenced to 25 years to life in prison.

Fleming's mother never gave up the fight to free her son. Over the years, she hired a couple of different private detectives, who took her money but did little. Finally, last year, the family found the PI team of Rahn and Anklin.

"We took a small retainer for a few weeks' worth of work," Anklin told me.

They started their investigation by poring over a boxful of old legal files, including the original police reports, which revealed solid leads never pursued. Rahn and Anklin visited the crime scene, took measurements and realized the eyewitness could never have seen the murder from her vantage point. After they tracked her down, she admitted she had been high on crack that night and had recanted her statement to police three weeks after the murder.

"We realized pretty quickly that Jonathan didn't do it," Rahn said.

"There just was no physical evidence except that one faulty eyewitness."

The retainer soon ran out, but this dogged team decided it just couldn't abandon the case.

"Jonathan's mother begged us to keep working," Anklin said. "And I told Bob, 'This case is going to haunt us the rest of our lives if we don't do something.'" During their frequent phone calls with Jonathan, they promised to keep working to help win his freedom.

The PIs discovered that buried within a police report was the name of a witness who was never mentioned in court. They tracked her down, and she said she had told police the murder occurred right outside her window. She had seen three men looking for the victim (one had a gun in his waistband) and heard the victim being menaced by them right before the fatal shot. She had given police two of the men's names, but detectives never followed up, thinking she was not trustworthy.

Rahn and Anklin also found a witness who swore that right after the murder, she had seen the trio and overheard their conversation.

"She heard them say to each other, 'Is he dead?' and 'How many times did you shoot him?'" Rahn explained. One of the men was her brother, and she said that when she later confronted them, they admitted to committing the murder. The jury never heard this witness, either.

The PIs reported their findings to the Brooklyn district attorney's Conviction Integrity Unit, and together they set out for South Carolina to question one of the three men. Almost unbelievably, he confessed to his part in the murder and identified the other two guilty parties. He also admitted he had been the one seen fleeing the scene that night in Fleming's car. Fleming had entrusted him with the keys while he vacationed in Florida.

On April 7, 2014 -- exactly one year after Rahn and Anklin took the case -- Jonathan Fleming, now 51, was exonerated by a judge and walked free. His lawyers are now suing "everyone," as they put it. If they win a monetary settlement, Rahn and Anklin expect they will finally be compensated for the more than 1,000 hours of pro bono work they put in on the case.

Naturally, not all private investigators are so honest and devoted. And most won't work without being paid. But this pair has suggestions should you ever need to hire a PI. First, check out PIs on the internet.

"Make sure they are properly licensed," Rahn said. "See if they have any complaints against them. Ask for references from the PI, and call them. And any investigator worth their salt is going to be a member of a professional organization -- probably more than one."

Also, check to see that the investigator has experience in working your type of case.

"Google is your best friend," Anklin said. "But use your common sense with what you find out. And ask a lot of questions -- just like the Flemings did with us."

Citizen Angels for Families of the Missing

Aug. 10, 2015

Sometimes out of tragedy comes triumph. Such is the case for Julie Pendley of Fayetteville, Arkansas.

In May, her cousin Ben Baber and his best friend Cody Parrick went missing. The two 20-year-olds had driven from their homes in Okmulgee, Oklahoma, to attend a concert in Pryor, about an hour-and-a-half away.

That was the last anyone heard from them. A devastating rainstorm had passed through the area about the same time the young men would have been driving home and it was feared that Ben, an inexperienced driver, might have had an accident.

Local news outlets around the tri-state area of Oklahoma, Arkansas and Missouri -- and then the national news media -- picked up the story about the best friends who were missing. Ben had a big smile and love of science fiction, and Cody was a young man who loved music and never let his cerebral palsy slow him down.

Days went by and no word from either Ben or Cody.

Law enforcement from several counties as well as the light horse rescue team from Creek Indian Nation were on the lookout for Ben's silver 2005 Pontiac minivan. But there was still too much standing water along the highways and too few officers to check every possible crash site.

Across the Oklahoma state line, in Arkansas, cousin Julie, 48, couldn't just sit and wait. In between her duties as a graphic designer and manager of a T-shirt company she hit Google Maps, charted out every conceivable route Ben might have taken home and sent out a social media call for anyone who wanted to help her search.

"I just posted where I planned to be ... and people showed up to help," Julie told me. "Total strangers turned out. It was amazing." Among the volunteers were those with airplanes, horses, boats, all-terrain vehicles and some with just two strong legs and a good heart.

Sadly, 16 days after they went missing, the bodies of the two friends were finally located in a flooded boat ramp near Lake Eufaula that had swollen to more than 14 feet above normal. Ben had obviously taken a wrong turn.

"I'm glad I wasn't the one to find them," Julie said.

"I'm not sure I could have handled that. But I sure learned a lot during our search effort."

Julie and her band of about 20 volunteers had bonded into a family. Julie says she felt a higher power guiding them somehow -- maybe the spirits of Ben and Cody.

So they have continued to look for missing people, forming a nonprofit group and setting up a Facebook page called "Bridging the Gap -- Search Team."

In early July, they assisted in locating a couple of teenage runaways from Pea Ridge, Arkansas. Lexi Nida, 15, and Tyler Raxter, 17, were returned home safely after about a week.

Bridging the Gap then helped a family in Talala, Oklahoma, locate the body of their missing 27-year-old son, Chazz Holly, who had disappeared about a month earlier. Julie's volunteers followed tips provided by a police informant (who was later arrested) and found Holly's body discarded along a highway near Antler, Oklahoma.

After attending Holly's memorial, Julie and her team hit Google Maps again and began piecing together information on the whereabouts of a man named Michael Fike of Cache, Oklahoma. He had been gone for two months.

After pinpointing a route they suspected Fike had taken the team set out on foot to scan guardrails and off-road fences to look for evidence of disturbance. Julie says local police officer tried to shoo them away claiming they had already searched the area. A short distance away, Bridging the Gap found Fike's decomposing body and his missing truck crashed into a creek bed about 800 feet off the road.

"I've seen and smelled things I never knew possible," Julie told me. "But as ugly and painful as it all is, I have never had such a full heart. I have found my calling," she said.

Julie and her team realize they will likely not continue to find every missing person they go after but they are willing to try.

"And while we'd love to get some financial help," Julie says, "For now we're doing it all on our own dime."

With so much of the news these days focused on political bickering and world strife, it's important to remember folks like Julie who are the fabric of our country, citizens who see a need and fill it. They don't demand police action or ask for fame. They dive right in themselves, because helping others gives them a full heart.

~~~

CHAPTER 15
Personal

Much of my professional career has been dedicated to telling stories about the strength and weakness of America's criminal justice system. I often try to focus on specific stories about folks unwittingly caught up in situations they could never imagine and how they have gotten through their ordeal. I feel the need to highlight the fact that random crime could happen to any one of us.

But every once in a while I'm compelled to write about my personal journey, situations I know my readers face as well. Issues of life and death -- the passing of a parent and fulfilling their last wishes. Sharing my craft and celebrating colleagues who are much smarter than I. Or, on the anniversary of some horrific crime (think the murders of Nicole Brown Simpson and Ronald Goldman), I ask readers to indulge me some grisly remembrances of being the first reporter on the scene.

I've had a fantastically interesting, jam-packed life, and I've collected lots of intriguing characters along the way. This chapter introduces you to one of them, a man who went from criminal to crime crusader who, I believe, deserves a presidential pardon.

I Confess

June 14, 2008

I have broken the law. Ironic, isn't it -- for someone who so righteously writes about issues of crime and justice every week?

Here's the deal.

When my dad died, Mom and I made that awful, painful trip to the funeral home to make final arrangements. We knew pretty much what we were going to do because Mom and Dad had both been adamant about drawing up living wills and writing down exactly what they wanted (an activity I highly recommend for the peace of mind of those you leave behind).

Among the "Do Not Resuscitate" declaration and the property disbursement directions was the request for cremation.

So, order given, Mom's next decision was how she want the ashes stored. There was an option for a lovely ceramic urn, a sturdy little oak box or, if desired, a container made of biodegradable material that would float for a time and then release its contents from the bottom as it slowly disintegrated into water.

That was it! Dad had been a Navyman, an avid fisherman, the owner of a boat. So the biodegradable container was the obvious choice. We chose the one that looked a bit like an oversized dinner plate with matching lid and a ship motif on the top.

Dad's long-expressed wish had been that his ashes be scattered at his favorite area of Navajo Lake in northern New Mexico. My parents and their fishing buddies had spent countless long summer days and nights there and it was a natural place for Dad to want to spend all of eternity.

Some time passed, and Mom died, too. Suddenly I had the ashes of both my beloved parents to take care of.

Mom's remains were easier to deal with, as she wanted to be in a private place that I'm not prepared to disclose. But Dad's remains, well, that was another matter.

We had to wait for the snow melt to give us the optimum opportunity at our appointed destination. And then there was the matter of whether it was even legal for us to release our papier mache contraption into a state-controlled waterway.

Being the researcher/reporter I am, I knew I should make some inquiries. I knew I should check the law. But I figured ignorance of the law might be considered some sort of defense (wouldn't it?), and besides, this was my dear father's final wish. How could I not do what he made me promise to do?

So, with my daughter, Jenna, and my husband, Michael, in tow, I drove northward from Albuquerque toward Navajo Lake with Dad in his biodegradable resting place in the back seat. We were bound and determined to make it a celebration but at times tears flowed.

My nagging suspicion that what we were about to do was not lawful continued. I worried that if some state officer happened by we would be in trouble. So, in a clandestine pattern we traversed the lake, unwilling to hire a boat to take us out, lest there be a witness to our crime. We zigged, we zagged, avoiding people as we saw them. To make the story of our hours-long journey short, we finally found the perfect place.

My daughter and I gently rocked the precious biodegradable package back and forth to heave it out into the stream of water that would swallow up my father's remains.

I don't want to give any details about exactly where we accomplished this, lest there be some sort of unlikely effort to undo what we did. But when it was over and we had watched Dad's temporary final resting apparatus melt and disappear under the water, I knew we'd done the right thing. The law be damned.

In the weeks that have passed, I've wondered whether scattering Dad's ashes the way we did really was illegal. Finally, I relented and contacted a top Navajo Lake Park official to ask, and received an email response.

"Navajo Lake State Park is owned by the Bureau of Reclamation and operated under a lease agreement by New Mexico State Parks," the email explained to me. "The B.O.R. does not allow any memorials such as the scattering of ashes on their properties."

Gulp. So my suspicions were correct. But why would such a profoundly soothing act be prohibited at a lake that spreads across 21,000 acres of land? I was referred to Section 423.28 of the B.O.R.'s public conduct rule, which said, "Such an allowance could result in Reclamation becoming responsible for long-term management of burial sites, a practice inconsistent with reclamation's mission."

Well, so be it. I had been on a mission of my own. My dad is where he wanted to be for all eternity. Mission accomplished.

O.J. Simpson's Baggage

Sept. 20, 2008

I had never seen so much blood in my life.

As the coroner's wagon pulled away, there it was. Puddles of it. Some of it had oozed down the cracks in between the pathway pavers and toward the sidewalk. As I looked closer, I could see pawprints from a large dog and patterned traces of wispy blood that its dragging leash had left behind. Up toward the gate of the fancy condo, statuesque Agapanthus stood, its purple flower heads dotted with drops of this blood.

It was about 10 a.m. on a sunny Sunday in June 1994 in Brentwood, California. My cameraman and I, the reporter on duty that weekend, had been assigned to go to the home of Nicole Brown Simpson. The word was O.J. Simpson's ex-wife had been murdered.

My first thoughts that beautiful morning were: Why didn't someone take a hose and wash away this horror? And where were the police?

With no one to stop us, and with the camera rolling, we gingerly tiptoed to the gate and opened it. Across a shallow courtyard was the plate-glass window behind which Nicole Brown Simpson had lived. We could see inside the cozy living room with its overhead balcony leading off to the side bedrooms. Candles were still burning, framed photos of a smiling Simpson and her kids were everywhere. Outside were bloody footprints and what seemed to be a bloody handprint on the side of the house. Eerie. And to this day, I remember it vividly.

A mostly black jury in downtown Los Angeles would ultimately find O.J. Simpson not guilty of the throat-slashing murder of Nicole Simpson and her Good Samaritan friend, Ron Goldman, who was simply returning a pair of glasses that fateful night. It was no matter that a drop of O.J. Simpson's blood was found on the toe-box of Goldman's boot.

Now, an all-white jury in Las Vegas, Nevada, is sitting in judgment of Simpson. This time the charges include armed robbery and kidnapping. They stemmed from an incident in which sports-memorabilia dealers say they were held in a hotel room and threatened by an angry Simpson and a group of goons with guns. The entire scene was immortalized on audio tape, including this opening statement from Simpson in which he snarled: "Don't let nobody out of here. Think you can steal my s*** and sell it?" And this charming statement from The Juice: "Stand the f*** up before it gets ugly in here!"

It's a sense of entitlement many famous people seem to adopt -- "I am different. I don't have to abide by society's rules. I can do what I want and explain myself out of trouble later."

Simpson's elevated sense of status in the world brings him to yet another courtroom, where he will once again have at the core of his defense the idea that when you're someone like him the rules of conduct should be different. His defense seems to be that he believed he was simply taking back what was rightfully his: artifacts from his past life.

It seems to me that if that's his defense, he should immediately be convicted because he's admitting what he did. The law clearly says that you can't take back items using threats and guns.

No matter. His faithful attorney will continue to claim that poor O.J. is just a victim of circumstance. The shoulder-shrug position will be that Simpson's celebrity attracts trouble, not the other way around.

In 1994, lawyers said that Simpson was the victim of a misbehaving ex-wife and overzealous detectives. This time, he'll claim he was victimized by unscrupulous sports dealers and overzealous detectives. He'll maintain he had no idea the men with him were packing heat.

This jury will not be allowed to hear testimony about the murders. They won't hear the more recent 911 calls by Sidney Simpson to Florida police about her out of control father, or about the December 2000 road-rage incident in which O.J. Simpson was charged with battery and auto burglary. (He was acquitted.) Also, there were the investigations (plural) that this Heisman Trophy winner may have roughed up his girlfriend and that he pirated signals from DirecTV. For that, a judge ordered him to pay a $25,000 fine. Gee. Trouble just seems to follow this guy, right?

Our system of justice does not usually allow a jury to take into account a defendant's past bad acts. But Simpson, by the very nature of who he is, drags baggage into that Nevada courtroom anyway. Some court watchers openly wonder whether he can get a fair trial. Others wonder whether he will ever face true justice.

I wonder whether justice will ever come for Nicole Simpson and Ron Goldman and that brutal, bloody scene I came across in Brentwood all those years ago.

UPDATE: On Dec. 5, 2008, OJ Simpson was incarcerated in Nevada after being found guilty of kidnapping and armed robbery. He was sentenced to a total of 33 years in prison. He is eligible for possible parole in 2017.

They Pardon Turkeys, Don't They?

Nov. 27, 2010

Watching President Barack Obama grant the traditional "pardon" to a Thanksgiving turkey got me thinking about my friend Dan Hanks. Dan has been asking for a presidential pardon since April 2003. I think he deserves one.

Since the early '80s, Daniel Joseph Portley-Hanks has conducted undercover investigations for our government, specifically the Drug Enforcement Administration and the Federal Bureau of Investigation. Along with his private investigation partner, the late Fred Valis, Hanks helped the feds crack a multitude of major cases that put away dozens of career criminals.

Dan Hanks was born on July 13, 1946, to an Irish Catholic family, the youngest of 10 children. They lived in Southern California, and after Dan's badly wounded and emotionally broken father returned from duty as a merchant seaman at the end of World War II, he committed suicide when Dan was still in diapers.

The widow and her children's hardscrabble life forced them to move constantly. When Dan was 10, his mom married a man who appeared to be an upstanding fellow. In private, Dan says, his stepfather was an alcoholic child molester who preyed on every one of the siblings. Dan quickly learned to make the streets his home, and as a result, he survived by his wits.

A second child predator -- another man who masqueraded as someone who cared -- got Dan in his clutches. Once again, the sharp thinking boy escaped with his emotional well-being damaged but intact.

Right before Thanksgiving 1963, at the age of just 17, Dan joined the U.S. Navy to escape the pain of his life. Unfortunately, a medical condition forced him to take an honorable discharge within a year, and his chance at a "normal" life was gone.

Back on the streets, Dan was arrested multiple times for auto and property theft, burglary and for being in possession of stolen checks. He served multiple sentences in prisons with names like Chino, Lompoc, San Quentin, Terminal Island and Soledad. But in prison he began to turn his life around, earning his high school diploma and teaching classes to others. Dan realized if he used his brain to rise from convict to crime fighter he might -- just might -- be able to make a new life for himself. And that's what he set out to do.

After his release, Dan worked closely with Valis, and they ultimately established Backstreet Investigations. They operated under Valis' P.I. license, since an ex-con like Hanks wasn't eligible for one.

After reading an article in Playboy magazine about federal law enforcement needing outsiders to go undercover, they enthusiastically applied to help catch "the bad guys." The pair was wildly successful in making drug, gambling, racketeering and even murder cases for more than two decades.

They first worked for the DEA and were later recruited by the FBI to infiltrate the bookmaking arm of the Gambino crime family, a four-year case that led to the arrest and convictions of more than 80 people.

It became important to Dan that he clear his record. He went after getting his own California P.I. license, and in 2004 a court finally ordered he be awarded one. Hank's petitions for both a state and presidential pardon have never been answered, however. For eight years he's heard nothing from the government he's worked so hard for as a crime fighter.

Interesting, when you look back at the history of those who have gotten pardons.

President Bill Clinton granted the favor to 16 members of FALN, a violent Puerto Rican terror group that detonated 120 deadly bombs across America. Richard Nixon pardoned corrupt Teamster's chief Jimmy Hoffa in 1971. President Gerald Ford then pardoned Nixon, although the disgraced president had never actually been charged with a crime.

California's Gov. Arnold Schwarzenegger has only pardoned six people during his term, but three of them, like Hanks, were men who committed nonviolent crimes back in the '70s and went on to become "contributing members of their communities." For goodness sakes, Florida's outgoing Gov. Charlie Crist is even considering a pardon for the long dead rock star Jim Morrison, who exposed himself during a wild 1969 concert!

But Dan Hanks, who's spent 25 years diligently working for the DEA and FBI, can't get a pardon?

I've known Hanks for more than 15 years. He is a trustworthy friend who, among other things, once dropped everything to travel thousands of miles on his own dime to help me track down a dangerous child molester for an article I was writing. I've known him to dig in his own nearly empty pocket to help others buy groceries and to help a kid with a dream of becoming a singer reach her potential. You'd want him for your next-door neighbor, and I'm thankful that he came into my life.

The turkey President Obama granted a ceremonial pardon to last year was named Courage. I hope this year Obama and Schwarzenegger have the courage to give Dan Hanks a break. He's long overdue for one.

UPDATE: As this book goes to print -- in the spring of 2016 -- Hanks has still not received a pardon from either the federal government or the state of California.

A Columnist's Favorite Column – Homage to Charley Reese

Dec. 14, 2013

Professionals of all types admire others in their field. Architects respect certain other architects, singers style themselves after singers who came before them, artists can find inspiration from someone else's work.

As a columnist, I have a favorite too. The best columns I ever read -- and ones I remember for their common sense ideas, written in common-man language -- were penned by veteran newspaperman Charley Reese. I didn't agree with everything he wrote, but I cherished his style. Although I write about crime and justice and Reese wrote about politics and international issues for the most part, I admit I have tried to achieve his simple way of communicating ideas.

Reese, who was born in Georgia in 1937 and died in May of this year, was a self-proclaimed conservative who jumped back and forth between the democratic and republican parties while admitting he was often drawn to libertarian ideals. To my mind, that meant he was smart enough not to swallow partisan political messages and kept an open mind about things. My father would have described him as, "his own man."

In 1984, while writing for the Orlando Sentinel, Reese came to national prominence when he wrote about the injustices he saw emanating from Washington, D.C. A particular target being Congress.

"Most politicians today are not human beings," Reese wrote in an article for the Conservative Chronicle. "You want to pry open their mouths and shout into the darkness, 'Hello! Is there a human being in there?' Buried under all that lust for office, is all that fear of offending a contributor."

See any modern day relevance to that 30-year-old remark? I sure do.

In my favorite Reese column, titled "The 545 People Responsible for all of America's Woes," Reese wrote that each of the nation's problems could be traced directly to the President, the members of the U.S. Senate, the House of Representatives and the nine justices of the U.S. Supreme Court.

"When you fully grasp the plain truth that 545 people exercise complete power over the federal government, then it must follow that what exists is what they want to exist," Reese wrote. "If the tax code is unfair, it's because they want it unfair. If the budget is in the red, it's because they want it in the red. If the Marines are in Lebanon, it's because they want them in Lebanon."

Just insert our modern-day conflict in Afghanistan in place of his mention of Lebanon, and Reese's words still ring true.

Updated copies of "545" began to resurface during the 2008 presidential campaign with names of modern-day politicians inserted and a reference to Iraq. It is still being passed around the Internet today with various unauthorized updates.

In a type of language every reader could easily absorb, Reese proclaimed that politicians are, "the only people in the world who create problems and then campaign against them."

About the ever-expanding government, Reese asked: "Out-of-control bureaucracy? Congress authorizes everything bureaucrats do. Too many rules? Blame Congress. The annual deficits? Congress votes for them. You don't like the IRS? Go see Congress," he wrote. "Don't be conned. Don't let them escape responsibility."

Over the years, Reese's syndicated columns were often quoted and sometimes entered into the Congressional Record by politicians ashamed of their fellow colleague's behavior.

One of the paragraphs he wrote years ago still resonates today:

"Have you ever wondered why, if both the Democrats and the Republicans are against deficits, we have deficits? Have you ever wondered why, if all the politicians are against inflation and high taxes, that we have inflation and high taxes?"

If the words you write still have meaning decades later, if you can cut directly to the core of a problem to help solve it -- isn't that the definition of wisdom? To me, Reese was a perceptive sage whose call to, "toss out the bums" should have been heeded by citizens long ago. Now look at the mess we've got.

To those who complained to Reese that the nation's ills were the fault of special interests or lobbyists, the columnist replied, "They have no legal authority. They have no ability to coerce a senator, a congressman or a president to do one cotton-picking thing. I don't care if they offer a politician $1 million in cash. The politician has the power to accept or reject it."

At the end of each year, I try to think back about those people who have touched my life. I never met Charley Reese, but I wish I had. Through his columns, he spoke about justice and fairness and practicality. He urged readers to care about important things like honesty, integrity and the need for a government that works for all the people and not for political self-interest.

Toward the end of his career, Reese told an interviewer: "It's not important to me if people agree or disagree with my point of view. What I hope my column does is provoke people into thinking about issues, about the world and their place in it."

My sentiments, exactly. I know that not every reader is going to embrace what I write, but I continue to write because it is vitally important that all Americans find time to contemplate the sphere outside their own life. With just 545 people controlling things -- and doing a pretty miserable job, in my opinion -- I think it is high time we wrest some of that control away.

As Reese said, "It seems inconceivable to me that a nation of 235 million cannot replace 545 people who stand convicted -- by present facts -- of incompetence and irresponsibility."

We're 314 million strong now. We can change things.

Thank You, Dr. Kevorkian

June 9, 2011

Hardly a day goes by that I don't remember holding my stricken mother's hand as she laid on a special hospital bed we had set up in her living room. It was there she took her last breath. Almost every day, I think about how my father died in the bedroom of the home he loved so much. Both my parents passed away exactly how they lived -- on their own terms.

They wanted no heroic measures to prolong their lives, and they adamantly told me -- their only child -- that they did not want to die in a cold, impersonal hospital room. They made me promise to abide by their wishes. And just in case, they signed a living will putting it all in writing.

I thank Dr. Jack Kevorkian for that. He started the national dialogue about death that opened up the topic for discussion in my household.

I never met the man and, yes, I know he was a convicted felon who served several years in prison for murder after he administered a lethal cocktail to a suffering man. But he changed the course of my life and the way I look at death. The intense debate he sparked likely touched a multitude of people who probably had never stopped to consider how they would die -- and on what terms -- until Kevorkian's quest became known to the general public.

When Kevorkian started down the path that ultimately earned him the nickname "Dr. Death," it was the early '80s. He wrote a series of articles on the ethics of euthanasia for a German journal called Medicine and Law. In 1987, he hung out a shingle in Michigan as a physician available for consultation on "death counseling." His first publicly revealed assisted suicide occurred in 1990, when he helped an Alzheimer's patient take her life. She, like many other of his patients, was not terminal. But she was suffering, and for Kevorkian that was enough.

"What difference does it make if someone is terminal?" he once asked during an interview with CNN. "We are all terminal." Truer words were never spoken.

Jack Kevorkian, the son of Armenian immigrants, believed every person held the ultimate decision-making power over his or her own life -- and death should be a dignified event. Yet his legacy will likely be focused only on his stand on physician-assisted suicide. Once asked what it felt like to take someone's life, Kevorkian said: "I didn't do it to end a life.

I did it to end the suffering the patient's going through. The patient's obviously suffering -- what's a doctor supposed to do, turn his back?"

Three states -- Oregon, Montana and Washington -- agree with the controversial doctor's stand and have passed laws allowing physician-assisted suicides.

Kevorkian wasn't perfect in his judgment as he assisted more than 130 people to end their lives -- but I'm not one who believes he had self-aggrandizement in mind. Like my parents, Kevorkian believed a mentally competent patient should always be in charge of his or her fate. The justice system may have branded him a criminal, but it is clear he single-handedly made generations of both young and older Americans think about their final moment.

When Kevorkian began to publicly preach about "the right to die" in Michigan in the early '90s, my parents in Albuquerque, New Mexico, became disciples. Both Mom and Dad were the type who didn't use 20 words if 10 would do. They sat me down and bluntly told me they believed they alone should be in charge of their own lives right up until the moment of their deaths. They showed me their living will and made me promise.

My parents never faltered in their resolve -- not even after Dr. Kevorkian had his medical license pulled by the state of Michigan or after he was sentenced to 10 to 25 years in prison on second-degree murder charges in 1999. Kevorkian's book, "Prescription: Medicide, The Goodness of Planned Death," was in my father's library. Included within was Kevorkian's idea that executed prisoners should be put to death in a certain way so as to preserve their organs for donation to others. You see, he wasn't all about death.

By the time Kevorkian was released from prison on parole in June 2007 on his promise that he would never assist in another suicide, both my parents were gone. But their life and death lesson remains indelibly etched in my soul. Because I watched them depart this earth marching to the drummer of their own choosing, I find I don't fear death like I used to. I'm now able to look at it as a next adventure.

It's ironic to think that at the end of his life Dr. Kevorkian did not choose the course toward death that he'd preached to so many. He died in a hospital in Royal Oak, Michigan, after a month-long battle with kidney problems and pneumonia. He was 83. He never married and had no children. His life became all about the death of others.

My Stalker, My Warning

Oct. 17, 2015
"I am a potential mass shooter."

That chilling line was written to me by my on-again, off-again cyberstalker.

He took exception to my opinion in June 2014 that the UC Santa Barbara shooter -- who killed six and wounded 14 before committing suicide -- was, "A young man of privileged means ... possessed by a demented, murderous and conniving mind." My stalker declared I was guilty of violating the Americans with Disabilities Act by maligning anyone with a mental disorder, and he began a letter-writing campaign to smear my name and terminate this column.

Boasting about his imaginary importance in media circles, he sent rambling, angry letters to a majority of my past and current employers (and some friends) telling them I was a bully and demanding they join in denouncing me. He called me vile names, threatened my safety and said it with language that caused me to think he had a mental problem. He soon confirmed that.

"Diane, I am mentally ill. I am physically disabled as well. My life is a living hell ... I am a prime candidate for committing a mass gun shooting ... and with the PTSD I am easily triggered."

After the rash of mass shootings America had endured I reported this disturbing language to an LAPD police detective I know. She forwarded it to a special cyber-crimes unit. I soon learned they couldn't do much. Neither could the LA district attorney's office or the FBI cyber-crime unit.

As a retired Secret Service friend of mine said, "There's just not enough manpower for agents to confront every nut on the Internet."

Now, more than a year later -- and with almost 50 school shootings so far this year -- my stalker's words came back to me.

Even though law enforcement can't seem to locate my stalker (he frequently moves), I know he is simmering out there somewhere, and I'm fearful he is a walking time bomb. I've learned of another dozen of his victims.

Three years ago the stalker picked an online chat room fight with an Emmy-nominated television producer who is also a film professor at an Ohio University. He is still waging a campaign to discredit the producer and demanding he be fired for "bullying the mentally disabled," which is the stalker's reference to himself. He's branded the producer a "serial killer" and "child abuser" online. He even went so far as to contact the Emmy committee and spew such violent threats that during an award ceremony extra security was hired to intercept him if he appeared. The producer got a Civil Stalking Protection Order, but it has done little to slow the madness.

A woman who ran a nonprofit group helping the homeless in California told me the stalker sent her emails out of the blue, declaring that she was ignorant about homelessness and bragging about his expert documentary on the issue. Once she responded to him that he launched a massive and prolonged internet smear that ultimately caused her funding to dry up. She was forced to shutter the organization and leave the state.

In Nov. 2013, the stalker threatened two female hostel workers in Los Angeles after they kicked him out for using foul language in the lobby. Within hours he asked for $10,000 as recompense for -- you guessed it -- their discrimination against the disabled.

Then, he turned his wrath to a retired police lieutenant the hostel hired to resolve the problem. Besides producing a barrage of vicious email and internet threats against the officer, the stalker also verbally attacked the man's wife. She was a top executive at a cosmetics firm, and the stalker publicly accused her of deliberately trying to disfigure customers. This self-described mentally ill man also posted photos and the addresses of the couple's California home and their new out-of-state retirement home.

Then, there was the successful television writer the stalker was once introduced to in California. He grandly declared online that she was his "writing partner," and he professed his love. When she protested, he turned on the woman, reportedly following her on dates, spitting on her companion and finally posting warnings like "Wouldn't it be terrible if on your way to work your brakes fail on the 405 (freeway)?"

I could relate other horror stories from this cyberstalker's victims from across the country and into Canada, but you get my drift. This is a dangerous man who has left a trail of police reports in Ohio, West Virginia, California, Indiana, Oregon and Washington. His alleged crimes include aggravated assaults, public drunkenness, violent domestic abuse, communications harassment, menacing and possession of drug paraphernalia. Yet he is allowed to remain free to wage war against accomplished people he obviously wishes he could emulate.

As the lieutenant told me from his retirement home in Oregon the other day, "This is not the crime of the century, but sitting around waiting for this guy to hurt someone again is not the right thing to do." And he ominously added, "He's giving all the same indications of past mass shooters."

Why don't we have a system to intervene with people like this? How many lives are they allowed to disrupt or destroy before the law can step in? I, for one, don't want to pick up a paper and read about a massacre with this stalker's name on it. He has given us ample warning.

~~~

Final Thoughts

As I mentioned in one of the columns in this collection, I became captivated by the issues of crime and justice as a young girl growing up in Albuquerque, New Mexico. My mother would routinely take me, her only child, to the local post office to buy stamps and mail packages. While she waited in line I, her voracious reader, would wander over to the community bulletin board (a standard display in all U.S. post offices back then) and gaze up at the FBI's Most Wanted posters.

Who were these people? What had they done? And, most important to a kid who grew up in a working-class home where character and integrity were stressed, why had they acted in the criminal way that they had? What would become of them? What was prison really like? That early exposure to an element so unlike my own sparked a lifelong interest.

The journalism of crime and justice has always fascinated me because it truly reaches into nearly every corner of life.

The system inserts itself in our lives when we marry, have children, divorce, fight over custody of our kids and when we die. Laws are in place that affect our homes, taxes, schools, workplaces, planes, trains and automobiles. Legislation guides how institutions that are vital to our well-being operate -- from hospitals, local governments and insurance companies to eating and drinking establishments, merchants and corporations. We live in a society with so many rules, regulations and legal restrictions that it hardly resembles the country our forefathers envisioned as they penned the U.S. Constitution and our Bill of Rights.

Crime is never going to go away, and justice is one of the cornerstones upon which this country was founded. So it behooves us all to pay attention to how it functions, to make sure our system is fair and populated by people who honestly care, not just in it for the paycheck and pension.

I hope to have sparked your interest with my columns. If you came away from any of them saying, "I didn't know that" or "I never thought about it that way," I've done my job.

~~~

Reviews

"She's a self-generating engine of nitty-gritty crime and justice coverage. ... In Dimond's columns, the reader gets not only a crime story, but a fast education in a new topic of the law. Dimond's ability to simultaneously captivate and edify is unique, as are many of the stories she chases down from every corner of the country. You never know what Dimond will produce next, you just know that it will be headline worthy." ~ *Dylan Skriloff*, publisher and editor-in-chief of the Rockland County Times

~~~

"In a world where every crime story gets reduced to 140 characters, no matter how complex the facts or the people, it's refreshing to read Diane's nuanced and insightful reporting. Those of us who do this stuff for a living prefer her in-depth analysis to the case summaries that barely list name, rank and serial (killer) number." ~ *Jack Furlong*, veteran criminal defense attorney and novelist

~~~

"Diane Dimond gives readers rare insight into the justice system and puts a human face on the intricate dealings of our court system, warts and all. Her columns are a winning combination of expertise and empathy, presented with great storytelling skills." ~ *Kent Walz*, editor-in-chief of the Albuquerque Journal

~~~

"Diane Dimond has spent her career thinking outside the box. This collection of stories reveals how her unique approach to covering the criminal justice system relies on several elements missing in journalism today: perspective, context, experience and empathy. Diane goes beyond statistics and reveals the human tragedies and challenges of both the victim and the accused. Have you ever heard of Jesse Shipley, Aaron Fisher, Janet Danahey or Betty Winstanley? Each of their stories will touch you and provoke thought and, more importantly, conversation. Once again, Diane Dimond shows us the value and power of going beyond the 'what' and revealing the 'why,' while offering this single challenge: Can we make things better? This collection demonstrates the transformative potential of simple, honest storytelling." ~ *Jim Moret*, chief correspondent of "Inside Edition," attorney and author

~~~

"Diane Dimond has dedicated her career to telling the stories and exposing the truths and the flaws in our justice system. The wide range of topics in 'Thinking Outside the Crime and Justice Box' will resonate with all readers, as Diane takes a deep dive where others rarely do. Kudos to Diane for her persuasive and clear presentation of topics that matter -- and for making us pause to think about how we can help." ~ *Beth Karas*, legal analyst, founder of KarasOnCrime.com and former prosecutor

~~~

"What I appreciate most about Diane's writing is that she spotlights the root causes of the problems that we have in our society, the rationales for the solutions that we've tried, the dedicated men and women on the front lines of implementing those solutions, the reasons why those solutions have or haven't worked well and the possibilities of alternative solutions that might work better. I wish that more Americans would spend more time thinking and talking about the kind of society we want to have and what we can do to improve it as individuals, parents, workers and citizens. Diane provides a valuable catalyst for those reflections and discussions." ~ *Dr. Brian Russell*, psychologist, lawyer and Investigation Discovery host

~~~

"Diane Dimond's columns consistently are among our most-read opinion pieces on Noozhawk, and they frequently generate vigorous debate among our readers.

Her insights on crime and the criminal justice system clearly have struck a nerve among our audience in Santa Barbara County. I suspect it's because many of these issues are overdue for a serious national discussion, if not outright reform, and our readers already have been thinking about them.

Diane's ability to spark that public conversation is something I admire, and I'm grateful she's doing it on Noozhawk." ~ *Bill Macfadyen*, Noozhawk founder and publisher

~~~

About the Author

Diane Dimond is one of the few journalists to have mastered the art of her craft across all platforms -- radio, television, books and internet publishing. As such, she defies a single category.

Dimond's greatest talent may be her ability to communicate complicated stories in an understandable, common-sense way. Her reputation as a fearless investigative reporter has won admiration from her peers, but she never lost the ethical and moral lessons she learned growing up as an only child in a middle class home in the Southwest.

"For a kid who grew up in Albuquerque, New Mexico, I feel fortunate to have found the calling of journalism," Dimond says. "I've gotten to roam the halls of Congress, report from the White House and be an eye-witness to several moments in history. I've also been able to concentrate on the issues of crime and justice in America and tell the often-forgotten human stories behind the headlines."

While working for Albuquerque's KGGM-TV and Radio as a receptionist during high school, Dimond was drawn to the newsroom in an odd and coincidental way. Late one evening the frantic news director came to the front desk holding a long trail of wire copy and urgently asked Diane whether she "knew how to write." He told her that the news writers had gone out to dinner (in between the early and late newscasts), been in a car accident and were hospitalized. Diane had won a few writing awards in school and immediately pitched in. This baptism-by- fire that night was the beginning of Dimond's passion for the news business and good old-fashioned storytelling.

After working in the KGGM (now KRQE) newsroom, Diane was recruited by the TV-radio station across the street. She joined KOB radio (now KKOB) and ultimately became both the crime and courts reporter and the morning newscaster. She was presented with the prestigious Silver Gavel Award from the American Bar Association for her intrepid multi-part series about political corruption within the Bernalillo County Sheriff's Department, which resulted in the sheriff being removed from office. In addition, Diane was awarded multiple APE awards from the Albuquerque Press Club for various other stories she covered.

In 1976, Dimond moved across the country to Washington, D.C., to anchor newscasts for National Public Radio's "All Things Considered."

In 1980, she became correspondent for the RKO Radio Network and was assigned to cover Capitol Hill, the White House and various Washington agencies. Dimond was named the network's national political correspondent and, in 1984, covered the presidential campaigns of Walter Mondale and his vice presidential nominee Geraldine Ferraro. Dimond was on the floor during both presidential nominating conventions that year -- the Democratic gathering held in San Francisco, California, and the Republican convention in Dallas, Texas. She was broadcasting live from the steps of the U.S. Capital when Ronald Reagan took the oath of office. Simultaneously, news broke that the American hostages held in Iran for 444 days were released from captivity, a final slap at the presidency of Jimmy Carter.

Dimond made her move into television in 1986. Her first on-air reporting job was at the CBS flagship station in New York. At WCBS, she earned several awards for covering such groundbreaking stories as the "Baby M" surrogate mother case, an investigative series on chromium poisoning in New Jersey and a sensational child molestation case on Long Island, New York.

Dimond was recruited into syndicated television in 1990 when she became the investigative reporter for the program "Hard Copy." Time magazine cited Diane's revelations and continuing coverage of the Michael Jackson child molestation story as among "The Best TV of '93."

While at "Hard Copy," Dimond also made headlines when she acquired and aired the actual interrogation tape of O.J. Simpson as he was being questioned by Los Angeles police detectives investigating the death of his ex-wife, Nicole Brown Simpson, and her friend, Ron Goldman. Diane sparked many national stories during her 7 years at "Hard Copy," including the William Kennedy Smith rape allegations in Palm Beach, Florida, exclusive interviews with Hollywood madam Heidi Fleiss and several sit-down prison interviews with notorious convicted killers. Among them were Kenneth Bianchi, the Hillside Strangler; Jeffrey MacDonald, the Green Beret Killer; James Earl Ray, the assassin of Martin Luther King Jr.; Pamela Smart, the teacher convicted of convincing her young student-lover to kill her husband; and Richard Allen Davis, who kidnapped and killed young Polly Klaas.

In 1997, Dimond moved to Warner Brothers/Telepictures, where she substitute-anchored the nationally syndicated program "EXTRA" and made headlines with her exposé of the deceptive practices of "The Jerry Springer Show," among other investigative reports.

In 1998, Diane moved back to the East Coast and joined NBC News. She partnered with Geraldo Rivera to co-anchor CNBC's nightly newscast, "UpFront Tonight." She anchored extensive live reports from Washington during the impeachment proceedings against former President Bill Clinton. After moving to MSNBC, Dimond hosted the series "Missing Persons," anchored major news blocks and, among other stories, covered the 2000 presidential campaign, traveling at various times with three of the candidates: George W. Bush, Al Gore and Ralph Nader. Dimond also became known as the correspondent who spent 35 straight days reporting live from outside the vice president's residence in Washington as the nation awaited the controversial recount of the disputed vote.

After the Sept. 11, 2001, terror attack in New York City Diane became a freelance anchor, hosting live programs on the Fox News channel, where she specialized in the network's continuing coverage of the war on terrorism. Her live interviews with military and policy newsmakers were often quoted by other news organizations. Dimond did double duty during this time as an anchor at Court TV, filling in during various day parts and the network's evening news program, "Catherine Crier Live."

In 2003, Diane joined Court TV fulltime and became the chief investigative reporter, once again, breaking the story of another allegation of child sexual misconduct against entertainer Michael Jackson. It was a story Dimond had followed since she first revealed Jackson's legal problems in 1993. In advance of preparing to cover Jackson's criminal trial in 2005, Dimond began to write a book about her decade-long involvement with the story. "Be Careful Who You Love: Inside the Michael Jackson Case" is seen by many as the definitive work about one of the most controversial figures in the entertainment industry.

Diane took time off in 2006 following the illness and death of both her father, Allen Hughes, and her mother, Ruby Hughes, in Albuquerque, New Mexico.

In late 2007, Dimond began to write a weekly crime and justice column for the Albuquerque Journal, the paper she grew up reading. By 2008 the column had gone national. The column is distributed to newspapers nationwide by Creators Syndicate. Dimond prides herself on writing about wide-ranging crime and justice topics designed to raise public awareness and promote outside-the-box thinking.

In 2010, the headline-grabbing story about the so-called "White House Gate Crashers," Michaele and Tareq Salahi, grabbed Dimond's attention. Having been assigned to the White House early in her career, she knew it was next to impossible to "crash" an official state dinner. Her investigation into what really happened -- and more importantly, how a simple story exploded into unnecessary handwringing and Congressional hearings -- culminated in Dimond's book "Cirque Du Salahi." The book was called "a riveting slice of contemporary anthropology" that exposed the gossipmongers masquerading as journalists who first peddled the "gate crashers" idea.

As a longtime contributor for Newsweek/The Daily Beast, Dimond covered multiple stories, including several high-profile criminal trials. Among them were the Casey Anthony murder trial, the political corruption trial of former Sen. John Edwards and the child molestation case against former Penn State football coach Jerry Sandusky.

In Jan. 2013, Dimond turned her attention to the technological future of media. As part of the senior management team at The Video Call Center LLC, she helped develop a whole new genre of television -- one which marries social media with mass media. Utilizing a patented console, the VCC was designed after the call-in talk radio model where the host runs their own control board. VCC technology created live, host-driven, call-in talk television. Guests and callers join the program by using their smartphones or tablets to access IP video services (Skype, Facetime, etc.), and the mostly automated system allows the host to control all aspects of the program. With a punch of a button the host can introduce callers, bring in preloaded stills and videos, and offer immediate access to everything on the internet.

Diane is currently in the planning stages for her next book, the topic of which remains under wraps -- for now.

Diane adores her cats, loves to be in the garden and lives in Rockland County, New York, with her husband, Michael Schoen, a longtime WCBS radio news anchorman and voiceover artist. They have one daughter and three grandchildren.

~~~

~~~

"THINKING OUTSIDE THE CRIME AND JUSTICE BOX" IS ALSO AVAILABLE AS AN E-BOOK FOR KINDLE, AMAZON FIRE, IPAD, NOOK AND ANDROID E-READERS. GO TO WWW.CREATORS.COM/BOOKS.

~~~

www.ingramcontent.com/pod-product-compliance
Lightning Source LLC
Chambersburg PA
CBHW070759280326
41934CB00012B/2973